Back to the Blanket

American Indian Literature and Critical Studies Series

Published through the Recovering Languages and Literacies of the Americas initiative, supported by the Andrew W. Mellon Foundation

Back to the Blanket

Recovered Rhetorics and Literacies in American Indian Studies

Kimberly G. Wieser

University of Oklahoma Press : Norman

RECOVERING
LANGUAGES & LITERACIES
OF THE AMERICAS

Back to the Blanket: Recovered Rhetorics and Literacies in American Indian Studies is published as part of the Recovering Languages and Literacies of the Americas initiative. Recovering Languages and Literacies is generously supported by the Andrew W. Mellon Foundation.

Publication credits and acknowledgments are listed as unnumbered footnotes where they apply in the front matter and main text.

Library of Congress Cataloging-in-Publication Data
Name: Wieser, Kimberly G., 1968– author.
Title: Back to the blanket : recovered rhetorics and literacies in American Indian studies / Kimberly G. Wieser.
Description: Norman : University of Oklahoma Press, 2017. | Series: American Indian literature and critical studies series ; volume 70 | Includes bibliographical references and index.
Identifiers: LCCN 2017011937| ISBN 978-0-8061-5727-6 (hardcover : alk. paper) | ISBN 978-0-8061-5728-3 (pbk. : alk. paper)
Subjects: LCSH: Indians of North America—Study and teaching. | Indians of North America—Ethnic identity. | Group identity—United States. | Rhetoric—Social aspects—United States.
Classification: LCC E76.6 .W44 2017 | DDC 970.004/97—dc23
LC record available at https://lccn.loc.gov/2017011937

Back to the Blanket: Recovered Rhetorics and Literacies in American Indian Studies is Volume 70 in the American Indian Literature and Critical Studies Series.

The paper in this book meets the guidelines for permanence and durability of the Committee on Production Guidelines for Book Longevity of the Council on Library Resources, Inc. ∞

1 2 3 4 5 6 7 8 9 10

Contents

Illustrations

Preface

According to the white man, the Indian, choosing to return to his tribal manners and dress, "goes back to the blanket." True, but "going back to the blanket" is the factor that has saved him from, or at least stayed, his final destruction. Had the Indian been as completely subdued in spirit as he was in body he would have perished within the century of his subjection. But it is the unquenchable spirit that has saved him—his clinging to Indian ways, Indian thought, and tradition, that has kept him and is keeping him today. The white man's ways were not his ways and many of the things that he has tried to adopt have proven disastrous and to his utter shame. Could the Indian have forestalled the flattery and deceit of his European subjector and retained his native truth and honesty; could he have shunned whiskey and disease and remained the paragon of health and strength he was, he might today be a recognized man instead of a hostage on a reservation. But many an Indian has accomplished his own personal salvation by "going back to the blanket." The Indian blanket or buffalo robe, a true American garment, and worn with the significance of language, covered beneath it, in the prototype of the American Indian, one of the bravest attempts ever made by man on this continent to rise to the heights of true humanity.

Portions of the preface, introduction, and chapter 1 were previously published in "Towards a Tribal-Centered Reading of Native Literature: Using Indigenous Rhetoric(s) instead of Literary Analysis," by Kimberly G. Roppolo, *Paradoxa* 15 (2001), 263–74.

> To clothe a man falsely is only to distress his spirit and to make him incongruous and ridiculous, and my entreaty to the American Indian is to retain his tribal dress.
>
> —*Luther Standing Bear, reflecting on his experiences at Carlisle Indian School (190–91)*

This book is a story of a journey across years and miles and language to a decolonizing of my own mind, a refusal, in Mohawk scholar Audra Simpson's terms, "to stop being myself." The title, *Back to the Blanket*, appropriates the mainstream pejorativism for captured American Indians returning to their people or their ways during the first few centuries of the settler colonial era. In using this term, I showcase my own paracolonial[1] refusal of "captivity" by mainstream culture's tools of empire. The attempted assimilation of Indian children like Luther Standing Bear in federal boarding schools was one such measure. In these schools, settler colonial educators, armed with assimilationist policies, aimed to inculcate internalized racism in their American Indian pupils so they would never "go back to the blanket"—never again value the knowledge and ways of their traditional cultures. Although I grew up with familial knowledge of tribal heritage, I received my education in "Indian ways," or traditions and cultural protocols, mostly from Namšem (Grandfather), the late Eugene Blackbear Sr. ("Tsis-tis-tas"/Southern Cheyenne). In other words, I went, as Standing Bear says, "back to the blanket."

When Namšem adopted me as a granddaughter, he was the oldest living Sun Dance priest, an Arrow priest, a fasting instructor, a sweat lodge leader, and a Native American Church roadman. He had what he called a "Ph.D. in Indian ways." Part of the process of becoming a part of the Cheyenne community and kinship network included Namšem taking me into the Sun Dance arbor, adopting me formally, giving me a medicine bag for protection, and later giving me a Cheyenne name. Most significant for learning Cheyenne ways, however, was instruction in the Cheyenne language, ceremonies, and cultural stories, spending at least four months of the year taking care of "Old Man," going around Indian Country with him, learning behavioral protocols and customs, and getting to know my new Cheyenne relatives. Once I became part of the Cheyenne people, they became part of me. In this way, my relationship to Cheyenne people is somewhat like that of intertribal captives of old. Well-assimilated war captives became relatives. Today those who assimilate into American Indian cultures, whether of American Indian ancestry or not, are *captivated* by Indian Country, "rez-merized," if you will, rather than forcibly captured.[2]

Because of these American Indian concepts of relatedness and identity, I cannot help but write from the position of a woman of multiple ancestries and intersectionalities. Among these are my familial oral traditions of having Cherokee, Choctaw, and Creek ancestry, instruction in culture by an adopted Cheyenne grandfather, and my daily life living intertribally in a household firmly grounded in the Comanche culture of my partner. Family in Indian Country is exponential. For instance, I am also the adopted granddaughter of the late Elizabeth Crow Flag, "painted into" the Blackfoot Beaver Bundle[3] she held, and have numerous close relationships in Southern Alberta. My Piikani and Kainai relatives are all dear to my heart, as are my Cree relatives who live among them. They affect who I am every day of my life and how I approach the world. My partner and I also have many relatives in Native American Church and in our intertribal community in Oklahoma and elsewhere. My experience in Indian Country has always been what some call transnational, what scholar Chadwick Allen says we should more properly think of as "trans-*Indigenous*" ("Trans-*national* Native American Studies" 1–2). My voice in *Reasoning Together* exemplifies this under the rubric of "Intertribalism," the name that Transindigenism goes by in Oklahoma Indian experience and throughout grassroots Indian Country, where the community views these interactions as relationships between kin groups rather than exchanges between Westphalian nation-states (Acoose et al. 303–24).

Tribal nations have always interacted with one another in ways that today would be labeled "Transindigenous," for purposes of war, trade, and other forms of exchange and contact. Many nations divided up leadership roles accordingly, with certain individuals trained for domestic matters and others for intertribal (as opposed to the non-Indian concept of "foreign") policy. Rhetorical devices grounded in tribally specific cultures and languages made their way into intertribal discourse in English in the eighteenth century on the East Coast. Historical practices of persuasion within and between tribes carried over to transnational exchanges with settler colonial figures and have, to some extent, carried over to contemporary exchanges both with U.S. government officials and in intertribal and tribally specific formal discourse. Tribal leaders trained in diplomacy as well as warfare added English to a linguistic arsenal that generally included at least some bi- or multilingualism and rich intertribal kinesthetic, embodied, visual, and material rhetorics[4] utilizing actions and material culture as mediums. This body of intertribal rhetoric in English still serves us transnationally and Transindigenously and can be observed in the writing, speeches, and other texts examined in this book by utilizing the paradigm of Intertribalism. Intertribalism, which differs from "trans" paradigms as it incorporates Native notions of relatedness, offers us rich possibilities as scholars of Native studies for developing knowledge and arguments grounded in Indigenous structures tied to Indigenous perspectives, allowing us to see relatedness and commonality while maintaining tribal specificity and sovereignty.[5] American Indian studies academics, instructors and students alike, are travelers across borders—we are intertribal, we are Transindigenous, we are transnational. Like all travelers, we bring with us news. We bring with us information that must be transmitted cross-culturally. In a traditional sense, we ask for the right and the responsibility to speak to the people, to be trusted that our intentions are good and our words are true.

One thing Namšem taught me to do—despite, and in fact because of, all my Western education—was to think for myself, to read the world around me, both the physical and the metaphysical, as is done throughout traditional[6] American Indian[7] cultures in the Americas. In doing so, he instructed me in a literacy that was new to me; that is, he gave me the ability to use a culturally grounded hermeneutic to make meaning for myself. Traditional American Indian people read signs in much the same way I have seen many American Indian people interpret texts—through synthesis as much as through analysis, if not more so. Muscogee Creek scholar Craig Womack says in *Red on Red*, "'Real life' and 'story' merge into a single identity. This synthesis marks the oral tradition" (99). From traditional American Indian perspectives, stories, signs, and symbols cannot be separated from the rest of reality; new information is added to preexisting cultural knowledge and context—decisions are derived in the confluence of ideas. Osage poet Duane Big Eagle says that synthesis—the putting together of ideas—is the more common problem-solving strategy for Native peoples.[8] Vine Deloria, the late, highly esteemed Dakota scholar, points out, "Tribal peoples are as systematic and philosophical as Western scientists in their efforts to understand the world around them. They simply use other kinds of data and have goals other than determining the mechanical functioning of things" (*Spirit* 41). Indigenous American articulation of philosophy and science—who we are and how we see the world, what our position in it is in relation to the rest of creation, how other aspects of creation relate to each other—has often been accomplished by indirect discourse, by saying something without directly saying it.[9] We are traditionally taught by story, and we typically explain by story, not merely by exposition. Stories, along with oratory, can rhetorically function as argument in Native cultures. Knowledge—cultural, familial, and individual—is often embedded in narrative and must be deduced by the individual listener. Because of this, the separation of American Indigenous literary and cultural studies—the courses in which the study of story, the study of narrative and oratorical structures, occurs—from other aspects of Native American and Indigenous studies is a false division that is unproductive for the discipline as a whole.[10]

This book examines how American Indigenous people read story, sign, and symbol (hermeneutics), how we encode meaning traditionally when we want to persuade (rhetorics), and how scholars of American Indian and Indigenous studies can apply traditional intertribal approaches to contemporary transnational and transcultural negotiation, debate, and decision making about key issues such as the rights of Indigenous and non-Indigenous people, natural resources, and environmental sustainability in ways that facilitate communication between the academy and the peoples and communities it studies. These key issues are pragmatic concerns that affect the lives not only of American Indian people but of all humans. In advancing this discussion, I use several terms in English that come from a long history of textual analysis, all of which were derived from Greek and first used in biblical studies: hermeneutics, rhetorics, exegesis, and eisegesis. "Hermeneutics" refers to the interpretation of symbols, usually those in texts. Rhetorics are organized systems of language whose primary function is to convey an idea or an argument in a way that convinces one's audience. "Exegesis" refers to the strategy scholars typically use in literary and rhetorical studies for "objectively" analyzing a text to make meaning. Most literary, rhetoric, and composition scholars likely know these three terms, but they might not know "eisegesis," which describes a reader's synthesis of the text with his or her own reality and preexisting knowledge to make meaning.

In biblical studies, eisegesis is considered a substandard hermeneutic through which a reader imposes his or her own meaning *on* a text, expressing reader bias that in effect silences God. I, however, would like to rescue this synthetic reading practice from its "inferior" status, as it strongly resembles the way holistic thinkers interpret data and reach conclusions. All readings, even those conducted by exegesis, are created *from* the schemata and biases of readers. The practice of eisegesis is based in ontologies and spiritual perspectives and is just as valid an interpretive strategy. In traditional American Indian cultures, everything, including every being in the seen and unseen world, is related and subsumed by spirituality; there are no truly secular epistemologies. Traditional metaphysics and ontologies do not include such a concept as secular. American Indian traditional logic, like other faith-based reasoning, is based more on synthesis than on analysis. Yet it has produced truths that scientists using strictly analytical reasoning—considered to be the only *objective* form of thought by many in the academy—are just now beginning to understand.[11]

Some readers might find my using non-Indian terminology to describe American Indian epistemologies problematic. I myself had some of the same hesitations, particularly when examining tribally specific discourse where it would be more precise to use specific terms in specific Indigenous languages. While, for the most part, American Indians have had no need to develop language for textual analysis, language for this could be created. For instance, Choctaws, with a significant history of biblical interpretation in the past two hundred or so years, have terminology that might lend itself for critical terms. *Holisso*, the term for "Bible," is also the word for any other book;[12] as with all Choctaw constructions, specific meaning—which book—is heavily dependent on context, from which the hearer is expected to make inference. *Holisso aiitimanumpuli* means to read aloud from or "talk with" a book. *Holissa pisa* (to study a book) might serve as a Choctaw substitute for "hermeneutic." Rick Billy, first-language speaker of Choctaw and former University of Oklahoma (OU) Choctaw instructor, offers that "holisso a^{n}li kiyo tuk ikana li anoli lachi"—"I read a book that was not real, and now I'm going to tell you about it"—is as effective a substitute for literary criticism as he can construct, since there is no concept for fiction in Choctaw (interview by author). Leroy Sealy, another respected, longtime Choctaw instructor at OU, suggests that "holisso anlhi hochefo li tuk kiyo cha chim anoli lachi" would also work (interview by author). In Choctaw-specific situations, either of these phrases would make sense to first-language speakers to describe offering a literary interpretation. Because of traditional ways of reading signs, symbols, and visions that I detail in the introduction of this book, I would suggest that this interpretive "talk," or *anumpa*, would include both exegesis and eisegesis.

However, the Choctaw critical terms would be useful only if all involved were Choctaw speakers and were discussing Choctaw texts or discourse. For the most part, in this book I describe intertribal discourse and rhetorics; when I describe tribally specific rhetorical practices—most notably in chapter 4 in regard to Cherokee rhetorics—I do so as they occur within intertribal discourse in English. Therefore, tribally specific terms simply are not appropriate. Using tribally specific terms seems to prejudice the potential for application of this critical rhetoric not only in this volume but also in future work by other scholars, because doing so would make it exclusive rather than inclusive. Either the material examined would need to be specific to a particular tribe or the audience for the analysis would need to be tribal speakers of that particular language. I also shy away from tribally specific terms, as I am reluctant to potentially offend people of sovereign nations by using their language for the framework of my analysis, indirectly implying that the people of those nations would somehow endorse or support my scholarship on this subject. From American Indian perspectives, I have the right to speak only for myself here. It is imperative that I do not appear to attempt to do otherwise. I have tried to restrict my use of tribal languages to proper names and to crucial tribally specific concepts. I want to make sure that when I do utilize Indigenous language, I am doing so because I am using the most precise language to communicate, not to exoticize my work by accentuating a false distinction or asserting a privileged epistemology, not to create a curio from language.

Indigenous languages offer the best specific terms for Indigenous concepts, but in our paracolonial reality, English academic terms are often the most precise language available to describe the process of how Indigenous Americans make sense of reality, to describe our conceptual praxis when making sense of the signs around us, to articulate how we learn, how we utilize language, particularly when describing in English how we do these things. Like everything taken into our cultures, English has become ours. As Acoma poet and scholar Simon J. Ortiz says, "The indigenous peoples of the Americas have taken the languages of the colonialist and used them for their own purposes" (122). If there is any English terminology with which I am familiar that is used by American Indian people to describe eisegesis, it would be the maxim given by elders in Native American Church on occasions when we as participants have a right to speak: we are given permission to "express ourselves" and are urged to "speak from the heart." When we do so, we strive to "talk in a good way," the way my Cheyenne relatives taught me.

Linguistic anthropologist William L. Leap considers the style of discourse built on the rhetoric we call "talking in a good way" to be part of American Indian English (3), what I term "Red English." However, Red English is not the "Me Tonto" gobbledygook portrayed in Hollywood westerns. The ever-changing rhetorical tradition of Red English springs from ontologies of relatedness that guide how Indigenous Americans reared and/or educated in these ontologies interpret signifiers, verbal and otherwise, and construct argument in ways cognizant of and respectful of those relationships. Colloquially, when we utilize discourse in this fashion, we "talk in a good way." No one has to speak monosyllabically to do this. That would only convince people who believe that American Indians are cardboard cutouts, historical stereotypes rather than contemporary human beings. It certainly would not convince Indians, traditional or otherwise. This discourse requires merely that I neither be rude nor walk through Indian Country in a way disrespectful of its customs.

Back to the Blanket

Introduction

> Each of us, in our spirits, is a council house. The traditional Cherokee council house was located at the center of a village atop an earthen mound. It was a meeting place where people sat around the sacred fire and discussed politics or took part in ceremonies. Our individual spirits compose a similar space: a place of memory where we gather our thoughts and the teachings of our elders to deliberate on how we should act, what we should believe.
>
> —*Christopher B. Teuton, Cherokee Stories of the Turtle Island Liars' Club (22)*

Over the millennia, truths were recorded in narrative and metaphor in American Indian oral traditions throughout cultures; stories, languages, artifacts, and ways, rather than academic discourse, carry this knowledge, making American Indian poetics, rhetorics, and other aesthetics overlap tremendously. Perhaps because the academy encourages the separation of the disciplines even in fields that are supposedly interdisciplinary, there is little study in this nexus. Nevertheless, some progress has been made in regard to increasing the body of American Indian rhetorical scholarship as a whole. Of course, any discussion of American Indian rhetorics must begin with Malea Powell (Miami descendant) and Scott Richard Lyons (Anishinaabe), the two scholars who did much of the foundational work in the field in the late 1990s. Their scholarship differs quite a bit from my own in terms of what it attempts to accomplish. Powell's has primarily focused on the rhetoric of "survivance" in the writings of nineteenth-century American Indian intellectuals and on American Indian material cultural rhetorics. Lyons's articles and recent book, *X-Marks: Native*

Signatures of Assent, have mostly dealt with how American Indians articulate and enact sovereignty in their discourse. My work details a wide array of American Indian rhetorical devices and applies these in close readings of writings and speeches by a variety of intellectual forebearers. It also examines historical discourse events as holistically as possible in regard to the multimodal rhetorics—oral, written, material, visual, embodied, and kinesthetic—that contribute to meaning making. Most significantly, not only do I argue for a resurgence of American Indian rhetorics in English in the academy, but I also incorporate elements of those in the structuring of this book. However, though my focus differs significantly from both Powell's and Lyons's, there are points of correspondence, and I engage them both throughout.

An important collection to which Powell contributed also deserves note: non-Native scholar and editor Ernest Stromberg's 2006 *American Indian Rhetorics of Survivance: Word Medicine, Word Magic*. In that text, contributor Karen A. Redfield's division of "external rhetorics" (directed at a non-Indian audience) from "internal rhetorics" (directed at an Indian audience; 151) is a useful paradigm for thinking not only about contributions to this book but also about the field in general. Still, the work of most of the scholars who contributed to Stromberg's book contrasts with my approach in this present volume. They are "external" and, in Stromberg's words, "examine the ways in which Native rhetoricians appropriate the language, styles, and beliefs of their white audiences in order to establish a degree of consubstantiality," for "across languages, beliefs, and traditions, Native rhetoricians have had to find ways to make their voices heard and respected by a too frequently uninterested and even hostile audience" (6). Powell's essay in Stromberg's text builds on her scholarship on late nineteenth-century Paiute author, public speaker, and Native rights advocate Sarah Winnemucca Hopkins, showing how Hopkins utilized performativity as well as literacy to position herself as both "civilized" and "authentically Indian," allowing her to persuade a white audience and evoke empathy in regard to American Indian issues. While Powell, here and elsewhere, provides the earliest models for examining multimodality in American Indian rhetorics, a couple of other essays in the collection deal primarily with "internal" rhetorics and are more similar to my work: scholar and poet Janna Knittel's essay on Dakota/Anishinaabe American Indian Movement leader Leonard Peltier's *Prison Writings: My Life Is My Sun Dance*, which in part examines Peltier's culturally based tropes and his use of the structural elements of oral tradition;

non-Native rhetoric and writing scholar Holly L. Baumgartner's essay, which analyzes the code switching in the autobiography of Charles Eastman, a Dakota physician, author, and reformer of the late nineteenth and early twentieth centuries; and Redfield's essay, which scrutinizes rhetorical structures from orality in American Indian "radio and television stations, movies, and newspapers . . . all forms of contemporary Native communication that exemplif[y] 'internal rhetoric'" (157). Baumgartner's contribution is also similar to mine in its indebtedness to Bakhtin's ideas on heteroglossia. Finally, Anishinaabe scholar Richard Clark Eckert's "Wennebojo Meets a 'Real Indian'" provides one of the most notable models in the field for discussing American Indian rhetorics while *using* American Indian internal rhetorics throughout, employing culturally specific references as well as those familiar to an intertribal audience.

There are other recent contributions to the field among which I see my work situated: Chickasaw poet and scholar Phillip Carroll Morgan's *Riding Out the Storm: 19th Century Chickasaw Governors, Their Lives and Intellectual Legacy*; Abenaki scholar Lisa Brooks's *The Common Pot: The Recovery of Native Space in the Northeast (Indigenous Americas)*; and non-Native communications scholar Jason Edward Black's *American Indians and the Rhetoric of Removal and Allotment*. Those texts, like this one, center mostly on what are considered early American Indian English-language texts, those of the eighteenth and nineteenth centuries, with Brooks in the eighteenth, Morgan in the nineteenth, and Black, like me, focusing mostly on those two centuries while incorporating a small amount of twentieth- to twenty-first-century material. All of these texts function in interdisciplinary space—Morgan's in the interstices of literary and historical studies, Brooks's and Black's between rhetoric and history, and this book in the space between all three. In doing so, our work fosters sensitivity to the political and individual human impact of texts.

As Morgan and Brooks were two of my coauthors in the Native Critics Collective who spent several years corresponding with each other as we wrote *Reasoning Together*, most critics of American Indian literature likely will not be surprised that we share some common ground. Morgan's work is similar to mine in its Indigenous logical structure as he examines the lives of three nineteenth-century Chickasaw governors, William L. Byrd, Cyrus Harris, and Winchester Colbert, synthesizing what might seem to be diverse knowledges, making indirect arguments about the impact of history on their lives and their politics. Morgan also incorporates the conversational, colloquial, and personal alongside the academic in his book, affirming community discourse as valid in the academy in a way different from, but just as significant as, Craig Womack's inclusion of Creek dialect sections in *Red on Red.* Lisa Brooks focuses, as I do, on "recovery," as shared references in our titles suggest. Brooks also stresses the importance of understanding the recording of knowledge and story in visual and material media meant to accompany or parallel verbal accounts. Similarly, Brooks invokes Indigenous epistemologies, depicting reading and writing as kinesthetic and spiritual actions that can change reality, with meaning as dependent on the reader as on the writer. Brooks demonstrates an ever-present awareness of the relationships—familial, intertribal, and political—that undergird texts and inform their potential meanings. Unlike me, however, my former coauthors write from tribally specific perspectives of their people (Chickasaw and Abenaki), falling into the school of criticism most associated with *American Indian Literary Nationalism,* by Womack and two other leading Native literary scholars and theorists, Jace Weaver and Robert Warrior (Osage). Nationalism also frames much of *Reasoning Together,* as most readers familiar with that volume are aware. In both that book and this, I position myself in the only way I can, as an Intertribalist rather than a Nationalist, seeking commonality that *does not* sacrifice tribal specificity but takes into account relationships that exist across and outside tribal lines. Finally Jason Black, who has a large body of work on American Indian rhetorics, explores the notion of relatedness between Indians and non-Indians in political discourse; however, rather than doing this from the context of a history of Intertribal relatedness, he does so through the Euro-American lens of "paternalism." He sees "an almost hybrid rhetoric at work in the circuitry of Native-US parley," in which "Native voices reflected, but also contributed to, US public culture" (*American Indians* 4), rather than framing this discourse as stemming from an already existing Intertribal diplomatic rhetoric into which "the Great White Father" entered. Nevertheless, despite significant differences in perspective, Black's work most strongly resembles my own, in being most clearly situated in American Indian rhetorical studies and in its close rhetorical analysis.

Last, but certainly not least, I must mention the 2015 contributed volume *Survivance, Sovereignty, and Story: Teaching American Indian Rhetorics,* edited by American Indian rhetoric scholars Lisa King, Rose Gubele, and Joyce Rain Anderson. This book is the first of its kind, adding pedagogy to analysis of internal rhetorics and application of American Indian rhetorics in its praxis. The volume grew out of the work of the American Indian Caucus (AIC) at the annual Conference on College Composition and Communication (CCCC or "Four Cs"), begun by Powell and Lyons in 1997 and since led by Powell, Anderson, and Resa Crane Bizzaro, another significant American Indian rhetoric scholar. Since 2008 the caucus has held a pedagogical workshop each year, and this collection emerged from that ongoing sharing of "critical sources, pedagogical practices, teaching demonstrations, sample units and assignments, and other materials on indigenous rhetorics and writing" (locations 190–208). While *Survivance, Sovereignty, and Story* serves a different purpose, it nicely harmonizes with and supplements my work here and hopefully addresses the concern many of us in the field have had that despite examples of solid scholarship like those mentioned above, American Indian rhetorics have been mostly neglected in the classroom, hindering greatly their application in the academy.

Particularly neglected are American Indian rhetorics in the many varied forms that extend beyond the verbal to the visual, including petroglyphs and Mayan and Aztec codices; to the material, in forms such as wampum belts and quipu; and to the kinesthetic or embodied, in forms such as Plains Sign Language or smoking a pipe, all of which I address in further chapters. This lack of attention to diverse Indigenous means of persuasion in Native studies classrooms means that after nearly fifty years, our discipline still has not been able to postulate what a more decolonized intellectual discourse truly looks like—something American Indian and Indigenous scholars can claim culturally that would be accepted by both tribal communities and the academy. Our discipline is faced with what I perceive as an ethical problem. Mainstream scholarship arises from both a philosophy and a rhetoric that is completely antithetical to those of traditional American Indian cultures, at least when that scholarship utilizes linear, analytical reasoning that argues for a "right answer" by creating misleading dichotomies and discounting other kinds of reasoning. As neither the discipline of American Indian studies nor the academy as it is today would exist in North America without settler colonialism, those of us in the discipline ought to give something palpable and pragmatic back to American Indian and Indigenous peoples. To create tribal-centered scholarship that is both culturally acceptable and identifiably Indian to traditional communities, Native studies scholars have to subvert accepted modes of academic discourse structurally as well as hermeneutically. We need the rhetoric of the argument to be more

"Indigenous" if we want the end result to be more Indigenous, because a good rhetoric and its epistemology are inextricably tied.

While ultimately, to be truly decolonized, this scholarly discourse would have to be constructed as something entirely different and in Indigenous languages, there is an intertribal body of intellectual tradition that can be drawn on. Written in English by one of the foremost American Indian intellectuals, Simon J. Ortiz's essay "Towards a National Indian Literature: Cultural Authenticity in Nationalism," from which I quoted in the preface, is part of that tradition and also claims English discourse as valid cultural expression despite its intertribal nature. Intertribal intellectual discourse in English allows for empowerment through alliances just as other forms of intertribal discourse did in the past. These alliances advance our right, as various Indigenous people of the Americas, to express ourselves *as ourselves* in our scholarly discourse. Ortiz asserts, "There is not a question of [Indigenous] authenticity here. . . . [T]his response has been one of resistance [to colonialism]" (122). Scholarship that likewise is both on and in this tradition has burgeoned over the past few decades. Archival studies by scholars such as Daniel F. Littlefield Jr., James W. Parins, and Bernd C. Peyer laid the foundation for much of this work.[1] Pima scholar David Martínez's *The American Indian Intellectual Tradition: An Anthology of Writings from 1772 to 1972* puts forth a survey of the corpus that has become generally accepted in the field since the publication of Robert Warrior's *Tribal Secrets: Recovering American Indian Intellectual Traditions*, the most pivotal work in this growing area of study. Martínez's article "Neither Chief nor Medicine Man: The Historical Role of the 'Intellectual' in the American Indian Community" offers important insights into this tradition, one that Martínez (29) asserts is generally agreed to have begun with Samson Occom, the early eighteenth-century American Indian writer whose work I examine in the next chapter. American Indian and Indigenous scholars who write in and about the tradition I have described here are seen by Martínez as cross-cultural communicators often peripheral to tribal communities, though recognized as relatives, and peripheral to the academy as well ("Neither" 30).

Despite changes brought on by colonization—the very changes that have created the cultural context in which American Indian literature and other discourse written in English have evolved, changes that necessitate explication in mainstream scholarship—tribal cultures in North America, as diverse as they are, remain heavily oral. In fact, existence hinges spiritually and culturally on remaining "storied peoples." "Listening" is a very important influence on readings of texts, ideas, and reality. Traditional ways of "talking in a good way" utilize the same oral rhetorics and poetics that are still very much apparent in creative writing—I argue that they also can be useful for oral and written scholarly discourse in Native studies.

Mainstream academic discourse depends on linear argument—an argument that proceeds through a series of points, each of which is a small chunk of information, connected by the sort of logic for which verbal thinking is most conducive. This is not so much the case with American Indian discourse in the communities. This contrast is perhaps best illustrated by metaphor, one from Laguna Pueblo author Leslie Marmon Silko's widely taught and studied novel *Ceremony*: the spider web. Now this image is extraordinarily appropriate, in my opinion, to illustrate Native ontology and epistemology and not just because of Spider's role in the stories of many tribes. The spider web, the work of the Creator-Grandmother in Laguna Pueblo ontology, is what is real, both seen and unseen. All of this creation is one story, the story that we humans inhabit. We can affect this story through our words, thoughts, and actions. And, like a web, if one strand is affected, the whole is affected. If someone wants to communicate something about this reality to someone else, there are an infinite number of connections between the speaker and the listener—and the story is all of the rest of the web. The speaker, knowing this, must pick a strand to follow. And the listener must meet him or her at the point of connection. The meaning of the particular communication act is affected by much more than merely what is said. A listener accustomed to this form of discourse realizes that the whole intent is not conveyed simply by the words themselves. Sometimes what is left out, what is not told, is just as important as what is told, if not more so. This is quite different from communication theory, in which the speaker (subject) is at one corner of the triangle, the audience (object) at another, the particular aspect of reality being discussed at the third, and the text in the middle.

I have been an avid reader all of my life, the kid who spent afternoons perusing encyclopedias or consuming detective novels. Twenty years ago, *Ceremony* was the first Indian novel that I read. I was, at that point, a beginning graduate student, dedicating my life to the study of literature, and this book was the first one that made *this* much sense to me. It was perfect. It reflected the unity of all creation. It showed a sense of the sacred that was familiar to me. Yet I felt I had absolutely no language to describe my understanding of this novel. In mainstream academic discourse, narrow theses are easier to work out, but my understanding of this text was holistic. In fact, for those who think broadly or holistically, who see reality as an interwoven series of relationships in which everything is ultimately connected, thought is difficult to convey linearly. Thinking in smaller verbal chunks changes the way the brain schematizes information, the way it stores and retrieves it. Verbal thinking allows and encourages a thinker to move from point A to the related point B, and so forth and so on to Z—or whatever point is at the end of a line of thought—because the brain schematizes bits of information in relation to the ones it has already schematized. Very broadly speaking, the line of connection is known as "logic." But I would assert that because this definition addresses only one kind of thinking, it does not encompass every kind of "logical" thought, though it may be that other forms of logical thought seem "illogical" to those accustomed only to mainstream discourse. As Silko said in her presentation "Language and Literature from a Pueblo Indian Perspective":

> For those of you accustomed to a structure that moves from point A to point B to point C, this presentation may be somewhat difficult to follow because the structure of Pueblo expression resembles something like a spider's web—with many little threads radiating from a center, crisscrossing each other. As with the web, the structure will emerge as it is made, and you must simply listen and trust, as the Pueblo people do, that meaning will be made. (*Yellow Woman*, 48–49)

Now with mainstream academic arguments, associational leaps are forbidden. It is not permissible to jump from point A to point Q, for instance, the way a holistic thinker forced to explain an idea linearly tends to do. The thinker sees the connection, sees the whole picture. The problem is that the mainstream reader or listener, trying to duplicate the thinking of the holistic speaker or writer, can't see the connection. It's not that the holistic thinker is illogical; he or she simply uses a *different* sort of logic.[2]

The academy has allowed for nonlinear logic in American Indian oral narratives by dismissing them as "exotic" or "quaint" "folktales" rather than rhetorical expressions of how the world works. Understanding American Indian texts means including more than one form of logical process. Narrative is a dominant rhetorical mode in Indian Country, but it is not the only mode. Hence, this book offers needed study connecting American Indian rhetorics in intellectual discourse and in oratory in English, addressing structuring of academic discourse and enabling American Indian students as well as non-Indians to study Native ways of thinking and expression. In most, if not all, American Indian traditional cultures, argument does not proceed the way it does in the kind of academic discourse in which the rhetor leads the hearer/reader to a specific conclusion. In many Indigenous rhetorical traditions, meaning making is equally distributed. The hearer/reader must make active choices, and cultural knowledge is a distinct advantage in making those interpretive choices, particularly when argument is done by analogy, by putting pieces of discourse into association with the actual context, what I earlier called indirect discourse. As seen with the Choctaw example in the preface, sometimes Indigenous languages actually *require* one to contextualize and infer. Even when utilizing English, Native communities value the rights of the individual to make his or her own interpretive decisions.

Cherokee scholar Betty Booth Donohue's explanation of Choctaw interpretive strategies[3] demonstrates why American Indian rhetoric is needed to express understandings so much more fluid and tied to the thinker than in mainstream scholarship. Donohue observes that "well composed American Indian texts" are intended to provoke thought in readers and that skilled storytellers intentionally leave out portions of stories known to the audience to highlight them by their absence, forcing the listeners to "supply the missing parts of a narrative and comprehend the point of the work by means of his or her own intellectual efforts" (68). This form of rhetorical practice highlights communal meaning-making systems. This is why American Indian narratives have less concern with chronology and causality:

> Events transpire, and the hearer/reader must infer possible cause and effect, significance, and chronology if such categories are necessary for comprehending the meaning of a narrative. . . . [N]arrative assumes different meanings as the interpretive abilities of the hearer/reader change with age and experience[;] narrative, like the hearer/reader, stays in a constant state of interpretive motion. . . . All of this is not to say that there is no truth to a story; it is to say, however, that truth or meaning must be perceived by a Choctaw in his own time and in his own way. (Donohue 68)

Similarly, the concept of tribalography put forth by LeAnne Howe (Choctaw scholar and creative writer) theorizes the synthetic practice of American Indian writers who do not "tell strictly autobiographical stories, nor memoir, nor history, nor fiction, but rather they tell a kind of story that includes collaboration with the past and present and future. Hence the term tribalography" (Acoose, et al. 333). Howe says, "Tribalography comes from the Native propensity for bringing things together, for making consensus, and for symbiotically connecting one thing to another" (42).[4] This holds true for the structure of the present book. Each body chapter contains an analysis of texts by American Indians and settler colonials that incorporate aspects of American Indian rhetorics in English or in American Indian visual, material, kinesthetic, and embodied rhetorics that transcend phonetic language. I contextualize these texts with information through a lens of American Indian studies—American Indian literary criticism, theory, philosophy, history, law, and politics. I also include fragments of larger historical documents and speeches and even a bit of family history and autobiography. My eisegesis at the end of each chapter allows me to apply the conclusions I draw from the synthesis or alliance-making of this material in a pragmatic way to give back to and empower Indian peoples and communities. Just like real-life formal speeches in contemporary Indian Country, these eisegeses can be long, opinionated, and highly tangential—especially those in chapters 1 and 2. What Daniel Heath Justice (Cherokee scholar and novelist) says of his own work is true of mine as well (with slight paraphrasing): "For those who might wonder if this [book] is more concerned with 'cultural studies' than 'literary studies,' I acknowledge that considerations of the literary [and rhetorical] are here embedded in the larger conceptual matrix . . . rather than being the sole focus of analysis" ("Rhetorics of Recognition" 238). In all the eisegeses, however, I speak from the heart and hope you will draw your own conclusions rather than merely accepting what I say. After all, as traditional people often say in making a speech, "I'm nobody. I only know a little bit about these things, not much, but me, this is what I think. I could be wrong."[5]

In other words, I intend for readers to draw their own conclusions from the penumbras, or blank spaces, of the pages, as it were, in synthesizing the analysis and eisegesis of each chapter. That is, I intentionally utilize "American Indian indirect discourse" myself in this work, a rhetorical technique I discuss at length in chapter 1. The quotation by Cherokee scholar Christopher B.

Teuton that I use as an epigraph for this chapter can be seen as articulating an Indigenous hermeneutic that calls for readers to do this: "Each of us, in our spirits, is a council house . . . a place of memory where we gather our thoughts and the teachings of our elders to deliberate on how we should act, what we should believe" (22). For readers who are unaccustomed to such a reading practice, this can be an adjustment. They do not have the necessary literacy to process Indigenous texts in a culturally grounded fashion. For instance, non-Indian students often find traditional oral narratives challenging when they encounter them in books, not only because of their nonlinearity, but also because of their open-endedness and the artificiality of including such stories in books where context is absent, as mentioned by Womack in *Red on Red* (62, 95). In order to prepare you better for this as readers, I'll share with you a story about one of my grandmother's stories, how I saw her meet a challenge when using indirect discourse cross-culturally. I share this same story with my students to help them utilize this culturally specific hermeneutic practice in my classroom, where I most often teach by using story. There I am far more animated and give far more detail than I do here, mostly because I want my students to be affected by this particular story in more than one way. I hope you will be able to deduce some of this animation and detail for yourself by the end of this telling.

My grandmother—my "Mammy," whom I discuss a bit more in chapter 4—became a registered nurse during World War II. The only one of eight siblings to complete high school, she had received a nursing school scholarship from an anonymous benefactor. Having grown up in a single-parent household in the Great Depression, first in the Hill Country of Texas and then on the outskirts of Houston, she and her sisters regularly experienced discrimination from other children, taunted as "poor, dirty Choctaws from Oklahoma." I have been able to document the family only as far as Chicot County, Arkansas, prior to their moving to Texas, but that's a different part of the story from the part I'm telling here right now. Anyway, my Mammy said she didn't plan on being poor once she grew up, and there's a whole lot of side stories about the why of that as well, about the days on end that they did without food and about how the ideas of poverty and Indianness were conflated in her head as child, particularly when she went into foster care. The long and the short of it for the moment, however, is that my Mammy went to Houston and became a nurse, and she was a hard worker and an excellent nurse. By the time I was born, she was about to retire from her position as head nurse at Gulf Coast hospital in Baytown, Texas. After that, we moved to my grandfather's—you guessed it, my "Pappy's"—hometown of Rosebud, Texas, and she became head nurse at the Heritage House Nursing Home, a position she held long enough to retire from as well.

During her many years as a nursing supervisor, she often used indirect discourse to speak to nurses and nurse's aides she supervised whom she suspected were victims of domestic violence. She would never be rude enough to directly tell these women to leave their partners. Instead, without referencing the particular woman's situation, Mammy typically told a story from her childhood in which a young married woman in her community used a practice akin to that which had developed among Cherokees, according to some, for addressing the alcohol abuse and domestic violence that came with colonization. In early years, this involved punishing a man for drunkenness and unacceptable behavior by having his wife publicly beat him.[6] *By my Mammy's time, this had evolved into women sewing up husbands in tarps or sheets during their drunken blackouts, before beating them with broomsticks, as the particular woman in my grandmother's story did (and, coincidentally, as did country singer Willie Nelson's first wife, a young Cherokee woman named Martha Matthews, as he relates in "Yesterday's Outlaw," a 1980 interview in* People *magazine).*

However, sometimes when using indirect discourse and telling this story did not produce the desired responses, my grandmother would ask, "Now, do you understand what that story means?" On those occasions, she would reframe her own understanding of the story in a way that a bit more directly suggested that leaving an abusive husband safely was possible if a woman planned carefully. My grandmother would simply say, "Every man has to sleep sometime."

In my classroom, I sometimes similarly "scaffold" lessons from stories more for students when I see confused looks on their faces, "splicing" the thinking I am asking the students to do—to utilize pedagogical terminology here. In other words, if the students don't appear to understand, I give other pieces of information a bit at a time as necessary to help them make meaning for themselves. In this book, the conclusions following the eisegeses at the ends of chapters act as this scaffolding.

This book articulates American Indian intertribal rhetorics that emerge from American Indian discourse in English, both in print and orally, and from American Indian visual, material, kinesthetic, and embodied discourse.[7] I posit a scholarly rhetoric and critical praxis tied to traditional rhetorics and American Indian hermeneutics (that require different "literacies") for the discipline of Native American studies as a means of better facilitating intertribal discourse between tribal peoples and the academy. The book also suggests that visual rhetoric, very much alive in contemporary Native literary works such as Silko's *Almanac of the Dead,* can be incorporated into our scholarly praxis as we write *toward* Native communities as well as academia. Additionally, this book interrogates how intertribal Native rhetorics in English can be and have been used by settler colonial figures historically and contemporarily to their own political advantage, sometimes working to empower Indian people as well as themselves, sometimes persuading American Indian audiences to be complicit in their own disempowerment. These rhetorical structures are neither good nor bad; their value lies in their persuasive ability. Finally, this book challenges static notions of Indigenous identity as I examine speeches given at the entrance into Westphalian nation-state relations for the Cherokee Nation from three related Cherokee leaders—argued by some to be my own ancestors and relatives—and offer application for today. Despite competing paper trails, I choose to write *viewing and treating* these historical figures as relatives for the purpose of seeing what the application of kinship rhetoric yields to discussion based on rhetorical alliance making. Ultimately, as humans, we must all see our relatedness to each other and our ecosystem, as well as our mutual dependence on one another for our collective survival.[8]

Scholars should ask which methodologies and theoretical frameworks respect a community's input in interpretation of texts about them and take into consideration their intended audience. Native epistemologies are multimodal and include oral traditions, individual lived experience, signs in the world around us, and knowledge shared by other biological and spiritual entities in the form of vision and dream. Therefore, my methodology is multimodal and interdisciplinary, incorporating both social science approaches from other branches of Native American and Indigenous studies and literary and rhetorical approaches from the humanities. To ground my theory in Native realities, I read American Indian material culture and cultural practices, known throughout Indian Country as "ways," connecting with the work of Malea Powell and her former students, scholar-poets Rain P. C. Goméz and Qwo-Li Driskill. They have long contended that material objects in Native cultures are texts themselves, constructed and embellished not merely for aesthetic purposes but with the intent of carrying meaning that can change other aspects of the shared narrative we live.

Chapter 1, "'I Speak like a Fool, but I Am Constrained': Emancipating Samson Occom's Intellectual Offspring with American Indian Hermeneutics and Rhetorics," looks at the relationship of theory to American Indian communities and to the field of American Indian literary and cultural studies, which examines multiple genres of texts produced by these communities, despite the field's being artificially separated from communities and from other areas of American Indian and Indigenous studies. I posit both a hermeneutic and a scholarly rhetoric for this field more in line with community need, following the call of Indigenous scholars such as Linda Tuhiwai Smith (Maori) and Kimberly Blaeser (Anishinaabe). My praxis is grounded in rhetorical analysis of the work of our intellectual elder Samson Occom, studying his "A Short Narrative of My Life" and exploring how examples of such a rhetoric have already been used by American Indian and American Indian–descended[9] scholars like Thurman Lee Hester Jr. and Patricia Penn Hilden. The chapter concludes with my eisegesis that examines how such a practice can affect American Indian and Indigenous students and communities in the future.

Chapter 2, "Vision, Voice, and Intertribal Metanarrative: The Amerindian Visual-Rhetorical Tradition in Leslie Marmon Silko's *Almanac of the Dead*," briefly examines the history of visual communication and rhetoric in the Americas. In the visual/oral-aural/holistic cognitive model, visually encoded story usually accompanies the oral tradition. This practice can be observed throughout the Americas both in visual and material texts like codices, glyphs, quipu,[10] wampum, winter counts, and ledger book drawings and in kinesthetic rhetorics such as Plains Sign Language. This practice of pairing verbal and visual communication survives in ceremonies such as the opening of the Blackfoot Beaver Bundle mentioned above as well as in other ceremonial and social situations throughout Indigenous America. I synthesize my argument regarding American Indigenous visual rhetorics with an analysis of the intertribal visual element of the snake in Silko's revolutionary text *Almanac of the Dead*. The snake is painted in a mural that acts as the graphic version of story contained in the book, much as a codex works to communicate with the oral tradition. I conclude this chapter with an eisegesis that calls for a revolution of relatedness that we must achieve to save the earth and humanity from environmental destruction.

Chapter 3, "The 'Great Father's' Tongue Is Still 'Forked': The Fight for American Indian Resources and Red Rhetorical Strategies in Settler Colonial Politics," demonstrates that throughout history and up to the present day, settler colonial political leaders sometimes learned Indigenous languages or parts of languages and Native rhetorical structures as they attempted to persuade Native peoples. Former U.S. president George W. Bush is no exception to this history. Chapter 3 analyzes a few of Bush's speeches and proclamations to and about Native Americans, considering the historical context of presidential rhetoric in such speeches and unveiling the false promises he made, particularly in regard to sovereignty, American Indian education, economic development and the Energy Policy Act of 2005, and American Indians in military service. This chapter suggests that Bush's speeches and the stances of Native American politicians in regard to Bush's policies should have been questioned by Native American constituents within a framework of specific tribal philosophies rather than having been accepted at face value. Bush's smooth use of pseudo-traditional oratorical devices serves as a reminder to us as American Indian studies scholars that the value of Native rhetorics is in reaching Indian Country with valuable, pragmatic contributions from our scholarly work, not that *any* rhetorical strategy can be a bearer of intrinsic truth. The chapter closes with my eisegesis exploring the idea of sovereignty in the context of these speeches and in current American Indian scholarship. I argue that the road to true self-determination might be found only with serious revision in tribal-governmental structures—replacing the federally molded "cookie cutter" constitutions and their subsequent revisions with traditional forms of leadership—and in intertribal and international alliances in the tradition of precontact confederacies.

Chapter 4, "'That Little Savage Was Insolent to Me Today': Ada-gal'kala, Idle No More, and the Perennial Problem of 'Our Mad Young Men,'" investigates how visual and verbal rhetorics worked together with kinesthetic, embodied, and material rhetorics in Cherokee diplomacy in the eighteenth century, through studying discourse by Ada-gal'kala (Little Carpenter), Tsi'yugûnsi'ni (Dragging Canoe), and Inoli (Black Fox). In order to better situate them as rhetors, this chapter presents Intertribalism as a way to approach American Indian studies from a lens of relatedness. It views relatedness from a Cherokee center looking outward, in a model I call Cherokicity, in an attempt to transcend static notions of time and fixed identity and instead examine beings in interaction with other beings. The chapter then offers a reading of the kinship rhetoric used by Ada-gal'kala as well as in that used by the settler colonial figures around him. To a lesser extent, the chapter also looks at speeches by Tsi'yugûnsi'ni and Inoli, contextualizing Tsi'yugûnsi'ni's speech as rebellion against a culturally specific form of what Scott Lyons calls rhetorical imperialism ("Rhetorical Sovereignty") within the Cherokee Nation that relegated Tsi'yugûnsi'ni and Inoli to the position of "mad young men" whom some might see as having no real right to speak on behalf of their people according to Cherokee ways. The division among Cherokee people that began over the American Revolution ultimately resulted from differences in viewing relationships with outsiders and how those outsiders behaved in relation to Cherokee people, compounded by a disagreement over who had the right to speak for the people. Though some of the relationships formed with outsiders were problematic, I argue that the intertribal, cross-cultural relationships themselves were not intrinsically the problem. The failure was in the inability to persuade settler colonials to view the world from Native perspectives. For our collective survival as Indigenous peoples, we *must* teach outsiders to see the world through an Indigenous view of kinship, because only people with a lens of relatedness have the foresight and the heart to create a sustainable future. The chapter ends with my eisegesis discussing Idle No More, an international Indigenous movement that models the type of intertribal relatedness put forth in the chapter, and the two rhetorical strains that have emerged within the movement, focusing in on an intergenerational disagreement and "rhetorical imperialism" similar to that considered in the first portion of the chapter.

My ordering of the body chapters in this book is intentional, giving readers a bit of information at a time in order to make the larger picture clear at the end. I see the body chapters as incrementally building toward chapter 4, examining three different strands that later come together—chapter 1 focusing mostly on written and spoken discourse; chapter 2 focusing mostly on visual rhetorics; and chapter 3 traveling to the realm of political and diplomatic discourse, where, of course, the practices of these rhetorics has perhaps the greatest real-life impact on the greatest number of American Indian and other Indigenous people. Understanding each of these strands separately first is useful in comprehending how verbal and visual rhetorics worked alongside kinesthetic, embodied, and material rhetorics in the intertribal diplomatic discourse for which individuals within tribal cultures were traditionally trained, as mentioned in the preface and described further in chapter 4. Those who prefer a holistic and encompassing explanation may first turn to chapter 4 before chapter 1 if they wish.

This book argues for a future American Indian scholarly rhetoric that positions scholars—Native, Native-descended, and non-Native alike—within relationships to tribal communities, nations, and humanity and that offers real-world application for people of those communities and nations and for the world. Through acts of intertribal and intercultural communication, just like those utilized by tribal captives, leaders, and diplomats, I try to fulfill my duties to my relatives. That is what real Intertribalism calls me to do. This book makes an attempt at a paradigm shift in this vein, moving toward an understanding of reading and writing from perspectives that are more Indigenous and embracing a sense of relatedness, in hopes that an ignored portion of our intellectual inheritance as Americans might be better understood, valued, and utilized both to give back to American Indian people and to make the world a better place for everyone. Finding space in the academy for intertribal ways of writing and thinking is simply an intellectual counterpart for the political vocalism based on commonality found in Idle No More, staking a claim for a more Indigenous model in the grove of academia that might open up innovative ways of solving tomorrow's problems.

Scholars can be most effective as cross-cultural communicators only when we refuse to sacrifice our ways of thinking, our ways of speaking, when we stake ourselves to our epistemologies, ontologies, metaphysics, and rhetorical structures. No one can be a scholar without speaking. A person can speak only from the position he or she is in. Formal ways of traditional discourse, even if translated into English, can still serve Indigenous scholars well while also serving the academy. Indigenous people benefit most when we "speak in a good way," but it is only through fighting for our right to do so that non-Native audiences can understand a different way of viewing the world, a way I believe is key to our survival as humans in this Anthropocene era as much as it is to survival as culturally distinct peoples.

ONE

"I Speak like a Fool, but I Am Constrained"

Emancipating Samson Occom's Intellectual Offspring with American Indian Hermeneutics and Rhetorics

> When outsiders can read between every stitch of beadwork, every wrap of quillwork and every brushstroke, then our stories will be told.
>
> —*Dakota artist Del Iron Cloud on his philosophy of art*

In 1997, I was sitting on a panel at the Native American Symposium in Durant, Oklahoma, listening to one of the other presenters, Clifford Crane Bear (Blackfoot), then director of the Glenbow Museum in Calgary. He said some words that I keep returning to in my ongoing theorizing about American Indian literatures: "Theories are somebody's guess. Through our oral history, we were told never to use theories. We were told to use what we were taught. The first thing my grandfather taught me was that the Earth is our Mother. Respect her." In the intervening years, very little has changed in the academy or in Indian Country regarding theory. Academics, Native or not, have been pressured to "jump on the theory bandwagon," as retired University of Oklahoma Native literature professor and my longtime mentor Geary Hobson (Cherokee/Quapaw

A version of chapter 1 was previously published as "Samson Occom as Writing Instructor: The Search for an Intertribal Rhetoric," by Kimberly G. Roppolo, in *Reasoning Together: The Native Critics Collective* (Norman: University of Oklahoma Press, 2008).

A version of chapter 1 also previously appeared as "An Incipient Study of the Indian Half of the Dialogic: Native Rhetoric and Occom's Use of Indirect Discourse," in *"Stealing/Steeling the Spirit: American Indian Identities" and "Smoke Screens/Smoke Signals: Looking through Two Worlds": Proceedings of the Third and Fourth Native American Symposiums*, ed. Lucretia Scoufos, Mark Spencer, and Chad Litton (Durant: Southeastern Oklahoma State University, 2003–2004), 41–47.

descendant) puts it, and many of us have subsequently learned to appreciate, use, and subscribe to the work of non-Native theorists and thinkers—Bakhtin, Foucault, Freire, Bhabha, Said, and many, many more. Moreover, in that twenty-year period, an increasing number of American Indian and tribally descended scholars have authored and are still producing a significant body of theory and criticism.[1] If people were ever under the false impression that there was only one "Native perspective" on American Indian literatures, surely they have been disabused of this notion by now. Clearly, we have *multiple* Native perspectives about multiple Native ways of reading and writing about American Indian literatures, and traditionally speaking, making room for a multiplicity of voices and perspectives is a positive value in American Indian cultures. As Craig S. Womack (Creek/Cherokee) pointed out in *Red on Red: Native American Literary Separatism*, "There *is* such a thing as a Native perspective and . . . seeking it out is a worthwhile endeavor. . . . Native perspectives have to do with allowing Indian people to speak for themselves . . . with prioritizing Native voices" (4). The field of American Indian literary and cultural studies has come a long way in that regard.

But theory, typically framed in circumlocuting, obfuscating, philosophical discourse, tends to feel alienating to those outside the academy. Grassroots American Indians, who quite arguably feel a more vested relationship in the work of the discipline of American Indian studies than the general populace does in other areas of the academy, have a similar relationship to theory, or rather the *idea* of theory. While Crane Bear disavows the *idea* of theory, theories themselves are certainly implicit in languages, ways, artifacts, and stories, and moreover, a theory is implicit in his statement. Scholars outside the field of Native studies may see no problem with this disconnect between community and academy. While many academics view their work as separated from communities outside the "ivory tower" of the university, Native and Native-descended scholars, among them myself, have in recent years staked a claim in the academy for pragmatic approaches to our research that have application for Native peoples and communities. If we are to follow the call that Maori scholar Linda Tuhiwai Smith set forth in 1999 in her foundational text *Decolonizing Methodologies: Research and Indigenous Peoples*—by "'reporting back' to the people and 'sharing knowledge'" (15)—then we need to find theory that is appropriate for Native studies subjects from the perspectives of the Native peoples and communities for whom we attempt to be useful. As Anishinaabe critic Kimberly Blaeser suggested in "Native Literature: Seeking a Critical Center," we need

> a way to approach Native Literature from an Indigenous cultural context, a way to frame and enact a tribal-centered criticism . . . [to] seek . . . a critical voice which moves from the culturally-centered text outward toward the frontier of "border" studies, rather than an external critical voice which seeks to penetrate, appropriate, colonize, or conquer the cultural center, and thereby, change the stories or remake the literary meaning. (53)

Traditional literary criticism posits both the artist and the product as objects to be analyzed, rather than recognizing the artist as an agent negotiating meaning with an audience, placing the critic in the role of archeologist or anthropologist, a role that historically has led, in the opinion of many Indigenous people, to cultural imperialism and exploitation. This "anthropologism" happens when well-meaning critics explain cultural aspects of American Indian texts, attempting to catalog discrete chunks, fostering misrepresentation of the whole in the same manner as museum exhibits of artifacts, and leading to the same sense of transferred ownership: the artifacts now belong to the exhibitors, to the viewers, and the cultural "knowledge" now is the "intellectual property" of the critic.

Though a great deal of the cultural literacy necessary for outsiders to understand Native American texts has come from critics writing in the mainstream, and though the scholarship has been done with honorable intentions, the appropriation, the cutting away, the splaying necessary to mainstream modes of criticism, is offensive to many Native people. Hobson says, "The assumption seems to be that one's 'interest' in an Indian culture makes it okay for the invader to collect 'data' from Indian people when, in effect, this taking of the essentials of cultural lifeways, even if in the name of Truth or Scholarship or whatever, is as imperialistic as those simpler forms of theft, such as the theft of homeland by treaty" (Hobson et al. 101). A good number of non-Indian scholars who have been part of the American Indian literary critical community for years have begun to see themselves as allies, acknowledging and adopting Native-centered theoretical approaches as they have recognized the validity of their colleagues' frustrations. Senior scholar David Payne's description of his experiences with American Indian literatures is a good example:

> Like most scholars old enough to worry about their cholesterol, I was taught to believe that good criticism spoke with the anonymous voice of a master rationalist, a sort of also-ran scientist, who dissected literary works like dead cats fresh out of the formaldehyde. I have since not only learned more ways to skin a cat, but to develop enough respect for cats to leave them fuzzy and contrary. I like them living in disdain of me (like stories) far more than splayed out on a lab table (like texts). And no matter how sharp a critic may hone in on a work/writer/movement, I now believe he's always telling me a personal story, not a universal narrative aimed at decoding a text. (85)

These comments, though, demonstrate that our issues with mainstream approaches are as much methodological as they are theoretical.

Some readers might argue that these distinctions apply only to the works of the New Critics. However, as I do not see either myself or the scholars upon whose work I build in this section—Kimberly Blaeser, David Payne, and Geary Hobson—as intending our critiques to be that narrow. Other theoretical approaches such as those of feminist, Marxist, and poststructuralist critics also have limitations in regard to Native studies. My discussions of Bakhtin later in this chapter, of Marxism's limitations regarding *Almanac of the Dead* in chapter 2, and of semiotics in chapter 4 demonstrate these limitations. Other readers might find my approach of incorporating eisegesis similar to reader-response theory. My discussion of the work of Graton Rancheria tribal chairman, scholar, and creative writer Greg Sarris later in this chapter explains what I see as the differences between reader-response approaches and eisegesis, in that Indigenous hermeneutics are grounded not merely in the individual experience but also in tribally specific and intertribal collective cultures, and their specific signifier sets and interpretive practices as tribal cultures can and have rejected individual interpretations—not all "readings" are accepted as "valid" in the way that they are in reader-response. While this admits a sort of "tribal hermeneutical imperialism" akin to Scott Lyons's "rhetorical imperialism" that I explore in chapter 4, a practice that occurs in culturally specific situations as well as extratribally, it also ultimately relates to this chapter's discussion of intellectual sovereignty and the United Nations Declaration on the Rights of Indigenous People as well.

As a body of scholars, we have not taken the time to consider that multiple generations of cultural practices not only are informed by the philosophical bases upon which theory is grounded but also perhaps give rise to different reading praxis, to a hermeneutic methodology that can differ from the mainstream and relies on other literacies. Though we have written and published much American Indigenous–authored literary theory and criticism, no one has articulated a more Indigenous hermeneutic or a corresponding way in which the readings offered by such a practice could be explained in writing. For that reason, before proceeding any further, I would like to posit such a philosophy of hermeneutics, a theory of reading and interpreting "texts" that is more in line with traditional American Indian teachings, without arguing that this is the *only* way American Indian readers make meaning from stories, texts, signs, and objects. My reasoning is twofold: (1) the separation between how we interpret meaning and how we encode meaning is artificially imposed, for the two are intrinsically tied in a meaning-making system; and (2) examining both hermeneutics and rhetoric is profitable for American Indian and Indigenous studies as a whole in validating models grounded in culture that serve not only American Indian and Indigenous scholars and students but also non-Natives. As scholar Donald Fixico (Shawnee, Sac and Fox, Muscogee Creek and Seminole) suggests in *The American Indian Mind in a Linear World: American Indian Studies and Traditional Knowledge*, teaching alternative models of thought opens up worlds of new ideas in the academy and beyond. This chapter, therefore, posits both a hermeneutic and a scholarly rhetoric for American Indian studies; examines how examples of such a rhetoric have already been used to some extent by American Indian and American Indian–descended scholars; grounds my theorizing in a rhetorical analysis of the work of one of our intellectual elders, Samson Occom; and concludes with my eisegesis that explores how such intellectual work can affect our greatest natural resource as American Indian and American Indian–descended peoples, our future generations.

Reading Red: American Indian Performative Hermeneutics[2]

An American Indian–based hermeneutic has to address several elements, all of which are intertwined. The relationships between text, reader, author, and "reality," which directly bear on the function of story—and thus literature—in American Indian cultures and what this implies about reading and purpose, must be articulated. The manner in which those relationships affect the way the reader makes meaning out of the text and how this way of reading is complicated by its contradictions with the needs of mainstream academic discourse about culture and cultural production must be explored. Finally, conclusions about this hypothetical American Indian hermeneutic and the ideas examined in this volume regarding American Indian rhetorics in English and postulate a scholarly rhetoric will need to be drawn together. This scholarly rhetoric must validate the ways traditional American Indian students discuss and write about American Indian literatures in college and university classrooms. It also must be helpful to critics of American Indian literatures who wish to create literary criticism that is acceptable and understandable to the grassroots American Indian people to whom this body of literature belongs, as well as be helpful to scholars whose work engages other aspects of American Indian and Indigenous studies.

An exploration of the relationships between text, reader, author, and "reality," I think, must begin with the distinct idea of the power of words in American Indian cultures. Unlike in speculative fiction, in which words can change reality by changing the way the reader perceives it, in Indigenous worldviews, words actually change reality. Unlike in structuralist and poststructuralist thought, words are not merely signifiers; they are *inherently* performative, *always* enacting meaning. Renowned Kiowa author N. Scott Momaday says:

> At the heart of the American Indian oral tradition is a deep and unconditional belief in the efficacy of language. Words are intrinsically powerful. They are magical. By means of words can one bring about physical change in the universe. By means of words can one quiet the raging weather, bring forth the harvest, ward off evil, rid the body of sickness and pain, subdue an enemy, capture the heart of a lover, live in the proper way, and venture beyond death. (15–16)

Because of this power, the role of the American Indian or Indigenous author—or storyteller or filmmaker or visual or performing artist—is quite different from the role of the mainstream author. S'Klallam poet Duane Niatum says:

> As a tribal poet, the word is a sacred object. . . . [T]he words are the carriers of the culture from past generations to the present, and on into the future. The values of the tribe are fused into the songs and stories. . . .

> [T]he word, if used respectfully, is invested with power and magic. . . . [Narrators] are merely the vocal reeds for the expression of their people, and . . . a higher power than themselves gave them the gift to give back to the people something they had lost long ago on the road we are forever following into the next century. (65–66)

These qualities of words are part of the reason why Namšem always taught me that, as "Indians,"[3] we try to say things "in a good way." Words and symbols have power. When we put them out into the universe, they have an effect. We have to be careful of the words we use because good and bad creative energies can be sent into the universe.

The author participates in the sacred act of creation, but this is not an exclusive role. As my late mentor Lee Francis III taught me, "Creator gave all of us a piece of the story. It is our responsibility to give it back." Vine Deloria says, "We are, in the truest sense possible, creators or co-creators with the higher powers, and what we do has immediate importance for the rest of the universe. . . . [T]he responsibility is always there for [all entities] to participate in the continuing creation of reality" (*Spirit* 47). Reality, then, is an ongoing metanarrative, one story that encompasses all story, in which all things are connected. This paradigm is evident in American Indian writings, such as *Almanac of the Dead* (see chapter 2), as well as in American Indian reality, showcased by the more radical rhetorical strand of the Indigenous activist movement Idle No More (see chapter 4).

I would suggest that this sort of thinking, which is far more holistic than discrete and linear, places those of us with this eschatology in a unique interpretative situation. On one hand, we are "listening" to the words of an author actively changing reality. On the other, we are co-creators, participants in change, synthesizing this "new" information with our previous knowledge/experience. In other words, we are actors in "ceremony," something Leslie Marmon Silko hit on very early with her first novel, *Ceremony,* which is still widely regarded as one of the most important American Indian novels. Deloria says the purpose of ceremony is "to make whole again what has now become disassociated and chaotic" (*Spirit* 55). In Cherokee terms, it is to restore *duyukta,* to put entities, including the self as a reader, in the proper place. Qwo-Li Driskill has already posited duyukta, or ᏚᏳᎪᏛ, as a part of a Cherokee methodology (*Yelesalehe* 28–29), but an explanation of this concept helps, I believe, to show why it would be applicable to an American Indian–based hermeneutic. Many American Indian languages have equivalent words. Laguna Pueblo scholar Paula Gunn Allen says, "Right relationship, or right kinship, is fundamental to American Indian aesthetics. Right relationship is dictated by custom within a given tribe or cultural grouping, but everywhere it is characterized by considerations of proportion, harmony, balance, and communality" (*Spider Woman's Granddaughters* 9). Seeing reading as evoking change in the reader and in reality, in the way ceremony evokes change in the participant and in reality, as all are interconnected, would certainly be in line with traditional beliefs regarding the role of story as delineated by Allen as well: "Stories . . . make pertinent points to some listener who is about to make a mistake or who has some difficulty to resolve, and hold the listeners' attention so that they can experience a sense of belonging to a sturdy and strong tradition" (*Spider Woman's Granddaughters* 1). We interpret as much, if not more, by *eisegesis*, through synthesizing story with what we already know and have experienced, than we do by analysis, or *exegesis*. As demonstrated above, pure analysis appears clinical and offensive in Indian Country. In fact, the epistemic function of narrative in American Indian cultures is *supposed* to lead to eisegesis. We should each derive a personal truth or truths when we are told a story, and we have the *right* as sovereign *individuals* to the validity of our personal truth.

So how does all of this affect our epistemology, the ways in which we learn from a text? For one, readers such as those quoted above are clearly holistic thinkers. Deloria quotes an old Crow chief who explains the difference between Indians and whites this way: "The white man has ideas, the Indian has visions." Commenting on this, Deloria asserts that "the true anarchism is the chaos of ideas that must compete against each other without having a context in which relationships can be established between them" (*Spirit* 15–16). "Ideas" are discrete—"visions" are holistic, encompassing many ideas and their relationships to each other, always part of an ontological context of infinity, the web of being. Narrative, present in all cultures, gains primacy as a rhetorical mode and functions not just as an analogue to, but also as a metaphor for, the listener's/reader's reality. And because American Indian epistemologies are open and polycentric, not closed as those of Western culture are, metaphor is fluid.[4] And because of this fluidity, syncretism–the phenomenon among all peoples in which metaphor becomes cultural currency–becomes a key means of both physical and spiritual survival.

We are co-creators and beings, creators of narrative and performers and interpreters of that narrative; the hermeneutic is polyreflexive both because of the epistemological base and because of the polyvocal nature of Native storytelling and communally made meaning in the oral traditions that have been living and growing for tens of thousands of years. Even today, despite urbanization and diaspora, gossip on what American Indians call the "moccasin telegraph" works in this way. Story is told and retold by communities until it assumes form and substance that fit within the body of tribal story and makes meaning of experience through the ontological and metaphysical lenses of the community, until it is embedded with, until it embodies, the values and ways of the community. This community protostory of each narrative is balanced by being told by individual tellers, allowing for individual variation as long as tribal Truth with a capital *T* is still told by the story. In novelist and scholar Thomas King's *Medicine River*, it is this aspect of Blackfoot culture that allows a woman to save her late husband's dignity by writing a fake suicide note that ennobles him in the eyes of the community as the warrior he could have been without their paracolonial reality. She reimagines him in story as having saved her from himself through his actions, instead of letting him be damned as a Christian and immortalized as a failure for his weaknesses.

In American Indigenous metaphysics, the immaterial is balanced with the material, and both are perfectly "seeable." Native people seek knowledge by "vision." But we also seek knowledge by "story," which in fact can change the material and the immaterial. The intertwining of these two concepts—vision and story—are reflected, even if indirectly, in the mission statement of Wordcraft Circle of Native Writers and Storytellers: "The Wordcraft Circle vision is to ensure that the voices of Native writers and storytellers—past, present, and future—are heard throughout the world" (Francis). Though the particular use of the word "vision" here means "what we'd like to see ourselves as in the future," the emphasis here is on vision and voice—not on text. American Indian writers are American Indian storytellers, putting words to what is seen in the mind's eye, what is envisioned in the spirit.

There is story ascribed to all that we see around us. As scholar Paul Beekman Taylor says, "Everything from stone and tree to eagle, coyote, and man contains story of its generic bond with all other created things. . . . The release of story from artifact is a hermeneutic act" (39). I'd also assert that sacred objects and the bones of ancestors—those things protected by the Native American Graves and Repatriation Act (NAGPRA)[5]—are all elements that likewise add to the story we inhabit; they act as images in the associational making of greater metaphysical meaning. In Indigenous worldviews, these objects and remains are protected both for spiritual reasons and out of respect—they are integral to our identities as peoples, to our being storied as peoples. For instance, the central concept of Cherokee thought mentioned above—duyukta, or balance—is represented in the Belt That Would Not Burn, a wampum belt with a man and a woman on one end (representing the Cherokee people); a beaded white path of life for them to follow (representing duyukta, or peace); a black strip of beads on either side of the white (representing the multiplicity of inharmonious actions that can cause the people to stray off the path); and a checkerboard of squares at the other end (representing the rewards of right living that come after death). The ideal place to be is in the middle, to be centered in one's ontology, so that one lives in the awareness of one's connection to all being, to the material, all a part of the Mother Earth and the Creator Spirit, both known by various names throughout American Indian cultures. Each human is (in) formed by his or her connections, connections that are both biological and spiritual in nature. I carry my ancestor's bones in my body and their beliefs in my blood. My ancestors dreamed me into being, and all beings are my relations. We are all agents negotiating the Story.

This concept of balance is not exclusive to Cherokees by any means, as I suggested earlier. Nor is it particular to that specific artifact. Across North America again and again, philosophies of living were held and/or recorded, not in texts, but in object, place, ceremonial space, and image. Many, if not all, tribes have or had a central sacred object, objects, or medicine bundles, and many, if not all, attach philosophical and theological significance to a sacred place, places, or space through story and ceremony. Meaning is encoded, inscribed, and ascribed throughout the Indigenous universe. In her theory of tribalography, LeAnne Howe incorporates the layered meaning of being in place as a people over the course of what Europeans call time. Internationally recognized and highly respected Kainai lawyer, philosopher, educator, and elder Leroy Little Bear asserts in his oral teachings that places and spaces hold readable or discernible meanings from which we can learn. And though Europeans prejudged America's First Peoples as inferior thinkers based on our lack of phonetic texts, I would assert that this lack was not due to any inadequacies in our ancestors' thinking capacities. The complexity of American Indigenous cultures itself belies that. Rather, Amerindian thought, being holistic, both visual and verbal, is more fully recorded through nonphonetic transcription in conjunction with the oral. The hermeneutic act Taylor refers to—storying the world around us—is continued in the creation of objects that reflect the same principles of balance found in nature, objects that in turn are storied, inscribed with and ascribed meaning. In our oral heritages and in our written literatures, the structuring of meaning evolves out of the same hermeneutic tradition. Not only are image and metaphor invested with much greater importance in the mind of the holistic thinker, but all elements of the story must be placed into a larger mental picture, so to speak, in order for meaning to be made. As with petroglyphs, meaning is in between, in the gaps of the story, as much as in what is explicitly written, if not more so.

That complicates things when we are forced to explain holistic, interrelated ideas concerning a text—our readings—in a linear fashion, especially when we are conscripted into service by the "publish or perish" culture of the academy. Deloria, speaking of Plains Indians in this case, describes holistic thinking:

> [They] arranged their knowledge in a circular format—which is to say, there were no ultimate terms or constituents of their universe, only sets of relationships that sought to describe phenomena. No concept could stand alone in the way that time, space, and matter once stood as absolute entities in Western science. All concepts not only had content but were themselves composed of the elements of other ideas to which they were related. Thus it was possible to begin with one idea, thoroughly examine it by relating it to other concepts, and arrive back at the starting point with the assurance that a person could properly interpret what constituted the idea. . . . The purpose of such an arrangement was to be certain that all known aspects of something would be included in the information that people possessed and considered when making decisions and reaching conclusions. (48)

I suggest that this kind of thinking is *still* what many American Indigenous people do when reading: synthesizing rather analyzing. And, in my mind, there is no reason—other than Eurocentric notions of the superiority of one way of thinking over all others—why it shouldn't be what scholars do when we argue in the academy. Traditional American Indian readings are constructed in the mind from synthesis. Forcing circular ideas into an entirely linear format *changes* readings, *changes* the meaning of the stories. It treats the story and the author as objects rather than subjects. It treats the story as a lifeless thing, worse than a dead thing—not as a living entity. And it makes us, as Indigenous scholars, into subalterns.

It is changing our children too, as I think the contrast in a couple of examples can show. Duane Big Eagle, who has developed pedagogical materials for teachers in California school systems, explains "Indian" problem solving this way:

> All peoples have developed many different ways of "knowing" about our world. In Western culture "analysis," taking something apart to know about it, is most prevalent. Traditionally-raised Native children may be more comfortable with "synthesis," or putting together bits of information to know about something. As an Elder once said, "We wouldn't be likely to take a drum apart to know where its sound comes from. We might knock against a hollow log and tap a hide stretched out for drying, then put those two bits of information together to know where sound comes from in a drum."

While change is not necessarily a bad thing, change that is too rapid, like the changes wrought by the onslaught of colonization in the Americas, can be destructive. In order for us to survive as culturally distinct peoples, we cannot tolerate changes to our children that completely sacrifice *who* we are, and it would be a loss to the intellectual diversity of the world if we did so.

"Talking Indian" and "Red Rhetorics" in Academic Discourse

How can we as critics of Native literature, film, or art engage in reciprocal relationships with Native communities and people? How can we give back unless we adopt a new scholarly rhetoric based on good ways of speaking in our communities so that our message is respectful and clear and can lead to actual healing and positive change? Furthermore, how can we model different ways of writing in the academy for those in other areas of American Indian and Indigenous studies? Our current ways of writing in the academy do not translate well. One of scholar Jeff Berglund's American Indian female students had this to say in the "second hour of the first day" of the National Endowment for the Humanities Summer Institute in 2001, after she had scanned "the packet of secondary articles, all authored by Native scholars and public intellectuals": "None of these writers seem Indian to me. Look how they write. This is not how Indian people talk" (81). Even those of us who are American Indian or American Indian–descended have not been fulfilling what Linda Tuhiwai Smith calls for when she asserts that the final results of studies, including research design, . . . should be "disseminated back to the people in culturally appropriate ways and in a language that can be understood" (15).

Although language revitalization programs have had a substantial amount of success throughout Indian Country, English is still our lingua franca. Nevertheless, as Craig Womack asks in his chapter in *Reasoning Together*, "might English *be* one of our Indian languages?" (Acoose et al. 404). I think the Creek dialect sections of his *Red on Red* in particular show that we have, as he suggests there, colonized English as much as it has colonized us. Considering *how* language is used to convey meaning is just as important in analyzing our English texts as considering *how* language functions in ceremonial ways is in understanding Indigenous beliefs in the efficacy of tribal languages to change reality. Award-winning writer Anna Lee Walters (Pawnee, Otoe-Missouria) says in *Talking Indian: Reflections on Survival and Writing*:

> It's for the old stories and songs that you grieve . . . That's what you want and need. . . . You came all the way back here for a story. You came all the way back here to hear someone, anyone, talking Indian, didn't you? . . . For what you are searching is right here. . . . This will give you life. . . . It is important and curious to remember that everything we two-leggeds know about being human, we learned from the four-leggeds, the animals and the birds, and everything else in the universe. . . . Everything we are was taught us, you see? This is what the stories are, the teachings of who we are. . . . That's why we need the stories. Without them we grieve. For ourselves, for direction, for meaning. . . . Now I sit here, sixty years later, telling you the exact same thing my old folks told me as a teenager. The only thing that's different is I'm talking a foreign language, one forced on us, but nevertheless, I'm still talking Indian. (30–41)

In our home communities or in urban areas where Indian Country can suddenly manifest itself when two or more of us are together, even in English some of us still "talk Indian." In my classrooms, my use of English has varied depending on the demographic composition of the class. In fact, my English varies throughout my daily life depending on whom I am with in the community. If I went to the towns of Watonga or Apache in Oklahoma, to either reserve outside of Lethbridge, Alberta (where I taught for four years), or *anywhere* in the heart of Indian Country and spoke in standard academic discourse, people *would* understand what I was saying, but they *wouldn't* understand *me*. In other words, non-Native use of English—and I mean that in a different way from English as a Second Language—would mark me as someone who doesn't know how to communicate in the community properly and doesn't want to learn—in other words, someone no one would listen to. Certainly, using Standard English in a Native American Church setting, where I might have the right to speak, implies a false sense of the speaker's own superiority. William L. Leap, in *American Indian English*, says that the choice to use what I term "Red English" is grounded in questions of "speaker identity and presentation of 'self.'" Moreover, Leap adds:

> At [some] sites, Indian English is the only *Indian*-related language tradition that community members have maintained or the only such tradition that older community members have been willing to transmit to the younger generation. When this is the case, Indian English fluency becomes a highly valued social skill, and the nonstandard features of the Indian English conversation have an even greater cultural significance for their speakers. (3)

Socially acceptable communication in American Indian culture had and has both tribally specific and intertribally common guidelines. Emerson College visual and media arts professor Thomas Cooper, who has written an entire volume on Native communication ethics, says, "Native Peoples had innumerable unique laws, rules, customs, and ethical practices that distinguished their communication from that of the European explorers" (79). For many, if not most, traditional cultures, these have included rules that limit free speech or that dictate who has the right to talk and when. For instance, Cooper says that the Shuswap tribe traditionally "believed free speech was somewhat modified by age, gender, and position" and that "chiefs, elders, and other authorities had the most freedom of expression" (134). Cooper also suggests that traditional Navajo communication has had many rules regarding who can speak and when (157), even down to a specific communication "pecking order" for the multiple wives a medicine man might have (152). The Nahuatl words for "speaker," "leader," "language," and "uncle" are all related, showing an etymological connection between concepts of who has the right to speak on behalf of the people that were manifest in early contact interactions. Even today there are ways and protocols within many American Indian cultures of either earning or owning the right to speak on certain subjects, in certain company, or at certain moments. For the Cheyenne, for instance, even aspiring powwow emcees have to "give away" at a specific time during the ceremonial year and earn the right to be a "town crier" in traditional ceremonies before speaking for people at powwow giveaways. This process has the prerequisites of being male and belonging to one of the traditional warrior societies, according to Eugene Blackbear Jr. Rarely have I traditionally had the "right to speak" to and for the people—I have had the right to speak in the morning when bringing in water in Native American Church ceremonies or at other times if I have "put up" the meeting. Similarly complex restrictions in different cultural contexts on the right to speak exist in many tribes. Chapter 4 addresses one of these, specifically in reference to Cherokee culture, and theorizes about such protocols as a sort of rhetorical imperialism, to use Scott Lyons's term, that actually works to protect tribal interests in a positive way. We should also, however, consider the implications for ourselves as academics. One of the dangers of a tribally specific approach to American Indian and Indigenous studies in terms of our own methodology is that if we are truly being "traditional" according to specific tribal rhetorical traditions, we may in effect point out our own lack of a right to speak. If we really wish to become "traditional" in our theorizing, we might write ourselves out of our right to say anything at all.

Our right, if any, is a responsibility to the people whom our writing is about. If academics expect writing in American Indian studies to be useful to this most significant constituency, then respecting Indian viewpoints about how discourse is pleasingly structured and politely conducted is important. While some scholars might perceive my assertion here as essentialist—the assertion that there *are* still viewpoints about discourse that could be considered "Indian"—my lived experience in Indian Country belies this. . . . And I am not alone. Womack also argues that suggesting Native viewpoints exist despite colonialism is not essentialist; rather, these "radical Native viewpoints . . . are called for to disrupt the powers of the literary status quo as well as the powers of the state—[because] there is a link between thought and activism" (5). Métis scholar and activist Howard Adams points out, "The state, rather than Indians, controls 'the mental means of production'" (qtd. in Womack 5). With this view in mind, Womack proceeds with a Creek literary analysis of Creek and Cherokee writing, with a tribal, in contrast to an intertribal, perspective. Womack structures his text by weaving narratives written in Creek dialect in between his chapters of literary analysis written in mainstream discourse mode—narratives that communicate, or are intended to communicate, the same point to a Creek audience that the chapters do to an academic audience. Although this discourse is "Creek English," I would imagine it is understandable by and profitable for a non-Creek audience to varying degrees. I have to say "imagine" here because I cannot know how much my familiarity with Creek discourse from community interactions informs my own reading. While I have no problem at all following Womack's dialect sections and find them much richer than mainstream academic writing, I am not sure how an audience unfamiliar with this dialect responds.

But I do feel that most potential readers can get at least the gist of the dialect sections and that this supports my notion that an even more intertribal mode of discourse might be developed for academic writing and speaking, by drawing on Rain P. C. Goméz's "Red Rhetorics" and communicating to a dual audience of Native and non-Native scholars, as well as to the general Native American community made up of people of various tribal origins. Similarly, as I demonstrate later in this chapter, Indian people have long structured discourse to a culturally mixed audience in this way. I see no reason why the same would not work for the audience I have in mind here. Both Choctaw scholar Thurman Lee Hester Jr.'s "*Pishukchi*: One Choctaw's Examination of the Differences in English and Choctaw Language Use" and mixed-blood scholar Patricia Penn Hilden's "Ritchie Valens Is Dead: *E Pluribus Unum*" are examples of works by American Indian and American Indian–descended scholars already written in such a manner. I would argue that this discourse not only can be understood by but also can be *constructed* by non-Native scholars who choose to become culturally literate in their field of specialty. Doing so would reduce the cultural barriers between the halls of academe and the communities and people on whom this body of work centers, making American Indian studies more profitable in every way for everyone involved.

Resolving "Oratorical Complications": An American Indian Studies Scholarly Rhetoric

Late nineteenth- and early twentieth-century traditional Lakota chief and author Luther Standing Bear says in *Land of the Spotted Eagle*, "Oratory receives . . . little . . . understanding on the part of the white public, owing to the fact that oratorical complications include those of Indian orators" (256). In delineating a scholarly rhetoric for American Indian studies, I hope to resolve such cross-cultural communication barriers. Further analyzing the term "rhetoric," an organized system of language whose primary function is to convey an idea or an argument, would be useful in making my explanation clearer. An intertribal scholarly rhetoric that utilizes the English language and crosses cultural borders—tribal ones and those that divide Native cultures from the mainstream, as well as those that divide academy from the larger U.S. society—falls into what communications scholar Colleen Burke calls a rhetorical borderland. In her definition, Burke incorporates prominent literary and cultural studies scholar Richard Ohmann's five patterns of classical rhetorics: "a way to persuade an audience to believe or to act in a certain way"; "the truth at which an author or spokesperson believes he or she has arrived and wants to convey to an audience"; "a vehicle that absorbs truth and abandons subterfuge"; "an avenue that embodies an author or spokesperson's character, voice, and style"; and "discourse that reflects a worldview" (qtd. in C. Burke). By contrast, I see a rhetorical borderland as a liminal zone where things are much murkier because of the lack of heterogeneity, because of a lack of shared beliefs, values, and assumptions, because of the lack of communal interests or goals, because of a lack of trust. Burke claims that in these borderlands, "depending on what the author or spokesperson wants to achieve, rhetoric can create a sense of well-being, incite an audience to action, propagate fear, engender trust, or . . . present a semblance of the truth." Working in this liminal area, we need to be cautious about creating the kind of fear that caused reactionary stances over the years in some non-Native critics, the kind that have given rise to charges of "essentialism." But we also need to keep in mind that this liminal area can be a zone of change, a space in which fuller readings of Native literature can develop, created by both Native and non-Native critics, and a space within which the kind of positive and productive interaction between Native and non-Native scholars and tribal communities that is needed in the field of American Indian studies can exist.

Though there are similarities, there is also a great deal of difference between Native American and mainstream arguments. In addition to differences in logos that arise from the inclusion of the kind of synthetic reasoning described earlier in this chapter and in the preface to this volume, there is a difference in the appeals to ethos. In Native culture, experience in general—whether derived from experiences of the culture encoded in story, those of an authoritative elder, or those of an individual who shares the same cultural values—is held as evidence. In fact, this is precisely what invests a person with "authority" in Native cultures: experience that leads to maturity. Deloria asserts that "maturity, in the American Indian context, is the ultimate goal of all human existence[,] . . . the ability to reflect on the ordinary things of life and discover both their real meaning and the proper way to understand them when they appear in our lives. . . . Maturity is a reflective situation that suggests a lifetime of experiences" (*Spirit* 13–14).

American Indian rhetorics also have differences in purpose. As I suggested above, American Indian oratory, when addressed to a culturally mixed audience, has carried messages intended for Indians and others intended for both them and those outside the culture. The messages intended for Indians carry the same purpose as narrative in Native cultures, to bring the people back into the circle, back into balance. The oratory, in other words, carries the intention of "homing" that literary critic William Bevis has noted in Native American novels, to give just one of many examples of the overlap between American Indian rhetorics and poetics. The messages intended for both those inside and outside the culture are intended to *do* something for the people, whether this is to obtain a boon, to negotiate terms of an agreement between cultures, or simply to express how some cross-cultural interaction has affected the people. In instances of extratribal communication, these messages are examples of American Indian and Indigenous history scholar Margaret Connell Szasz's "culture brokering," texts coming from someone serving as a cultural go-between. While I do not want to relegate those of us who are American Indian or American Indian–descended scholars to the role of the mixed-blood in the 1950 film *A Man Called Horse*—"I've got a lot to learn, and you, Metis, you are going to teach me"—it is one of the roles we do fall into by nature of our association with the academy. Perhaps more importantly, it is a relationship obligation within a "network of writing Indians," if we see ourselves working in much the same way that Lisa Brooks sees the Indian writing community of Occom, Brant, Aupaumut, and others in *Reasoning Together* (Acoose et al. 254).

There are also many other differences in these rhetorics, not the least of which is the valuing of paradox in the argument, as opposed to the need to resolve it definitively. Confusion *can be* a positive value; it is the nexus of growth, as it makes people think for themselves. Duane Big Eagle puts it this way: "Many American Indian people have a greater acceptance of paradox than is common in many European and Western cultures. Pointing out to a Native American that they have just said something contradictory might only bring the response: 'So?' . . . Paradox may be seen as the essential nature of existence." Deloria says:

> American Indians . . . [recognize] that premature analysis will produce anomalies and give incomplete understanding. When we reach a very old age, or have the capability to reflect and meditate on our experiences, or even more often have the goal revealed to us in visions, we begin to understand how the intensity of experience, particularity of individuality, and rationality of the cycles of nature all relate to each other. (*Spirit* 14–15)

Before proceeding with an analysis of two articles mentioned earlier in this chapter as rhetorical models, I would like to summarize the other elements I envision as possibly being included in a critical rhetoric, a scholarly discourse mode designed for American Indian studies. Later in the chapter, I demonstrate how some of these elements create meaning in Occom's "A Short Narrative of My Life" so that my claims are grounded in examples from the first well-known, educated American Indian writer of English. A rhetoric for American Indian studies would be tribally centered, with intertribal connections. In fact, it would recognize the connectedness of All My Relatives. Saulteaux and Métis scholar Janice Acoose does just that in *Reasoning Together* when she says: "I introduce this paper by honoring *Ni'Wahkomakanak* from both a writing and speaking *Koochum* place that, like Nêhiyaw-Métis-Nahkawè ceremonial traditions, invokes the spirit-presence of ancestors as well as the living presence of 'all my relations'" (Acoose et al. 220). Scholar Tol Foster (Muscogee Creek), moreover, reminds us in his analysis of Will Rogers in that same volume that our predecessors writing in English did this as well: "Rogers engaged in a rhetoric, and I would argue, a pedagogy of relation by imagining himself in relation to his colonizers, and imagining a relation between his colonizers and the colonized of the world" (287–88). In fact, Foster claims that "relations are the primary axis through which we can understand ourselves and each other" (277).

This rhetoric would incorporate American Indian "indirect discourse."[6] *It would be based on* synthesis as much as analysis and would be nonlinear/holistic, with meaning-filled gaps, rich lacunae, which in the oral appear as pauses and appear in my writing here as divisions between sections of text. Our penumbras, in other words, are the universe, are all of creation, for a Native worldview would posit scholarly writing as part of the ongoing story of reality. Structuring our discourse holistically allows it to encompass more and facilitates our work in American Indian studies, which as a discipline is interdisciplinary in nature.

Scholarship written in this vein would show an awareness of the power of words, much like the work of First Nations scholar Neal McLeod. Acoose says of McLeod: "He . . . bundles medicined Nehiyâwiwin words into the fabric of written English. As the medicine-powered words transfuse the text, organisms within the cultural body become revitalized. McLeod's ritualizing critical performance adheres to important cultural protocol that honors Nehiyâwiwin being, both spiritual and physical" (Acoose et al. 223).

This proposed Native scholarly discourse would include repetition and recursivity. Poet and scholar Ron McFarland, who describes repetition as "perhaps the fundamental tool of rhetoric," points out that it "is one of the basic features of traditional Native American poetry and is typical of oral poetry in general." This carries over to the contemporary, as McFarland observes in regard to well-known Spokane and Coeur d'Alene writer Sherman Alexie's work. Muscogee Creek writer and musician Joy Harjo's poems and Silko's poetry and prose are other excellent examples.

Like Native literature, our Indigenous literary critical work and other scholarly discourse would defy genre boundaries. Greg Sarris's *Keeping Slug Woman Alive: A Holistic Approach to American Indian Texts* exemplifies this and is seminal to all progression toward changing the terms of discourse in the field, though I do feel it is closer to reader-response than it is to what I am envisioning.

Our criticism would allow for paradox, recognizing it as a nexus of growth. As a Native reader, Acoose does not feel she *has to* resolve Cree writer Paul Seesequasis's Uncle Morris/Malcolm Norris. She allows the character to retain his shapeshifting identity as well as his religious and sacrilegious nature. An even better example is the analogy of the two fires used by George E. Tinker:

> Imagine two Indian communities who live in close proximity to each other, separated by a mountain. A non-Native visitor arrives at the first community [and] . . . is informed that the tribe's council fire is the center of the universe [and] . . . [t]he following day, the outlander and representatives of the first tribe travel to the other community. The elders of the new tribe declare that their council fire is the center of the universe, and the members of the first tribe nod their assent. Confused, the visitor asks her host, "I thought you said that your fire was the center." The Indian replies, "When we're there, that is the center of the universe. When we are here, this is the center." (Qtd. in Weaver, *That the People Might Live* 33)

This polycentric ontology that allows for paradox matches Leroy Little Bear's Native Paradigm, taking into account a world of constant flux, where balance is maintained through reciprocal, respectful relationships that are periodically renewed in ceremony and in material and cultural exchange (Cajete ix–xii).

The Native scholarly discourse I desire would value communally made meaning, as Native cultures have since time immemorial, just as the Native Critics Collective did in *Reasoning Together*. In connection with this characteristic, it would utilize an experiential-based auctoritas. In Native discourse (using myself as an example), authority is centered in my experiences primarily, but I can refer to what I know of my peoples' experiences—those both my tribal peoples and my peoples in my field. This authority appears in Native discourse as "what I've been told," often preceded by "they say" or a similar construction based on tribal language devices for referring to an authority beyond one's personal realm of knowledge.

This discourse would have an accruing context of meaning, one that mimics the continual acculturation that occurs with maturation and results in elders being those who are the most acculturated, the most mature, who have the greatest body of contextual knowledge. This is what is so impressive to me about Acoose's work in *Reasoning Together,* despite the differences between our approaches. Her positioning of herself as *Koochum* reflects not only her individual and familial identity, not only her cultural grounding and use of communally made meaning, but also her own growth as a writer during the course of developing that volume. Her chapter itself *layers* meaning, mirroring the development of the very knowledge it conveys. I honor her here as my critical elder, deserving of our respect in the American Indian studies community as our elders are in our traditional communities.

Like American Indian oratory and everyday discourse, this scholarly framework would not only take into account, but be grounded in, the identity of the speaker. Who I am has a direct bearing on what I know, as I can know only what I have experienced personally. I can *believe* what I have heard from (read of) others, but I can report it only as such. My literary scholarship now puts forth an intertribal critical mixed-race theory that draws on Lumbee scholar Bryan Brayboy's Tribal Critical Race Theory, Daniel Heath Justice's Kinship Criticism, Cherokee anthropologist Robert K. Thomas's Peoplehood Matrix (popularized after his passing by his coauthor Tom Holm), and LeAnne Howe's tribalography. I draw on them because I have to ground my work in my background, experiences, and relationships to others, and these frameworks all allow me to incorporate this and other aspects of the scholarly rhetoric I describe; additionally, they can encompass the kinds of readings described in the previous section. Self-awareness of positionality and disclosure of that to an audience reflect traditional introductions in American Indian formal public discourse, which identify the orator by qualifications he or she has to give the speech at hand, as well as provide a context for listeners that explains who the orator is in terms of relationships. As a powwow emcee who regularly is called upon to speak for people publicly in American Indian social contexts, Eugene Blackbear Jr., says,

> I just follow [the] standard format. I talk about good deeds. I talk about the credentials of that person. I talk about the reputation of that person. I talk about genealogies. In regard to good deeds, what I usually like to do is give some information about hospitality and etiquette. As far as reputation, I give some information about accomplishments, ceremonial standing, belonging to a traditional group, warrior society, or traditional chieftainships. Genealogies depend on tribe. For instance, for the Cheyenne, this would be paternal relationships, going back for four or five generations, so that people in the crowd will know how they are related to that person.

Traditional introductions let the hearer/reader know who the person is and what he or she has accomplished in relation to his or her people. This is why Mary Crow Dog (née Brave Bird) starts her book by saying, "I am Mary Brave Bird. After I had my baby during the siege of Wounded Knee they gave me a special name—Ohitika Win, Brave Woman, and fastened an eagle plume in my hair, singing brave-heart songs for me. I am a woman of the Red Nation, a Sioux woman. That is not easy" (*Lakota Woman* 3). Crow Dog lets us know who she is—in intertribal terms, because of her involvement with the Indian movement, and in tribally specific terms—and gives us a recounting of her coup that marked her as a warrior among her comrades.[7] She spends the rest of her first chapter building on this, giving histories and genealogies of both her and her (now ex-)husband's families, as well as personal history in regard to what she is about to relate. She gives us the context from which she is speaking, what gives her the right to say what she is about to say.

This does not mean that only Indian or descended scholars should write about or teach American Indian studies. University of Nevada Las Vegas professor Patrice Hollrah says of non-Indian scholars of American Indian literatures:

> They are limited by their position, but at the same time, not all of them attempt to speak with the authority of cultural insiders. There are white scholars who consciously listen to what the Native scholars and critics prescribe in terms of approaches to the literature, whether they are tribal-specific cultural and historical contexts, issues of sovereignty and connections to the land, and/or literary criticisms developed from the literature of the tribe in question. (32)

Hollrah quotes Wahpetonwan Dakota history scholar Angela Cavender Wilson, who suggests "that white scholars consult American Indian sources for the cultural insiders' perspectives," and that "if they do not, they should acknowledge the limitations of their white perspectives in their work" (qtd. on 33).

As I mentioned earlier, Womack's *Red on Red* includes within its analysis of Native literature some very insightful rhetorical suggestions for our scholarly discourse; I would like to return to it as a source for two additional elements, both of which I feel are very important. In *Red on Red*, Womack claims "that Native literary aesthetics must be politicized and that autonomy, self-determination, and sovereignty serve as useful literary concepts." He further explains:

> I will seek a literary criticism that emphasizes Native resistance movements against colonialism, confronts racism, discusses sovereignty and Native nationalism, seeks connections between literature and liberation struggles, . . . roots literature in land and culture. . . . This criticism . . . attempts to find Native literature's place in Indian country, rather than Native literature's place in the canon. (11)[8]

Or as the character Stijatti says in one of Womack's interchapter sections:

> How can Native Lit Critters carry on a discussion of Creek culture as a conversation *with* Creek people rather than speaking *for* Creek people? How can white Lit Critters become helpers, rather than Indian experts? How can they promote the work of Native people over their own, and still was keep up their own good efforts at contributing to Native literary development? How can Indian Lit Critters do the same thing—encourage the budding talent in their own tribes, the young ones who have new things to say, the kids singing themselves back together? (127)

Womack's work suggests, and I agree, that a Native literary discourse must be political, must be mimetic, as the literature is, and must be a radical act of love for the Peoples.

Based on his study of Muscogee Creek and Yuchi storyteller and writer Louis Oliver's work, Womack proposes that the inclusion of humor, an essential element of Indian discourse even when the subject matter is serious or sacred, can aid in "analyzing Native literature in a manner that Indian people can immediately recognize and relate to" (210). Womack's examination of Alexander Posey's writing, moreover, gives a breakdown of some of the rhetorical devices used in Indian humor—the humorous situations that often arise because of cultural differences when Indians have to function in a "changing world"; the humor that can be found even in the dark circumstances of Indians cooperating in settler colonial assimilationist actions against their own tribes; the humor derived from naming (i.e., a character's name can have humorous implications regarding personality); Indian slang; "unusual expressions"; "reworked clichés"; "botched English"; onomatopoeic puns; sexual humor (many Native cultures traditionally took a very relaxed and natural approach to sexuality, both hetero- and homosexuality, and sexual situations and humor are a vital part of the oral tradition); and, finally, "understatement" (136, 156–58).

Let me add one last note on a rhetorical element of Indian humor that Womack mentions later in his book, an element that not only is illustrated in the Creek dialect passages between his chapters but also is a function of Indian joking on a daily basis—Indian "talk" is filled with "Indianized" allusions (178). In short, contemporary Native American discourse continually takes in and absorbs dominant culture by making elements of it Indian.

Finding Precedents: Hester and Hilden, Writing Red in the Academy

As I have mentioned previously, I believe our strongest rhetorical models in print have come from other areas within Native studies. Thurman Lee Hester Jr., Choctaw philosopher and coeditor of *Ayaangwaamizin: The International Journal of Indigenous Philosophy*, uses a traditional Native rhetoric in his article entitled "*Pishukchi*: One Choctaw's Examination of the Differences in English and Choctaw Language Use." This article illustrates the same principles and rhetorical structures seen throughout Native American written and spoken discourse.

Hester begins by briefly contextualizing who he is: "I must admit that I am Choctaw, a citizen of the Choctaw Nation of Oklahoma" (81). He admits his limitations: "I'm . . . a learner. Though I learned some Choctaw at my grandmother's knee, she had already lost much of her language and I was forced to learn it more as a second language" (83). Throughout, Hester employs indirect discourse combined with humor, all the while being "polemic," in a positive sense of the word. For instance, he explains that the word "Choctaw" was once used colloquially in English to refer to unintelligible speech, but he adds:

> It turns out that even when Choctaws speak English, it is still "strange or incomprehensible." If you look at historical documents and are at all familiar with how Choctaws talk, you see instance after instance where the Choctaws fail to make themselves understood. Officials of the United States government, try as they might, have been unable to crack the Choctaw code and are as much in the dark now as they were 200 years ago. (81–82)

Moreover, the whole purpose behind Hester's article is double-edged; while it is ostensibly about language differences, the choice of outside material he uses to develop his argument—the words of government officials during the removal process and Choctaw oratorical reactions to them—at the same time builds a case that his people were wronged in this process. As most academics are unfamiliar with this style of discourse, and as the article *is* about language use differences, Hester directly points out his use of indirect discourse; he "culture-brokes," he scaffolds the lesson for readers. After employing a personal narrative about something he learned from Choctaw elder Aleckton Davis to his support his argument—another aspect of a tribal-centered discourse—Hester says,

> This story in itself probably explains all the differences between Choctaw language use and English language use. Indeed, if this were a completely Choctaw paper, I would only smile and thank you for your attention at this point and consider the presentation over. . . . It would be almost insulting you if I were to presume to continue and explain the differences. Politeness—respect—would prevent me from ever being so presumptuous. . . . [T]he key here is thought and context. (83–84)

Hester suggests that the more context someone has, the greater someone's understanding is, that meaning is made by the listener/reader through synthesizing a message with context and experience. Hester also claims that sometimes what is not said is more important than what is said, a construct he asserts is "hard for an academic" to accept, much less process. Determining what is not said is something only someone who knows context can do (84). Correspondingly, Hester claims that more can be said than what is said through indirect discourse. He argues that a well-constructed Choctaw discourse act contains meaning that takes years for listeners/readers to discern (84). In conclusion, Hester uses, at least in a modified form, a tribally centered style of discourse to convey an academic message, one that—though the presenter is Choctaw and his language use is based on Choctaw English models—is, I would suggest, familiar to most other speakers of Red English. Unlike dialect writing, such as *The Fus Fixico Letters* of Alexander Posey, Hester's writing is understandable to an intertribal audience (even if they've never met a Choctaw or heard a Choctaw talk) as well as to academics.

The anthology *As We Are Now: Mixblood Essays on Race and Identity*, edited by author and American Indian literature professor William S. Penn, offers yet another model that I see as appropriate. Penn says of the selections in the book:

> [They] cross boundaries in the fields of storytelling, ethnography, history, psychology, dance, music, and art—[and] are often narrative and nonlinear: rooted as they must be in the overwhelming respect for the power of words and the oral tradition of "telling" or "saying," the new generation of Native American writers is appropriating the genres and modes of the Western tradition to its own purposes. . . . This narrative mixture of modes is often produced by the act of reclamation, an imaginative act of identity and selfhood that must be reenacted every time the mixblood writer sets out to write, an act that always involves recognizing the gap, entering the dialogue between disagreements (European or Native American, linear or circular, direct or indirect, historical image or historical actuality), and then finding a way to bridge that gap—or to express it. (3)

Of particular note in this collection is Patricia Penn Hilden's "Ritchie Valens Is Dead: *E Pluribus Unum*," a synthesis that epitomizes Penn's description above and, at the same time, is recognizable within a traditional tribal framework. Hilden's essay, for me, is the best written example of a mode of discourse I label as "ndn," postmodern but not postcolonial (as we are indeed still colonized), a polycultural outgrowth of tribal discourse, layered with code-switching allusions in the spirit of California Indian diarist and artist WaWa Calachaw Bonita Nuñez: "I am a seeker of Truth. / And [I] search out all things regardless where" (qtd. in P. Allen v).

Hilden, like Hester, introduces herself at the beginning of her essay, acknowledging in a sense her limitations—she is a mixed-blood and three-quarters Anglo.[9] Also like Hester, she employs indirect discourse throughout the essay, but she does so in more structural terms, using multiple headings and subheadings, leaving the reader to fill in the gaps between sections of the essay such as pieces of law, quotes from elders, a negative review of Disney's *Pocahontas,* bits of poems by Sherman Alexie and Wendy Rose (Hopi/Miwok descent poet), and her own expository prose and personal narratives. Additionally, she appropriates allusions from mainstream culture and makes them her own, the title being a perfect example of this, her indirect commentary on the subject of her essay, California ideals of "real" American identity and whiteness and the reality of its mixed-blood past and present. As Hilden says in the introduction to the volume:

> The classical Maya wrote their histories by recording and *giving context to* the events considered to be most important to the people. Narrative essays, I suggest, do the same. Thus, in contextualizing ideas, they may well seem loose, nonlinear, fractured, or digressive. But in reality they are carefully structured, and each structure may be both described and defended. They are not loose, but oral and even conversational—as though talking to a really imagined audience; they are nonlinear only in the sense that for most of us all things are connected, and thus to give the proper context dialogue rarely follows from A to B to Z; they are not digressive but, as I have begun to insist, "augmentative"—and augmentation . . . adds connection and context, gives life to dull "facts," and celebrates the power of imagination, metaphor, and the cross-connections between the speaker and the listener, which is another way to claim that narrative essays work toward community, toward inclusion and not the exclusivity of colonization. The narrative essay is, in my opinion, where scholarly or academic writing is heading, or where it will head if it wants to revive its relation to an audience greater than seven. (5)

I believe that readings based on models such as these offer possibilities for a more tribal-centered discourse, one that is both open-ended and respectful of the texts and authors as subjects negotiating meaning rather than dissecting them as objects and, moreover, one that might relate to our communities.

Samson Occom as Writing Instructor: The Search for an Intertribal Rhetoric

Born in 1723, Samson Occom was a Mohegan Indian who became a Christian minister following his conversion during the Great Awakening. Occom studied under Eleazar Wheelock, an American Congregationalist pastor, speaker, and teacher who founded Dartmouth College. During a four-year period with Wheelock, Occom learned Latin and Hebrew in addition to expanding his English. Occom was later sent by Wheelock on a preaching and speaking tour of Great Britain from February 16, 1766, to July 22, 1767, to raise funds for an Indian charity school. Wheelock misdirected these monies, some £12,000, instead providing initial funding for Dartmouth. This experience, however, brought Occom into the Transatlantic discourse of the day regarding Christianity and American Indians, as he preached between three and four hundred sermons abroad. Occom is thought to be the first American Indian to publish his or her work in the English language. He is the author of *A Sermon Preached at the Execution of Moses Paul, an Indian,* which esteemed American Indian literature scholar emeritus A. LaVonne Brown Ruoff calls "the first Indian best-seller" (62), in addition to other writings that include hymns, letters, an unpublished manuscript on herbs and roots, and his autobiography, "A Short Narrative of My Life."

Much of the critical writing on Occom centers naturally on his role as a mediator between Indians and whites in the colonial era and on the role Christianity played in colonization and assimilation. The works of non-Native scholars Dana D. Nelson, Eileen Razzari Elrod, David Murray, Michael Elliott, Margaret Connell Szasz, and Bernd C. Peyer have all focused on some aspect of how Occom manages to address both colonizing and colonized audiences at once, offering a plurality of meaning in one piece of discourse. All of this scholarship grew out of the then popular interest in applying a Bakhtinian dialogic to the study of written Native literature, a literature that for a variety of reasons is inevitably cross-cultural. But as Blaeser points out in "Native Literature: Seeking a Critical Center," even in studies that attempted to create a "dual vision to adequately appreciate the richness of Indian literature, the native half to that vision was still . . . conspicuously absent" (57).

To a reader familiar with American Indian rhetorics in traditional cultural settings, what is "conspicuously absent" in the studies of Occom's heteroglossia is any mention of indirect discourse.[10] Though several scholars arrive at interpretations similar to those that can be derived with an awareness of this phenomenon in Native speech, often their cultural distance has caused them to arrive at conclusions divorced from a Native reality. Even when their interpretations are more harmonious with those based on Native rhetorics and epistemologies, studying how Occom uses—or more accurately, adheres to—this "rule" of politeness enriches and expands their readings. When someone has done something wrong or foolish, when an error needs to be addressed, care is often taken, at least traditionally, that this person does not feel "put on the spot," that he or she can remedy the mistake without losing honor. Implication, rather than explication, is the usual means of conveying this message. Barbara Duncan, education director at the Museum of the Cherokee Indian in Cherokee, North Carolina, recalls the time she told her Cherokee friend Hawk Littlejohn about some relationship difficulties she was experiencing. Rather than telling her she was codependent, Littlejohn told her a story about an old man crossing a mountain pass on a cold autumn day. After he reached the top and was starting down, he say a near-frozen rattlesnake next to the trail. The old man "was ani-yunwiya, one of the real people," and so "he had compassion on his relative." He placed the snake inside his shirt so that it could get warm. As he continued down the pass, the air got warmer and warmer, and so did the snake. It moved more and more vigorously and eventually bit the man: "[The old man] said, 'Why'd you bite me? I picked you up and saved your life, and now you've bitten me and I might die!' And the snake said, 'You knew I was a rattlesnake when you picked me up.'" When Duncan asked Littlejohn what the story meant, he replied, "'If you know somebody's a rattlesnake, . . . you don't have to pick them up'" (*Living Stories* 16).

Straightforwardly saying that the person in question was bad for Duncan would have been rude, not only because talking badly of people is typically considered so, but also because Duncan's foolishness would have been pointed out. Additionally, despite the emphasis on the group among tribal peoples, Native Americans have a great deal of regard for an individual's autonomy in making personal decisions. Littlejohn, though he obviously cares enough for his friend that he would like to see her out of a destructive relationship, avoids directly telling her what to do. Had Duncan been accustomed to indirect discourse, the story alone would have sufficed. Even when she indicates with her question that she does not see how the story relates to the earlier portion of their conversation, Littlejohn finds another way to imply that it does, rather than fully explicating his "reading" of her situation.

Violating the rule of polite speech brings censure. Choctaw attorney Scott Kayla Morrison tells of the time her aunts were giving her advice after she had graduated from college, and one of them, Aunt Opal, who rarely contributed to these sessions, joined in with a comment.

> Aunt Little Al's raised eyebrow at Aunt Opal's remark was the only indication of surprise. Aunt Opal was still able to be coherent, as this

> rare moment of sharpness indicated. The aunts exchanged bare glances, not at Aunt Opal, but at Little Al for showing surprise. She was still not ready to be called plain "Alice," and a helluva long way from being called "Big Al." Children seeking counsel from elders called for a certain decorum, decorum which comes from internal control over individual emotions. This solemn discussion concerned the collective interest of the community. It did not relate to the individual concern of Aunt Opal being sober. "Big Al" would have known that. Even plain "Alice" may have suspected that. But Little Al did not, and thus had acted on her impulse. She had a long way to go, but the aunts were in no hurry. (94–95)

Alice's foolish or childish behavior in showing surprise, albeit without actual speech, was enough to be impolite.

Knowing that Occom uses indirect discourse as a way to avoid offending anyone's honor, even when this meant he had to show respect to those who had shown him none, can make a great deal of difference in how we understand his intentions. Near the end of "A Short Narrative," Occom parenthetically interjects, "I speak like a fool, but I am Constrained" (618), a phrase that has been commented on by various scholars. Eileen Razzari Elrod suggests that Occom makes an association here between himself and the apostle Paul by alluding to 2 Corinthians 11, making a related association between the white missionaries and "the ungrateful and recalcitrant Corinthians" (142). Nelson reads the interjection as evidence of "Occom's own sense of self-division . . . a pained awareness of the contradictions that finally may have no resolution within the (mono)logic of colonialism." She argues that "the cultural hegemony of colonialism . . . undercuts Occom's attempt to argue his own worth . . . exactly at that moment that he compares himself to a white missionary." Occom makes this self-commentary right before he mentions his having acted as his own "interpreter," one example of how he should deserve at least as much, if not more, pay than white missionaries. Nelson feels it ironic that "as he asserts a fuller worth *because* of his ability to speak his native tongue, he finds himself compelled to apologize for his lack of eloquence in English" ("'I Speak'" 58). While both Elrod and Nelson may have valid points, I feel that Occom makes this interjection because he feels forced to speak rudely—that is, directly—in pointing out the un-Christian behavior of his superiors on the missionary boards. Despite his repeated appeals to

Wheelock for help, despite the hardships he had endured in "Instructing [his] poor Kindred" because of his "uncommon Pity and Compassion to [his] Poor Brethren According to the Flesh" (615), Occom has been treated abominably. The round of accusations leveled at him after his breaking with Wheelock—that he was not really Mohegan, that he was only recently converted for the purposes of the fund-raising tour—along with accusations of drunkenness and family troubles, leave Occom feeling as if he must defend himself forthrightly. But like "Little Al" in the excerpt from Morrison above, Occom would look *foolish* within his own cultural context for speaking so frankly, and he indeed seems to feel so.

The next section of his narrative, the anecdote of the "Poor Indian Boy" beaten by a young man in his white master's family, is evidence of Occom's use of indirect discourse as a rhetorical technique. Even though in this context he somewhat explicates himself—having already "made a fool of himself" anyway—Occom avoids pointing out that the ministers who have beaten him metaphorically, by complaining of his service, are not his masters. Rather, they, like the young man in the story, are subject to answering to the master themselves. David Murray's interpretation of this passage, that it is "almost . . . an expression of solidarity" for Indians mistreated by whites, is too cursory. Realizing that this passage of an Indian rhetorical device used in a Christian religious context, albeit a syncretic one, makes clear that Occom is suggesting that whites will have to answer to God for their treatment of him based on nothing more than his race, and he refuses to sacrifice his dignity any further by spelling out for them the moral that derives from their own scripture.

Occom clearly used indirect discourse in communicating with other Indians in ways that they recognized. In a letter to Wheelock regarding his work among the Oneidas, Occom relates the following speech, in which the Oneida leaders give their consent to having him stationed as a missionary among them.

> Father, We are very glad you have come among us with the good Word of God, or God's News: And we think we are thankful to God, and give you Thanks, and the good Men who assisted you up here.
>
> We will, by the Help of God, endeavor to keep the Fire which you brought and kindled among us; and we will take our *old Customs, Ways, and Sins,* and put them behind our Backs, and never look on them again; but will look straight forward, and run after the Christian Religion.

> Whenever we shall attempt to erect Schools among us, we beg the Assistance of good People your Way.
>
> *We intreat the great Men to protect us on our Lands, that we might not be encroached on by any People.*
>
> We request that the great Men would forbid Traders bringing any more Rum amongst us; for we find it not good; it destroys our Bodies and Souls.
>
> This Belt shall bind us together firm in Friendship for ever. (Qtd. in Blodgett 63–64; my italics)

The belt, a gift of wampum, places the exchange in an Indian context, the gift sealing what we now must view as an oral and written ("in shell" rather than "in stone") contract. And clearly Occom has implied to these chiefs, leaders who at this time were finding it impossible to fulfill their traditional obligations to their people, that the agreement to become Christian would do more than provide for their peoples' spiritual salvation, as the colonizers purported it would. Both sides for which Occom was a go-between had expectations not detailed in this oral contract. Occom recorded in his diary just prior to this event that the English had been demanding to extradite an Oneida accused of killing a Dutchman (qtd. in Blodgett 60). While we cannot know what Occom's intentions were, we do know that a similar case, that of Moses Paul, involved alcohol, and we do know how devastating alcohol was and is to traditional Native cultures and in the lives of individual Native people. Additionally, Sir William Johnson, who negotiated with the Oneida regarding this incident, reports in his diary that the Oneidas were "in a very wretched situation . . . for the want of provisions" and were starving (qtd. in Blodgett 61). Wheelock's own correspondence suggests that his real reason for sending Occom and his brother-in-law, David Fowler, was not to establish a mission, but rather to recruit more students: '"a fine Opportunity this to obtain Boys Judiciously chosen for our Design from remote Nations'" (qtd. in Blodgett 55). The collusion of Christianity in the form of missionizing and capitalism in the form of alcohol trade once again *really* add up to merely methods of colonization.

While Bernd Peyer indicates that the Oneidas might expect the "requests" they make in this "meeting," as he terms it, would be fulfilled by Occom's residing among them as a missionary, an understanding of indirect discourse in combination with the knowledge that this is an oral and written contract reveals even more. Obviously, Occom has implied to the Oneida leaders, whom he would not wish to offend by pointing out directly their failure to fulfill traditional obligations to their people, that whites will tolerate their continued existence if they will assimilate, that this will be the only way in which they will now be able to care for their people. *Sin,* for these Indian Christians, is the maintenance of traditional *Customs* and *Ways.* Occom's strictness with the Oneidas in this regard—noted by Gideon Hawley, a white missionary, as stricter than necessary (qtd. in Blodgett 64–65)—is his attempt to save them physically by making them appear less Indian. And Occom's concern over the alcoholism induced in the people by the machinations of empire, referred to by Wheelock in a letter to Rev. George Whitefield (qtd. in Blodgett 67) and admittedly one likely cause of their impoverished circumstances, also is a concern that they are being stereotypically Native in the eyes of the colonizers, making them even more susceptible to attacks on their sovereignty.

An experience Occom had on the way to the Oneidas offers convincing evidence that Occom himself could not have believed that acting white necessarily made one a Christian. Having traveled on the outskirts of New York City, Occom records his shock in his diary, a forum in which he is obviously much more straightforward about his opinions:

> But I never Saw a Sabbath Spent so by any Christian People in my Life as some Spent it here.... Drunkards were Realing and Stag[g]ering in the Streets, others tumbling off their Horses, there were others at work in their farms, and if ever any People under the Heavens Spoke Hells Language, these People did, for their Mouths were full of Cursings, Prophaning Gods Holy Name—I greatly Mistake if these are not the sons and Daughters of Belial....
>
> I have thought there was no Heathen but the wild Indians, but I think now there is some English Heathen, where they Enjoy the Gospel of Jesus Christ too. Yea, I believe they are worse than ye Savage Heathens of the wilderness. (Qtd. in Blodgett 56–57)

Occom, in this state of mind, cannot truly believe the Oneidas should give up their mode of dress and change their hairstyles in order to be more Christ-like. Rather, as the agreement between them implies, Occom believes these changes necessary to prevent whites from uprooting the Oneidas.

These few examples of how the Indian rhetorical tradition of indirect discourse informs Occom's writings suggest to me that further examination of his works from a Native viewpoint to see what we as Native studies scholars can learn for our own writing is warranted. Like Occom's other works, his *Sermon Preached at the Execution of Moses Paul,* delivered to a mixed audience, does offer itself up to a dialogic examination, as the scholars mentioned in my introduction to this section indicate by their methods. But including the Indian half of this equation is the only way we can access a fuller interpretation. Michael Elliott asks of the sermon, "Did Native Americans understand that Occom was delivering a different message to them than to his Anglo audience? Could Anglo-Americans see that he questioned their treatment of American Indians? To what degree did any of his listeners or readers question the sincerity of Occom's Christian faith?" (235). While Elliott acknowledges that Occom uses a "pluralistic rhetoric," a familiarity with Indian rhetorics is plainly needed to answer his questions fully. Only then will Occom's role as "cultural broker," to borrow Szasz's term, be more comprehensively understood.

Eisegesis: Reading and Writing Red for Indian Nations across Generations

By no means is this book meant to be taken as "anti-white" or opposed to Euro-American modes of analysis and study. Just as I did in 1997, I believe that European and Euro-American theories have their use in Native studies, but if these approaches are truly compatible with Native metaphysics, epistemologies, and ontologies, these theories should be explicable through specific tribal and/or intertribally common lenses; we as scholars should be able to draw connections between them to languages, ways, artifacts, and stories; we should be able to test whether or not these theories "fit" from Native perspectives. Moreover, their end products should not be offensive or alienating to more traditional American Indian community members. Perhaps even more importantly, the academy needs to make space for and recognize the validity of thoughts derived from more traditional American Indian hermeneutics and epistemologies and constructed in more traditional modes utilizing more traditional rhetorical techniques. Native and Native-descended scholars have obligations, after all, to their relatives and communities, not merely to the academy. I believe non-Native critics have obligations to Native people and communities as well.

Native literature and Native literary criticism *do* serve a purpose in Indian Country. Stories are essential to survival. The American Indigenous body of story includes both our oral traditions and the written tradition that predates English and continues to live through that language. Stories, like functional and sturdy baskets,[11] are the bearers of our theories and our knowledge. Our stories can be admired as culturally distinct works of art. As scholars, we can analyze the ways these stories are put together and see what that says about our cultures and beliefs. We can find patterns—points of alignment between languages, ways, artifacts, and stories—and use inductive reasoning to produce theory, rather than recklessly applying outside theory and using deductive reasoning to force our stories to prove it. However, while baskets, like literature, have design, have aesthetic qualities grounded in culture and spirituality that we can analyze, they are also vital for their usefulness, for what they carry and what they do. Oral stories, and even some stories written in English, either recount or have embedded within them traditional cultural or ceremonial knowledge and/or local and Indigenous knowledge about things such as geography, ecosystems, methods of harvest or hunting, or knowledge of other survival skills for that particular group in its homeland or other areas its people frequented. Stories can also be performative—they themselves can effect change through their use in ceremony. Contemporary stories today can also be performative—reading Native American literatures can effect change in people, Native and non-Native alike, and in the reality that we all share. In a 2013 speech, Linda Tuhiwai Smith proposed a way in which research justice paradigms can be used to effect change (in this case, in public policy):

> Much of what we do in research . . . has to be more than just documenting "the truth," or "our story," or "our truth." That's one part of it. Part of it is about mobilizing others who believe that truth to be truthful. It is about mobilizing knowledge resources. It's about mobilizing opinions and experience and leadership in the community. It is about mobilizing language and discourse. It's about having community leaders—doesn't matter if they've read the research or not—having them stand up and support the researchers, having them stand up and support the activists. It's about coming together despite huge differences in our community. (DataCenter)

The stories of American Indian people, carrying truth about history and contemporary lived reality, have the power to mobilize students, and they have the power, if shared, to mobilize communities. In more ways than one, stories can literally save us.

For our survival as peoples, not only do we need the knowledge that stories contain, both old and new—think of all the social and political issues embedded in contemporary American Indian literatures—but we also need the acts of reading and writing themselves, acts that American Indian children are increasingly finding challenging in mainstream schools. We need all this even though we are working in English, a nontribal language. As Joy Harjo said way back in 1997 in *Reinventing the Enemy's Language*:

> We have come to life in an age in which we are aware of ourselves as native [people] . . . in a language that we have chosen to name our own. When our lands were colonized the language of the colonizer was forced on us. We had to use it for commerce in the new world, a world that evolved through the creation and use of language. It was when we began to create with this new language that we named it ours, made it usefully tough and beautiful. (Bird and Harjo 23–24)

Every single act of Native writing, every single act of reading from a Native perspective, is an act of resistance. If colonization were perfected, if it were complete, Native people would either be all dead or entirely assimilated into the mainstream. Native people living and thinking and creating and speaking and writing as Native people in *any language* defy colonization. This is why Steven Paul Judd's Indian pop art and Daniel Heath Justice's fantasy trilogy, though tied in many ways to American popular culture, are acts of Indian resistance. Their art may engage heavily with the mainstream, but it asserts cultural difference and a Native perspective on history within the milieu of popular culture is a statement: we are still here. This is why the popularity of Indigenous science fiction, what we are now calling Indigenous futurisms, spurred on by Judd's art (such as *Powwow Rangers* and *Invaders*), Joseph Erb's animated short films, the scholarship of Grace L. Dillon and Brian K. Hudson, and the works of Native Realities/INC Comics' artists such as Arigon Starr and Roy Boney Jr., is so significant: we will continue to be here in the future. To me, the single biggest way we as literary critics can encourage this form of resistance is to get written Native literature into the hands of Native people and enfranchise grassroots Native people as significant participants in the Native literary discussion. Written Native literature is as much a part of the Native tradition as oral literature is; it grows as surely from the same source, along with sign language, petroglyphs, codices, winter counts, birch bark scrolls, painted tipis, quipu, and ledger book drawings. Returning ownership of Native literature to Native communities and people is empowering. As one American Indian college graduate said upon receiving her bachelor's degree in education: "'I struggled in school for a long time, not knowing whether or not I was able to do this work. Now I know I am . . . Now, I see a need in our community to have our students read, have their parents read with them, and to recognize that there is power in both the written word, and [our] stories. We can, and must, do both'" (qtd. in Brayboy 426). Wordcraft Circle of Native Writers and Storytellers national director Lee Francis IV, who did his Texas State University doctoral work on school improvement, says,

> What I have experienced over and over again in working with Native students is the continued need to enhance their writing and reading skills, not simply for postsecondary success, but to draw out the language and articulation passed to them by their ancestors, to bring forward the joy of understanding and communicating. All our people should be reading more and writing more, if only to confirm our continued existence in a world that would rather we just disappear.

Native people need stories, and that means that Native people need Native literature. If Native literature doesn't get to Native people and communities in meaningful and pragmatic ways, isn't it all, on a material, literal level, just a continuation of the series of images of Natives produced for consumption by non-Native people, no matter who made it and for what reasons? The corpus of Native written literature that utilizes Latin letters stretches at least as far back as the Nahuatl codices, and it is growing exponentially. With Native mysteries, vampire novels, literary novels, serial novels, short story cycles and collections, erotica, poetry collections, plays, historical fiction, young adult novels, children's literature, nonfiction, and, yes, comic books, there's something for just about everyone. However, many people in the communities continue to be unaware that this literature *about* them and *for* them even exists. Admittedly, those of us who are either tribal citizens or tribal descendants in the academy have knowledge about and access to this work, but we're relatively elitist. If we do not take our work and the body of literature on which it is based out of academic isolation, it does no good for American Indian communities, and if we do no good for American Indian communities, what indeed is the use, from Native perspectives, of Native American literary theory and criticism?

I firmly believe that in carrying out scholarship in Native literatures or in any other field within Native American studies, we as scholars must give back to the community. Therefore, the subject of criticism must have a pragmatic impulse; it must do something for or give back to the Native people and peoples whose cultures, histories, and individual life experiences give rise to this body of literature. It must give back to those whose very oppression and genocide—in its multiple forms delineated in the United Nations Convention on the Prevention and Punishment of the Crime of Genocide—give rise to the Native literature written in English that we study to make our livelihoods and continue our own survival. Colonization, among other things, is consumption. It is unethical from Indigenous perspectives for the academy to consume Native literature for profit, for individualistic career advancement—with accompanying personal renown and hegemonic control; that practice does not demonstrate respect or reciprocity. We, as scholars of American Indian literatures, Indian and non-Indian alike, have an ethical obligation to consider what Native people might want of Native literary studies and what it can do for them, not just what we want and what it can do for us—just as scholars in other areas of American Indian studies have similar obligations.

That ethical obligation exists, moreover, from the perspective of the international community. American Indian peoples, like other Indigenous peoples around the world, have a right to their literatures if we take into consideration the words of the United Nations. Before the United Nations Declaration on the Rights of Indigenous People (UNDRIP) was adopted, those working on notions of sovereignty in recent years had suggested that we in the academy had been using terms like "intellectual sovereignty" too loosely. Article 31 of that document suggests, however, that from a legal perspective intellectual sovereignty does exist internationally for Indigenous peoples and nations, or at least the global community believes that it should.

Article 31

1. Indigenous peoples have the right to maintain, control, protect and develop their cultural heritage, traditional knowledge and traditional

cultural expressions, as well as the manifestations of their sciences, technologies and cultures, including human and genetic resources, seeds, medicines, knowledge of the properties of fauna and flora, oral traditions, literatures, designs, sports and traditional games and visual and performing arts. They also have the right to maintain, control, protect and develop their intellectual property over such cultural heritage, traditional knowledge, and traditional cultural expressions.

2. In conjunction with indigenous peoples, States shall take effective measures to recognize and protect the exercise of these rights.

As scholars, *we* also need to consider that intellectual sovereignty.

Another issue that I think we as Native American studies scholars might need to consider is what I see as a gap between our theory and our practice. Most of the work we have done, whether tribally specific or intertribal, has focused on *analyzing* the philosophical tipi stakes of Native cultures—the things that are "holding us secure" as cultures in a windy world—ontology, epistemology, metaphysics, our cosmologies. This is necessary and important, and, in fact, I spend quite a bit of time analyzing these later in this text. To produce work grounded in Native perspectives, scholars need to work in the nexus of Robert Warrior's "intellectual sovereignty," Scott Lyons's "rhetorical sovereignty," Weaver's "hermeneutic sovereignty," and Santa Clara Pueblo filmmaker Beverly Singer's "cultural sovereignty" while paying attention to the actual inherent sovereignty of tribal nations, as Chickasaw scholar Amanda J. Cobb cautions us we ought (129–31). If scholars are simply doing mainstream academic argumentative analyses using pieces of tribally specific literature as a lens for reading, are we really doing anything very different? I think we as scholars need more focus on *employing* Indigenous cultural epistemologies and hermeneutics to decode texts, written and otherwise. I also think we need to further examine rhetoric—how do Native people construct meaning within their respective cultures? What particular rhetorical devices are used in specific texts to develop the argument in specific tribes, between tribes, extratribally? Robert Warrior's call to read Native works against each other is a place to start, along with Christopher B. Teuton's three functions of tribal oral traditions, which are epistemological functions (both in *Reasoning Together*). But I also think Teuton's emphasis on the *structure* of oral tradition narratives gives the discipline room to grow—the rhetorics that underlie these narratives and other

Native texts have application, I believe, for Native studies methodologies and our praxis. From the inception of the Native Critics Collective, the contributions of LeAnne Howe, scholar Jim Ottery (Brothertown Indian), and Kimberly Blaeser to the conversation that evolved into *Reasoning Together* utilized some of those structures that I suggest change intrinsically the kinds of arguments we as scholars make and their implications. Janice Acoose's chapter evolved in such a way as to employ some of these as well.

Traditional Native rhetorics, manifest even in literature and oratory recorded in English, certainly have more in common with one another than they do with the sort of rhetoric taught in freshman/first-year composition classrooms in colleges and universities across the English-speaking world. For Native American students who go there to "get an education," the privileging of Standard English in the academy can cause complications when they try to come back and work with their peoples—some once very traditional young people come home and are impatient with tribal modes of discourse, the time traditional speaking takes, and the communality of decision making when dialogic discourse *is* used, as it also takes more time than even the sometimes seemingly endless competing monologues. If Native American communities are sending their young people away *so that* they might come back and help their own peoples, then those of us who are scholars need to academically validate our own English discourse that grows out of our home communities. The words of those young people who have excelled in the dominant culture's educational system, who have learned to change the way they think, those who have graduated from universities, who want to go home now and "improve" conditions on the "rez," are evidence of the discrepancy between Native and mainstream rhetorics and of the cultural divide it is causing between generations and between those from varied educational backgrounds. In an article titled "Two Worlds Collide," Associated Press writer Matt Mygatt quotes Gene Humeyestewa, a twenty-four-year-old Hopi student at the University of New Mexico, as saying:

> "We want to go back out there and start new economic developments. . . . But we have to make sure we can speak our language because that's how we're going to communicate our politics with tribal government.
>
> "[I am] often . . . frustrated at Hopi Tribal Council meetings, where the elders bring up some good points, but they never find a solution to a problem. They're sitting up there the whole day and then you walk

> out at the end of the day and say, 'OK, what's the point? What have we accomplished here today?' They're just sitting there and regurgitating the same thing over and over and over." (Mygatt)

Now, it is *not* that learning another way of thinking, learning another way of communicating that thought, is causing Native American children to lose their ways. Rather, it is the *value* the dominant culture places on its own ways of communicating to the *exclusion* of all others. With *no value* placed in the classroom on a Native American way of speaking, *no value* placed on discovering a Native American way of writing—a way that both structurally and hermeneutically parallels Native ways of thinking—and with a *high value* placed on the discourse modes of the dominant society, our children's *minds* themselves become colonized. We lose the last vestiges of what is ours as peoples—our identity—when we lose control of our stories, when we stop re-creating ourselves with words. Teaching children to use words to continually give life to their culturally specific peoples reasserts sovereignty and ensures continuance.

Conclusion

For me, claiming our own Native intellectualism means valuing Native ways of reading, Native ways of communicating, in our work as scholars. It is an issue as important as tribal language preservation—and it is one we share as Indigenous peoples because it is about the use of the language we share with one another as well as our non-Native relatives, the one we use to preserve *shared* culture for our children. Moreover, I believe that utilizing Native rhetorics in constructing our criticism changes our arguments, their means and ends, and that rhetorical analysis of the models left by our elders, such as that of Occom's "A Short Narrative," can guide us in constructing criticism that is part of our cultures, not apart from them. Because Occom spent much of his life teaching intertribally, I think it is particularly appropriate that we study his writing to see what we can learn from him today as we theorize a scholarly rhetoric in our shared language of English.

I would also suggest that further studies of Native rhetorics in other texts, written and otherwise, might be fruitful in developing our own methodologies and praxis. Moreover, this kind of study would give us as Indigenous scholars the support we need to validate Indigenous ways of constructing arguments in the academy. In an early draft of *Reasoning Together,* Acoose bemoans an absence of Native elements in some Native writing:

> With great expectations, I fervently search the pages for reflections of an author's nation of origin, ancestors, language, and expressions of national sovereignty. Often I'm saddened to "discover" Natives, Indians, full-bloods, half-bloods, and Aboriginals (to use just a few choice nomenclatures) who have ceded not only vast territories of land, but also the territories of imagination and of voice.

If we want our texts, our scholarly works, to "reach home" in the communities and not just in the academy, we need to speak to those communities in ways that are culturally *acceptable* and *recognizable.* By doing so, we will also reinforce to our Native students, no matter what tribe, that *their* ways of arguing, their elders' ways of speaking, are productive, are useful, and offer up different results from those produced by mainstream arguments. We can send our Native students, as well as their and our texts, back home with intellectual, hermeneutic, rhetorical, and cultural sovereignty intact.

TWO

Vision, Voice, and Intertribal Metanarrative

The Amerindian Visual-Rhetorical Tradition in Leslie Marmon Silko's Almanac of the Dead

> Those who can't learn to appreciate the world's differences won't make it. They'll die.
>
> —*Calabazas, in Silko's* Almanac of the Dead *(203)*

Anna Lee Walters's *Talking Indian: Reflections on Survival and Writing* contains a story entitled "The Web." In this story, a character named Hilda suddenly has her life invaded one morning by numerous spiders. Hilda, a waitress, ponders the significance of this phenomenon with another waitress, who, like Hilda, is American Indian: "'Do you know what your problem is, Hilda?' Lou asked with a tired raised eyebrow. 'You're always thinking like an Indian. Always noticing things like how many spiders there are all of a sudden. You have to stop doing that. There's no place for that kind of thinking in the world anymore'" (109–10).

Hilda, however, ignores Lou's advice and, at the end of her tiresome day, proclaims to herself in her spider-infested abode, "Time to think, Hilda, old girl. . . . Time to think. Even if it is 'like an Indian'" (112).

Hilda's thinking comes about in a fashion to which mainstream readers are unaccustomed. In order to think, Hilda falls asleep, having abandoned logical analysis, which she concludes is "not thinking like an Indian at all" (112). The

Portions of chapter 2 were previously published by the University of Nebraska Press in "Vision, Voice, and Intertribal Metanarrative: The Amerindian Visual-Rhetorical Tradition and Leslie Silko's *Almanac of the Dead*," by Kimberly G. Roppolo, *American Indian Quarterly* 31.4 (2007), 534–58.

ghosts of elders circle her in her sleep. One particular spider, who has perched on her earlobe to rest, whispers to her, "Sleep, Grandchild . . . but listen as you sleep. . . . I've got a story to tell. . . . But do not listen with your ears and mind. Listen with your hands, listen with your feet, listen with your skin and hair" (113). Hilda awakes, fully knowing the implication of the spiders, which has to do, not with the spiders themselves, but with a problematic person in her life. What is important here, for our purposes, is *how* Hilda gains that knowledge. For American Indians, knowledge can be gained and transmitted visually, through signs, symbols, and dreams, as well as verbally. As mentioned in the introduction, visual recordings or transmissions of language were often meant, historically, to be accompanied by the oral tradition. However, to those who understand the symbols and the visual rhetoric[1] they utilize, these symbols can communicate on their own. Furthermore, these symbols have power; they are performative in an American Indian worldview, just as words are. The visual rhetoric in Silko's *Almanac of the Dead* performatively communicates a revolution in our sense of relatedness as human beings, a recognition of kinship as a means of sustainable survival. *Almanac* certainly is timely in terms of its approach to the kind of revolutionary change sought after by social justice movements today, particularly if it is read in light of comments made by activists Grace Lee Boggs and Angela Davis (discussed in my eisegesis). This chapter examines the history of visual communication and rhetoric in the Americas briefly; synthesizes my argument with an analysis of Silko's "polemical," revolutionary text *Almanac of the Dead*; then concludes with my eisegesis, which explicates a revolution of relatedness. From a perspective grounded in both tribal worldviews and the novel, we humans must achieve this relatedness to counteract the detrimental effects of environmental destruction on ourselves and the earth.

The Amerindian Visual-Rhetorical Tradition

Though not exclusive to American Indian cultures, one way in which American Indians have traditionally gained knowledge is through "visions" and dreams. This facet of Amerindian epistemology requires holistic thinking that embraces a network of relationships. Personal vision is always conjoined with the knowledge handed down by one's elders. This holistic thinking is more than a "mental" phenomenon—things can be "known" not only with the mind but with the heart, body, and spirit as well, just as Hilda understands in the example above. Lying about a vision is taken to be a serious violation of protocol and has equally serious implications.

It is important to note that vision is a private enterprise and not always a matter for public consumption. Visions are shared with appropriate audiences at appropriate times. For instance, though others have occasionally shared their "dreams" or "visions" with me, I do not have the right to share those. The only visions or dreams I have the right to share are my own. A few I have used in my poetry, most significantly perhaps the dream I had that started my publication career:

> *It was a beautiful dream. Aunt Ruby and I were in this log house that was part of a fort-like structure, and she could walk and talk again like she did when I was younger. Her hair was down, and the ends of it were green stalks with maize heads. But it was the European kind of maize, milo. She and I decided to make up a new corn ceremony. We felt like it was an okay thing to do. She said she would walk outside, and I would follow her. As we went, we picked up all of the old corn lying about with the husks attached, but pulled back. It was Indian corn. I kept thinking to myself in the dream that I wanted to cut off the ends of her hair, the green parts, but I knew she wouldn't be okay with me cutting her hair. It is still very long and black for her age of 84. Anyway, we were supposed to throw all of the old corn out before the newly harvested corn was brought in. It was clear that very many more people lived there, but I don't know where any of them were. We were alone as far as I can tell. But this wasn't a green-corn ceremony. It was a harvest.* (Roppolo, "Selections" 193–94)

It took me a while to understand the entire significance of the dream, which I now see as a sign of my aunt's impending death. I believe that my Aunt Ruby, the woman who taught me how to read and write at age three and who stressed my Cherokee and Choctaw heritage, sent me the dream. For many American Indians, as elderly people drift in and out of consciousness or even in and out of what the mainstream calls reality, we believe that they are "crossing over" or "visiting the other side"—the afterlife. I saw this as my aunt's way of taking me with her on one of these journeys, of giving me a sense of comfort about the place she was going to and preparing the rest of the family. My aunt indeed did cross over shortly after the dream. I believe that the dream has brought me good things. My view of its significance, just like that of the character Hilda's "thinking," might seem bizarre or superstitious to those outside Indigenous cultures, but not so to tribal people.

As Chief William Berens (Berens River Anishinaabe) taught his close friend and collaborator A. Irving Hallowell, "Dreams [are seen as] active forays into the world . . . [and] the dream experience . . . [is] interpreted as actual experiences of the self. . . . Social interaction in terms of the Ojibwa [or Anishinaabe] outlook involves no vital distinction between self-related experience when awake and experiences during sleep" (qtd. in Bower). Anishinaabe scholar Lawrence W. Gross takes this one step further, saying, "In some ways dream experiences are more important than waking reality. In the dream state, according to Anishinaabe thinking, one is able to interact with the spiritual world more directly" (178). Likewise, Lee Irwin's "Cherokee Healing: Myth, Dreams, and Medicine" relates that "the spiritual dimensions of Cherokee religious identity [are] constantly informed by personal experience through dreams, visions, and healing rites that [work] in conjunction with the sacred word [ritualized incantations] . . . and sacred world." Irwin claims that, among Cherokee people, dreams have multidimensional power that is manifested in a variety of ways in the lives of humans: they can cause illness and death, can be used in diagnosis and curing, can divine the right course of action for an individual or the Cherokee people as a whole, can indicate the predestined life-span of an individual, or can be a conduit for *ulanigvgv*, what might be loosely translated as "medicine power." Irwin also notes that early ethnographers David Bushnell (1909) and John R. Swanton (1925) recorded the importance of dreams among the Choctaws and the Creeks, respectively.

Two academic studies on Indigenous knowledge acquisition are of particular note. Leanne Simpson (Anishinaabe/Chippewa) explains in "Stories, Dreams, and Ceremonies: Anishinaabe Ways of Learning" that, for the Anishinaabe, learning occurs over the course of a lifetime. Some methods are experiential and empirical—but empirical within a Native worldview. One can learn both by doing—that is, actively participating in everyday tribal life and culture—and by observing nature. Plants, animals, and other aspects of the environment are considered teachers, as are children and close relatives.[2] Other methods of learning that Simpson notes are storytelling, dreaming, ceremonies (including the individual aspects of singing, dancing, and praying),[3] experimenting, and apprenticing with elders or spiritual leaders. These are the pedagogical media of prophecy and spiritual revelation. Highlighting the importance of learning by dreaming, Anishinaabe sweat lodge leader Garry Raven says:

> Dreams
> Remember your dreams
> They tell you what you need to do
> Ask elders what your dreams mean
> You will learn more about
> Choices
> Meaning in Your Life
> The Contributions you should make. (Qtd. in L. Simpson)

In "Dreams, Theory, and Culture: The Plains Vision Quest Paradigm," Lee Irwin shows that dreaming and vision are primary means of gaining knowledge among Plains tribes. Irwin suggests that the type of cognitive process by which knowledge is acquired in dreaming differs vastly from the linear model of the dominant culture. He observes that because of the primary differences in the ways that knowledge is acquired, people from mainstream culture tend to be left-hemispheric dominant (have more activity in the left hemisphere of the brain) while those from tribal cultures in which dreaming and vision are valued as means of knowledge and power acquisition tend to be right-hemispheric dominant. Other research, Irwin says, "has suggested that the accessibility of right-hemispheric activity to left-hemispheric processing is minimized in culturally left-hemispheric individuals," particularly after those individuals reach adulthood. This may account for the skepticism with which mainstream scholars have encountered the alternative cognitive processes of non-Western cultures. While nonlinearity and nonrational thinking are acceptable in literary expression in Western culture, they are not acceptable in its academic discourse.

The tendency of American Indian cultures to be right-hemispheric may also account for the propensity to *record* and *transmit* knowledge in holistic, nonlinear ways. Donald L. Fixico (Shawnee, Sac and Fox, Muscogee Creek, Seminole) says in *The American Indian Mind in a Linear World*:

> "Indian Thinking" is "seeing" and "listening." . . . Listening does not necessarily involve only hearing sounds. . . . [L]istening involves hearing and realizing as a receiver while understanding the objective of seeing. It is the counterpart of Indian "seeing," . . . [which] involves trying to

> understand the significance of relationships. Without listening, seeing only provides images to the mind with limited information and hearing sounds adds substance or more pertinent knowledge to the visual experience. . . . [I]t is imperative for [both] traditional and linear thinkers to look around themselves while trying to understand the natural and man-made environments.[4] (4)

Over the thousands of years that American Indian peoples have lived in the Western Hemisphere, strong visual rhetorics were developed, I believe, because of this tendency to engage in visual thinking and because of social and economic needs to communicate with others who either might not speak the same language or who shared situations in which speech was either inappropriate or dangerous. Growing out of the study of semiotics, a scholarly analysis of visual rhetoric focuses on how the images, rather than words, communicate or create arguments. Primarily, this sort of study has examined the relationships of visual tropes in Western art history. It has also been used by non-Native scholars to look at the relationships between images and texts. Because of the unique cultural developments in Native America and because of the relationship of that heritage to Native contemporary literature, I think it is important to examine how image *has acted and continues to act as* and *with* text in our cultures.

Birgit Brander Rasmussen's *Queequeg's Coffin: Indigenous Literacies and Early American Literature* gives broad coverage of the topic of precontact alternative literacies—some of which are still used by various Indigenous nations of the Americas today—that were/are often at least partly, sometimes wholly, visual in nature. Rasmussen, who offers unprecedented readings of pictographs, petroglyphs, ledger drawings, birch bark scrolls, wampum, quipus, and Polynesian tattooing in dialogue with alphabetic texts, says:

> As long as literary scholars continue to think about writing predominantly as the alphabetic system used by Europeans, we uphold that legacy by defining other forms of recording knowledge and narrative out of existence. . . . As the field is currently configured, writing is too often conceptualized as synonymous with alphabetic script. The common equation between writing and the alphabet relegates other forms of recording and transmitting knowledge outside the boundaries of literary inquiry, leaving uncontested the monologues of colonial agents and diminishing our understanding. (3–4)

Though the scope of this chapter is too narrow to explore this topic in depth, following are a few examples of how some visual rhetorics have evolved over the years and how they are still important in Native American life and culture today. My interactions with many people from Plains tribes, including Comanches, Cheyennes, Blackfoot, and Crees, have introduced me to the ongoing use of Plains Sign Language (PSL) in both intra- and intertribal interactions. Storytelling on the Plains, even among speakers of the same language, has also often been accompanied by sign (Davis 5, 7). In the Blackfoot Beaver Bundle ceremony, PSL accompanies each of the many songs the ritual requires. The documentary *The American Indian's Sacred Ground* demonstrates that PSL even has a direct correspondence with some of the petroglyphs found over much of North America. For instance, the sign for "snow" is made by extending both arms from the elbow slightly above the waist with the fingers loose and making a wavy motion downward. The petroglyph for snow can be made by applying paint to the fingers and making the sign over the surface of the rock (figure 1). Similarly, the sign for a sacred place is made by placing the hands close together, bringing them apart in a downward motion, and then bringing them together again, literally meaning "to go around" (figure 2).[5] This correspondence, in my opinion, offers proof that this system is ingrained, having been used for an extensive period of time, and is highly organized and systematic, being pervasive across many tribal lines.

Figure 1. Petroglyph for "snow." Drawing by Marlena Roppolo.

Figure 2. Petroglyph for "sacred place." Drawing by Marlena Roppolo.

Although some scholars, from Garrick Mallery in 1881 to William Samarin in 1987, have argued for a European origin of PSL with a transmission to American Indians during colonization, visual narratives scholar Patricia Kilroe has cogently argued for the Indigenous origins of PSL. In "On the Probable Origin of Plains Indian Sign Language," Kilroe reviews—as proof—the European notations of PSL in early contact, gives evidence of other gesticular and visually based communication devices among the tribes, examines the functions of PSL and its possible relation to speech taboos,[6] and investigates its relation to precontact Indigenous pictorial records. As in the documentary film noted above, Kilroe mentions the connection some archeologists have found between North American petroglyphs and PSL. In particular, she notes a glyph at Tule River, California, that includes the signs for "rain," "nothing here," and "hunger"; an Alaskan wood carving from the late nineteenth century that shows the signs for "nothing" and "winter lodge," made by two men in a boat; and Dakota petroglyphs with an ear of corn representing the Arikaras, signed in PSL as "corn shellers," and a figure making the Kiowa sign for "rattle-brained," made by circling the hand or hands horizontally on one or both sides of the head.

More surprisingly, Kilroe lists at length correspondences between PSL and Mayan and Mixtec pictography. As opposed to some of the glyphs found in the continental United States, all the Mayan and Mixtec figures seem to be of the sort of the sign for Kiowa above—a figure gesturing the sign rather than a reproduction of the pattern of the sign like that for "snow" or "sacred place" first noted above. In the Dresden Codex, a figure signs the PSL for "yes" and one signs "the same"; one Mixtec figure makes the PSL for "fire"; another makes the sign for "to give"; and connections exist between the signs for "sun," "moon," "accession," and "water" or "drink." Kilroe further points out Helen Neuenswander's 1981 finding that some contemporary Mayans seem to use signs, at least in regard to lunar cycles and seasons, that bear a correspondence to ancient lunar series glyphs.

These correlations suggest a network, perhaps once extensive, of a widely used, visually based linguistic system. The Mayan codices and other ancient Mesoamerican "writings" themselves bear remarkable proof for the degree to which semipermanent visual recording of knowledge might have been part of the precontact past, with possibly as much cultural importance as the alphabetic system of recording has for mainstream culture today.[7] Eminent pre-Columbian art historian and archaeologist Arthur G. Miller—building on the work of George Kubler, one of his most esteemed predecessors in the field—says in the introduction to *The Codex Nuttall: A Picture Manuscript from Ancient Mexico*: "Ancient Mexican screenfolds are remarkably versatile as forms of information storage. It is possible to view several pages simultaneously and even to consult the obverse at the same time as the reverse. Clearly the screenfold format was devised as a solution to the need of non-Western, nonlineal patterns of thought" (viii).

Although anything that I can include here about the breadth of Mesoamerican writing systems must be oversimplified, an overview of them is necessary to understanding both the history of the visual recording of thought in the Americas and the relation of this issue to Silko's *Almanac of the Dead*. Ancient writings on materials that resemble what our contemporaries recognize as texts are extant from several cultures: Mayan; Aztec, or more properly, Mexica (pronounced "Me-shi-ka"); Mixtec; Zapotec; and possibly others. Scholars agree that the Mayan glyph system has "evolved" into a phonetic system, while the Mexica, Mixtec, and Zapotec systems remain pictographic. Pictographic screenfolds in particular are thought to have been intended to accompany, not necessarily to replace, the spoken word, as PSL often does in contemporary Plains discourse.

Plains ledger books are a more recent form of Indigenous pictographic writing. Though Plains peoples had previously recorded pictographs on a variety of surfaces—notably hides, in addition to the petroglyphs mentioned above—accountants' ledger books were used between 1860 and 1900 to create a number of pictographic books illustrated with crayon, colored pencil, and sometimes watercolor. The books at first held recorded war exploits and then later ceremonial information and details from daily life. Accurate accounting of war deeds is extremely important in Plains cultures, as warrior activities play key roles ceremonially. Even today, veterans are called upon to recount their coups during the Cheyenne Sun Dance, the world-renewing ceremony for the tribe. Military service is greatly esteemed in American Indian communities because it is one of the most common ways for young people to succeed off the reservation and the only legal way to earn war honors, a necessary function in the ceremonial continuance of the universe from many American Indian perspectives. The ledger books continued a long tradition by the warrior-artists of the Plains. As Senator Ben Nighthorse Campbell, one of the forty-four chiefs of the Cheyenne, points out, "Coups and battle honors *had* to be confirmed by witnesses."

Then and only then were they recorded pictographically to aid their preservation in the oral tradition of the people. Or as an old saying, repeated by Senator Campbell, puts it, "The picture is the rope that ties memory solidly to the stake of truth" (qtd. in Masich et al.).

One of the earliest of these ledger books was created by Cheyenne Dog Soldiers in the years following the Sand Creek Massacre of 1864. Although the blank book as originally produced held 144 pages, 114 pages remain in the illustrated book as it is. The Colorado Historical Society (CSH), where the ledger is housed, has determined that the book is the work of fourteen author-artists. Several issues, such as sequencing and a seemingly patterned order of blank pages, complicate interpretation for scholars. The CHS states that the largest problem, however, is that scholars are "severely limited by an incomplete oral tradition."[8] The pictographic method is similar to that of the codices, with pictographs for the names of the warriors whose deeds are recorded in it and for objects associated with those deeds. For instance, the symbol shown in figure 3, painted in red, stood for the name "Red Lance." The symbol shown in figure 4, painted in black, stood for the name "Bear Man," and the symbol in figure 5 stood for "house" or "building." Another symbol, shown in figure 6, represented "bushes," "trees," or "branches." Like the other media written of in this section, the Plains ledger books provide ample evidence of a strong visual recording tradition in the Americas, a tradition in accordance with the right-hemispheric tendencies of cultures that revered and still revere the visual receiving, encoding, and transmitting of knowledge.[9]

Figure 3. The Plains ledger book symbol for the name "Red Lance." Drawing by Marlena Roppolo.

Figure 4. The Plains ledger book symbol for the name "Bear Man." Drawing by Marlena Roppolo.

Figure 5. The Plains ledger book symbol for "house" or "building." Drawing by Marlena Roppolo.

Figure 6. The Plains ledger book symbol for "bushes," "trees," or "branches." Drawing by Marlena Roppolo.

Silko's Visual Rhetorics and *Almanac of the Dead*

Silko's writing on ancient visual recordings of knowledge, in the first half of an essay entitled "Books: Notes on Mixtec and Mayan Screenfolds," does match the scholarly record. She points out:

> Books were and still are weapons in the ongoing struggle for the Americas. . . . In 1540, the great libraries of the Americas were burned by the European invaders, most of whom were illiterate but not stupid. They burned the great libraries because they wished to foster the notion that the New World was populated by savages. . . . International law regulated the fate of conquered nations but not of savages. (*Yellow Woman* 155–57)

Moreover, Silko's novel *Almanac of the Dead* provides a contemporary example of both the visual/holistic receiving of knowledge and the visual/holistic recording of it. In a personal interview, Joy Harjo, noted Creek poet and close friend of Silko's, shares that Silko felt compelled by the spirits to write the novel; she said the "spirits rode her" until the text was complete. Robert Nelson, a longtime Silko and Native literature scholar and friend of the family, says that he heard a story from one of Silko's family members that suggests Silko possesses an actual almanac, a "book" of oral history and prophecy painted on leather pages that has been handed down in the family for generations. It is this almanac that inspired her book (Nelson, e-mail). Although Silko does not mention this in describing the book's genesis in the essay "Notes on *Almanac of the Dead*," she attributes the novel's origin to her interest in similar texts—the codices with their "prophecies that predicted the invasion by the Europeans . . . [and] say that all things European will gradually disappear from the Americas" (*Yellow Woman* 137)—as well as to her dreams and the injustices faced by many Native Americans today. Since visual signs are imbued with power in American Indian worldviews, Ashley Argyle suggests that *Almanac*, like the artifact it is named for, can be read as "code" for "survival" (21). Unquestionably, Silko herself sees the novel as a part of the prophetic and visually encoded tradition; the "old almanac" she re-creates, *rebirths*, in the novel "correctly predicted the Zapatista uprising . . . [and] even purports to explain the unfortunate assassination of Señor Colosio[10] in Tijuana" (*Yellow Woman* 158). According to literary scholar Robin Cohen, Silko claims that Zapatista leader Subcomandante Marcos contacted her after the novel's publication because he shares her sentiment about the novel's prophetic nature (Cohen interview). Moreover, in an interview with Ellen Arnold, Silko drew connections between the unplanned November 2 publication date and its coinciding with Día de los Muertos, as well as other connections:

> January 1, 1994, I pick up a Sunday paper, and it says that the Zapatistas were in the mountains outside of Tuxtla Gutierrez. . . . The spirits had a sense of time and things about dates and time. . . . That's what happened in terms of . . . that pub date, for [people] to be reading it when the riots happened, for the Zapatistas. . . . [Subcomandante Marcos] went to the mountains in 1980, and that's when I started to have transmissions. I started to have to spontaneously write down things from the *Almanac*. So there's a real parallel there, which works on that plane that extends across the universe, where stuff travels faster than the speed of light. (Qtd. in Arnold, "Listening" 8)

Silko has placed herself within a long tradition of both prophets and warriors engaging in a battle for the survival of Indigenous peoples and the earth.

The critics' reactions to *Almanac* were virtually a counterattack. William Dinome—compiler of the Silko bibliography published five years after *Almanac*—points out in *American Indian Culture and Research Journal* that the reviews were "largely negative" (211). John Skow's review, which appeared in the December 9, 1991 issue of *Time*, is one of the most vituperative, labeling Silko "self-righteous" and her novel "vengeful." However, like many of the negative reviews, his outburst is fueled by both misunderstanding and just plain sloppy reading, perhaps caused by the first half of the novel's being "long" and, in his opinion, "a dull headache" (86).

Admittedly, *Almanac*, with its more than 750 pages, is not an easy novel for academics to work with. And maybe, after *Ceremony*—likely the most analyzed and studied of all contemporary Native American novels—Silko partially desires this. Maybe a bit of Silko is showing through in the *Almanac* character Seese, who "hated people who marked books" (55). In an interview with Kim Barnes, Silko does, after all, admit that *Almanac* is "long and complex to the point of being foolhardy." She adds: "I don't want to write something that the MLA will want. I want something that will horrify the people at the MLA" (Barnes 47–48). *Ceremony*, 262 pages long, is centrifugal, grounded in Laguna Pueblo; *Almanac* is centripetal, moving outward in concentric circles to encompass the universe and all of history. As Adam Sol says:

> *Ceremony* focuses on one man's struggle; *Almanac* tackles the struggles of whole peoples—Native American peoples especially, but also African American peoples, Latino peoples, women, the poor of all races. And, perhaps most significant, where *Ceremony* uplifts, *Almanac* overturns. *Almanac* similarly calls for a return to Native ways of viewing the earth and mankind's place in it, but this is only one aspect of a whole system of change. Instead of invoking the healing ceremony, *Almanac* calls for an upheaval in the world order and a dramatic revision of world history. (24)

And *Almanac* is multilayered, with an immense amount of textual interweaving between plots, between images. In a testimonial quotation in the front of the 1991 Penguin paperback edition, Richard Erdoes calls *Almanac* "epic . . . a landmark in Native American literature—the Indian *War and Peace*." I agree with Erdoes that it is that, and more. Craig Womack proclaims *Almanac* as "one of the most important books of this [the twentieth] century" (252). I would suggest that *Almanac* could be compared to *Paradise Lost, The Iliad,* or *The Odyssey* in that it is directed toward an audience who are intended to see themselves as inhabiting the same mythos as that of the story. Like *Ceremony, Almanac* fits itself into an intertribal metanarrative, the story in the novel being the ongoing story that humankind is living, the story that is living itself and not a dead thing on a shelf.[11] *Almanac* situates itself within history, within prophecy, and it reaches forward into the future. In order to succeed at that, all aspects of *Almanac* must be interdependent; it must, like life, be a web of relationships. And the story of *Almanac* must find the commonalities in the stories of the peoples and the symbols within them and make these, not an individual, not an individual culture, its center. As Silko has said, "I knew *Almanac of the Dead* must be made of myths—all sorts of myths from the Americas, including the modern myths" (*Yellow Woman* 140).

Although many aspects of the novel are visual,[12] I would like to examine the visual rhetoric of the novel by focusing briefly on one image: the snake. I choose this image because I see it, along with Silko's novel and the ancient almanac within its pages, as being metonymic for the intertribal metanarrative that I discuss in my eisegesis at the end of this chapter. That is, the snake is the almanac, is the narrative of the novel, is the narrative of human lives. Because of this, I believe that there is a great deal we as readers can understand by isolating, temporarily, the strand of Silko's web (or the fold of her codex, if you will) that is the snake motif. Silko lets us know that the inspiration for this motif is the actual carved stone snake that "reappeared" at Laguna after centuries of being hidden by dirt shortly before her filming of *Arrowboy and the Destroyers* in 1979.[13] This snake is part of the Laguna Pueblo visual rhetoric and requires interpretation to understand its significance in the story of the people. As usual when a community is trying to make meaning of something or someone different within its midst, Silko says that "rumors circulated":

> One rumor said it was a sign that the uranium mine and the people who depended on it and things of its ilk had won, and the snake was pointing at the next mesa the open pit would devour. But the next thing I heard was that the Jackpile Mine had closed because of a worldwide uranium glut; that meant the rumor about the mine winning had been wrong. . . .

> It was a relief to think maybe the mine and all that it symbolizes [the destroyers] had not yet won. (*Yellow Woman* 138–39)

In trying to work out just how the snake functions in her story, in the Story, the story of Indigenous peoples, of our lives, she begins to paint the mural, now unfortunately gone, on Stone Avenue in Tucson:

> Gradually, in 1988, I began to realize the relationship between the mural of the snake and the latter part of my novel. The snake in my mural is a messenger. He emerges out of a rainstorm and is surrounded by flowers, birds, and other creatures. His belly is full of skulls. Above the snake I painted the words in Spanish as if they had blossomed out of the flowers and plants that grew around the giant snake. . . . "The people are hungry. The people are cold. The rich have stolen the land. The rich have stolen freedom. The people demand justice. Otherwise, Revolution." (*Yellow Woman* 143–44)

But the snake in the mural requires a bit more interpretation as well. On one hand, he appears to have eaten the dead, just as the snake at Laguna can be seen as eating the land. On the other hand, he (or she) appears to be pregnant with the dead, just as the male figure at the beginning of *Ceremony* appears to be pregnant with the story, just as the character Tayo at times appears to be pregnant with his own new beginning. The snake, the messenger of the dead, is giving birth to their tale; he, like the ancient almanac, like Silko's *Almanac*, carries the story, the story that she as an author, a ceremonial co-creatrix with her ancestors, rebirths performatively, reinvigorating the metanarrative, reanimating the prophecies. *Almanac* truly enacts the power of words from an American Indian perspective. Therefore, it should be no surprise when we as readers open the novel to find it contained by the snake: a smaller image that echoes the mural is on the title page, and the last words of the novel are the message of the snake at Laguna.

In examining the images in the novel, it is important to remember that the snake seems to have a double message, one that can seem either positive or negative. As a scholar who specializes in the work of women of color, Ann Folwell Stanford asserts, "Part of the complexity of *Almanac* arises from Silko's refusal to identify one group as completely evil, another as completely good.

What Silko makes clear, however, is that those who distance themselves from indigenous origins become . . . heartless, passionless machines of greed and destruction" (28). But ambiguity is necessary for at least three reasons. First, Silko's work on the whole shows binaries to belie the complexity of reality. In *Ceremony*, Betonie says, "Nothing is that simple" (128), and Josiah teaches Tayo, "Nothing was all good or all bad either; it all depended" (11). These quotes are reflective of the worldviews of many Indigenous peoples. Second, the story, being the very metanarrative humans inhabit, is not over. If the novel is to stand in for it, ambiguity is imperative, for the fate of the planet is uncertain in our Anthropocene era. In the words of an e-mail posted by Ecotrust, a major conservation organization, at the passing of Hopi spokesman Thomas Banyacya:

> [The cycle we are in will] culminate either in total rebirth, or total annihilation—we don't yet know which, but the choice is ours. War and natural catastrophe may be involved. The degree of violence will be determined by the degree of inequity caused among the peoples of the world and in the balance of nature. In this crisis, rich and poor will be forced to struggle as equals to survive. That it will be very violent is now almost taken for granted among the traditional Hopi, but man may still lessen the violence by correcting his treatment of nature and fellow man. (Tarbet)

The third reason for ambiguity is directly connected to the snake motif I will examine throughout the remainder of this chapter. Across world mythologies, the snake as a symbol almost always has two aspects—like Janus, it is two-faced. The various venoms of snakes have long been used to both heal and kill. The double serpents of the caduceus—the symbol of Hermes and that used on the staff associated with physicians—are a symbol of the unification of dualities, of life and death as part of one cycle.

No matter how the Laguna people interpreted the stone snake when it was rediscovered, the Lagunas have a clear tradition that Silko connects with in the novel.

> Maah'shra-True'-Ee is the giant serpent
> the sacred messenger spirit
> from the Fourth World below.

He came to live at the Beautiful Lake, Ka-waik,
that was once near Laguna village.
But neighbors got jealous.
They came one night and broke open the lake
so all the water was lost. The giant snake
went away after that. He has never been seen since.
That was the great misfortune for us, the Ka-waik'meh,
at Old Laguna. (*Almanac* 135)

But interestingly enough, the story of the snake at Laguna does not come from Sterling, the Laguna representative in *Almanac* and the character whom Silko calls its "moral center" (qtd. in Perry 330). This story, a very important one that is part of the history of the Laguna people's name, is in the character Yoeme's almanac, a Yaqui inheritance of pre-Columbian origin, connecting the Mexican Indians of the past to contemporary Pueblo peoples. The almanac also links the ancient ancestors with the present Laguna people through ritual. In a time of drought followed by flood—in short, in a time of disharmony and upset balance, "[The ancient] priests sprinkle corn pollen and meal and bits of coral and turquoise on the stone snake's forehead. They whisper to the stone snake leaning close so no one may see their lips" (*Almanac* 576). When Sterling returns to Laguna at the end of the novel, we see the same picture: "The ground near the snake's head was littered with bits of turquoise, coral, and mother-of-pearl; there were streaks of cornmeal and pollen on the snake's forehead and nose where those who came to pray had fed the spirit being" (761).

But the stone snake, carrying spiritual knowledge, also causes problems for Sterling. The movie crew that wishes to film the snake epitomizes the destroyers: "The movie crew people seemed only to understand violence and brute force." They believe that their money, their "rent" pays for everything, even the reservation itself and all that is sacred to its people—just as their forefathers believed they "paid" for this country (*Almanac* 90). Sterling feels that since the movie crew doesn't understand the stone snake's secret, it doesn't hurt to let them film it (36). However, Edith Kaye, a woman whom Sterling has sexually rejected and Aunt Marie has warned him about, convinces the council that "Sterling had conspired to steal the giant stone snake" (92–93). This brings up bad memories from the tribal past. Sterling ends up being punished for white theft of the sacred in Native communities; his involvement with the stone snake is conflated with the anthropologists' theft of the "Little Grandmother" and "Little Grandfather" figures given to the people by the Kachina spirits at the beginning of the Fifth World (the present epoch) (31, 92). And even though Sterling regrets mentioning the stone snake to the film people, he feels that they probably would have found out about it from one of the Laguna young people they had hired anyway (95).

Literature and theology specialist Gregory Salyer suggests that "Sterling is . . . very much like Silko" (103)—perhaps why Silko considers Sterling the "moral center"—but Salyer fails to point out their similarity in sharing tribal knowledge with the outside world, something Silko came under heavy attack for from Laguna Pueblo author Paula Gunn Allen. In a question-and-answer session during a reading at the University of New Mexico Bookstore on April 16, 1999, Silko responded to a question about Allen's accusations that she had used sacred clan stories in *Ceremony*. The Lagunas are a matrilineal society, however, and Silko, whose mother is not Laguna, was never initiated into a clan. Therefore, no sacred knowledge was ever shared with her that she would have had to hold secret. The traditional stories told in *Ceremony* are based on versions already in print, Silko explained. Although some in the community might fault her use of these stories, Allen, a cousin of Silko's, surely knew that she was not initiated. Sterling's and Silko's critics fail to take into account that this metanarrative requires a reaching outside the community in order to protect the world, that this story purports to be not just local but global. The almanac records Spirit Snake's message that he tells the people so that they can prepare and protect themselves, because "this world is about to end." This message is followed by an entry that foreshadows the end of the novel: "One day a story will arrive at your town. It will come from far away, from the southwest or southeast—people won't agree" (135). At the snake's appearance, the old people had argued over its meaning, but the last words of the book tell us that Sterling now knows what the meaning is: "The snake was looking south, in the direction from which the twin brothers and the people would come" (762–63). Sterling knows that survival depends on the oppressed banding together.

In conjunction with this hope for continued life, there is another reference in the almanac to the stone snake, or to one very much like it, that connects a large stone reptile to the human sacrifices of the Aztecs. In this image, an "old priest" sacrifices a boy on a stone lizard, "Lord Iguana," who "carries all the seeds of the World in his tail." Unlike sacrifices made by "barbarians," who might offer "prisoners of war" or "slaves," this boy is of the upper class, as "the spirits only listen when the bloodshed is royal from the rich." Like Silko's snake in the mural, the lizard carries life, both vegetative, regenerative life for the earth and life for the human story: "The lizard's head is full of fruit and flowers. / Each day has its own name and spirit. / Days form like buds" (*Almanac* 593).

All of the snake images have two aspects that are part of a whole, a cycle. Joseph Campbell, another scholar who sought to find human commonality while celebrating our diversity, mentions that "the serpent eating its own tail . . . [is] an image of life." Campbell points out, "Life sheds one generation after another, to be born again. The serpent represents immortal energy and consciousness engaged in the field of time, constantly throwing off death and being born again. . . . And so the serpent carries in itself the sense of both the fascination and the terror of life" (53). As Silko's project reaches out to greater humanity, it is important that she uses this symbol to carry meanings in ways that make sense to the larger audience while simultaneously preserving local meanings for smaller audiences.

Silko uses variations on the snake image to repeat this pattern and make links between cultures. Unlike Navajo poet and writer Luci Tapahonso, who uses the Diné version of this story in "The Snakeman" (92–96), Silko cannot limit herself to one tradition and simultaneously remain true to the intent of her work. In *Yellow Woman and a Beauty of the Spirit,* she tells of cross-cultural associations she made between the snake stories of the Americas and those of Africa (143). In *Almanac,* it is perhaps natural that Quetzalcoatl is one of the dominant manifestations of Snake-man, given Silko's own mixed heritage and that Quetzalcoatl traditionally signifies rebirth.

In an article entitled "The Myth of Quetzalcoatl in a Contemporary Setting: Mythical Dimensions/Political Reality," prominent Chicano novelist Rudolfo A. Anaya compares the Toltec Mesoamerican world and America today. Anaya recounts that the Toltecs flourished "under the benign rule" of the historical king and deity Quetzalcoatl before he entered the world of myth. "A great deal of their prosperity," Anaya tells us, "was taken by the warrior class to conduct war on the neighboring tribes. Toltec civilization rose to its classical apex, then fell." He goes on to assert that this story "speaks to us across the centuries, warning us to respect our deep and fragile communal relationships within nations and among nations, and our meaningful relationships to the earth" (199).

Silko's depiction of the Quetzal is in total accordance with Anaya's urge for writers to draw on the myths of the past to inform our present and future. Early in the novel, the Quetzal and Jaguar tiles in the ranch house kitchen (*Almanac* 21) show sister-mothers Zeta and Lecha's connections with the people's history, despite the atmosphere of criminality and the witchlike symbols that surround them. The twins, Zeta and Lecha, who on the surface might appear to be out of balance, have inherited a role from their grandmother Yoeme of being warrior-mothers for the people as a whole, on both a spiritual and a physical level. This is tied to the snake image by more than just the Quetzal. Yoeme teaches Lecha and Zeta what she learned from the big bull snake that acts as one of her spiritual guides: "Snakes crawled under the ground. They heard the voices of the dead: actual conversations, and lone voices calling out to loved ones still living. Snakes heard the confessions of murderers and arsonists after innocent people had been accused. Why did Catholic priests always kill snakes?" (130–31). It is tempting to see Lecha and Zeta as both responsible for Ferro's out-of-balance nature. In many American Indian traditional ways, including those at Laguna, he would be seen equally as their son because they are sisters, even if they had not been twins. Moreover, Lecha "abandons" him to Zeta when he is a week old (19), and Zeta rears him to traffic drugs. They appear to be "bad mothers" and, therefore, "bad" characters. However, they do both "listen" to the voices of the ancestors and spirits as Yoeme did through the snake, just as the people need to "listen" to the snake at the Jackpile Mine. Lecha and Zeta's actions, however morally questionable, advance the intertribal metanarrative, the story told by the snake.

While Ferro clearly has psychological problems, they more likely arise from his internalization of the dominant culture and its individualism and property concepts. Women and their children are owned and thus controlled. Rather than finding his connection with the eternal feminine and understanding the larger role his "mothers" play in the course of history—the importance of the story they are responsible for—he rejects Indigenous principles and the feminine, siding instead with the destructive forces around him. Remembering the mother, through the act of storytelling, through Indigenous people's control of their own histories, is the cure that will literally (re)member, put the people back together and in control of their future.

Silko uses the Gorgon as a Greek cognate for the Quetzal, serving to connect another character, Root, to the people through his great-grandfather

(*Almanac* 168).[14] The book shows these ancient connections to have been discouraged by colonialism, capitalism, and Christianity because the connections remind "the people"—in the larger sense of the oppressed as a whole, not only the Indigenous—of who they are. *Almanac* also shows that Marxism, which presents itself as an alternative to the paracolonial state in which the characters live, discourages the people from making the connections of which the Quetzal reminds them, even though both Marx and Quetzalcoatl had been reviled by the nuns at the mission school that the Indigenous female resistance leader Angelita attended as a child: "The old Castilian nuns at the mission school had called Marx the Devil. . . . The nuns had [also] taught the children that the Morning Star, Quetzalcoatl, was really Lucifer, the Devil God had thrown out of heaven. The nuns had terrified the children with the story of the snake in the Garden of Eden to end devotion to Quetzalcoatl" (518–19). Both Bartolomeo (Angelita's and Alegría's double-dealing European lover) and the Marxism he espouses fail within the novel. Bartolomeo signifies Bartolomé de las Casas, the first priest ordained in the "New World" and a "defender of the Indians." Thus, Bartolomeo must be associated with well-meaning non-Natives who cannot "save" Native people, because of their own lack of power over the colonizing institutions of which they are a part, whether that is mainstream Christianity or European Marxism. Bartolomeo's secular non-Indian Marxism fails for these Indians, not only because of its denial of the human need for spiritual grounding, but also because of its elimination of divergent thinking. Bartolomeo and the Cuban Marxists, who take issue with "native religion" and "primitive bugaboos," deny tribal histories and attempt to annihilate them (515). Ultimately, however, the greatest failure of Marxism as a political system that can subvert the colonized state for Indians is its lack of a kinship obligation and sense of relatedness, because of the inability of Western culture to create what it sees as true kinship through any venue other than marriage. For secular Marxists, political coalitions do not constitute kinship of equals. Bartolomeo and the Marxists believe that "tribalism" limits the Indians' beliefs about the world; because Indigenous worldviews value kinship and regard life as a sacred totality, Angelita sees herself and her people as "tribal internationalists" who have sacred alliances and relationships worldwide (515). Moreover, this Indigenous worldview is necessary for the success of the tribalist movement. Ideas of equity are destroyed by the reality of human greed, and reciprocity goes by the wayside in structures where relationships are not built on kinship obligations and respect. Angelita sees Marx himself as having some understanding of Native American communities: "[He] had learned about societies in which everyone ate or everyone starved together, and no one being stood above another—all stood side by side—rock, insect, human being, river, or flower. Each depended upon the other; the destruction of one harmed all others" (519–20). But Bartolomeo and the Cuban Marxists behave in ways that are in opposition to their stated beliefs.

The Quetzal, too, has two aspects. The renewal he brings is inherently connected with violence and sacrifice: "Quetzalcoatl gathered the bones of the dead and sprinkled them with his own blood, and humanity was reborn" (*Almanac* 136). The people will have to undergo the "cruel years" about which old Yoeme had warned Zeta and Lecha (702–3). The images of the Quetzal in the ancient almanac are hybrid, just as he is as a portent. For the Antepasados (Those Who Have Walked Here Before Us), Venus, the Morning Star, was Quetzal, the returning deity, but with "carnivorous teeth and a body withered like a rabbit," the Trickster of Cherokee and other Southeastern Indian traditions. Venus was "the Celestial Dragon with eight heads," with his "dogface partially blackened" and "a fish in his headdress." And this, the Death Dog aspect of this figure, brings "plague, earthquake, drought, famine, incest, insanity, war, and betrayal" (572).

Through the character of Clinton, a homeless, black Vietnam War veteran, Silko enriches and magnifies her snake motif further: the African snake god, Damballah, "great serpent and keeper of all spiritual knowledge, joins the giant plumed serpent, Quetzalcoatl" (*Almanac* 429). The descendant of "black Indians," Clinton sees the benefit of drawing the connections between his peoples' spiritual histories to help all: "Damballah, the Gentle[,] . . . excluded no one and nothing" (416). In a study of the Afro-Native presence in literature, Sharon P. Holland claims that "Clinton achieves agency and a move toward sovereignty because he can see himself in solidarity with other oppressed peoples" (345). Clinton comes to see those "screaming 'Black only! Africa only!'" as "fanatics or extremists" (742).

Silko makes connections between several of the African and Native deities in *Almanac*—the Giant Serpent, the Twin Brothers, the Maize Mother, and Old Woman Spider (416, 742), all of whom have multiple manifestations in the novel. Like his Native American counterpart, Damballah acts as a connection between the people and the Earth Mother. This is symbolized in the feminine imagery of the costume worn by the black Indian queen in the Mardi Gras parade: a "huge snake of pearls writhes on [her] gold-lame cape" (421). Asserting her sexuality and fertility in response to a challenge from another black Indian woman, "the queen darts her tongue out like a snake's, and her hips and stomach writhe like a snake's because black Indians still keep in touch with the serpent spirits Damballah and Simbi" (422).

Like Quetzalcoatl, Damballah has dual aspects. On one hand, "pure-hearted Damballah" is the only African god not made "short-tempered" by the bloodshed in the Americas (423), the only one not angry and not causing "anger and fear" and "madness and meanness" in the people, people who had "forgotten . . . the spirits of all their ancestors who had preceded them on these vast continents" (424). In fact, Damballah is "so shy and apart from the world that he [does] not involve himself in the trials of humans except as a messenger" (424). On the other hand, Damballah is also associated with death. As Legba-Gede, the Lord of the Crossroads, or Gede Ge Rouge, he "has always been a cannibal": "*Ge Rouge* [red] is synonymous with the Americas. The power of Gede and spirits of the dead is original to the Americas. . . . Master of the Dead, protector of small children, tricksters, and sexual athletes . . . who connects the living people with distant ancestors and forward in time to descendants yet unborn, Gede belongs to the Americas." And we learn that Gede is an aspect of the same snake, an aspect of Damballah: "Old crippled Gede sometimes has only one foot; then they call him Congo Zandor because a snake has only one foot, which is his belly that he crawls on" (429). This "old bent-man, Cinq-Jour Malheureux," is a Quetzal figure; he is "Gede-the-dying-sun-soon-to-be-reborn," and he "represents the unnamed, empty, and unlucky days at the end of the Native American calendar" (430).

As with the Quetzal and with the stone snake, the death face of Legba-Gede is necessary for the rebirth; they are both part of an unending cycle. In *Almanac*, the Barefoot Hopi addresses the "International Holistic Healers Convention":

> In Africa and in the Americas too, the giant snakes, Damballah and Quetzalcoatl, have returned to the people. I have seen the snakes with my own eyes; they speak to the people of the Americas; they speak through dreams. The snakes say this: From out of the south the people are coming,

> like a great river flowing restless with the spirits of the dead who have been reborn again and again all over Africa and the Americas, reborn each generation more fierce and more numerous. Millions will move instinctively; unarmed and unguarded, they begin walking steadily north, following the twin brothers. (735)

Just as the snake in the mural carries the dead in its belly for rebirth, the snake as a story has brought the rebirth of Indigenous relationships with the land and other humans. Decolonization is a death of the capitalist, exploitive relationships of empire and a birthing of a new people grounded in ancient ways of respectfully and sustainably interacting.

I have neither exhausted the snake images or even the *kinds* of snake images in Silko's *Almanac of the Dead.* There is still the bull snake who advises Yoeme and to whom Zeta later learns to listen; there are the drawings in the almanac; there are the Barefoot Hopi's connections with the snake; there are the rattlesnake images in Menardo's dreams; there are the lizard-skin pumps of Alegría and other wealthy women—over and over the snake motif occurs. Nor have I investigated any of the other numerous images in the text, many of which, like the Twins and the Maize Mother, are also culturally shared and part of an ancient visual rhetoric. However, demonstrating the correspondence between the ancient stone snake as the inspiration of the novel, the snake *as* the novel, and the snake *as* the mural with the underlying visual rhetorics allows us to see how Silko's mural acts to enrich and alternatively record her story. The novel is thus much like a codex, a ledger book, or a PSL sign as it enriches and alternatively records the oral tradition; it is firmly grounded in the American Indian visual tradition. Moreover, the story it records is an intertribal one, one that shows the need for connections between the tribes and other oppressed peoples, along with the need for individual tribal sovereignty. The ideas that were once communicated visually in the Americas through the lingua franca of sign and symbol ground this novel today as it reaches out for unification against the oppressive forces that unfortunately are as much a part of the world we live in as they are a part of Silko's story. The story of the dead and the story of the living are indeed one; it belongs to the ancestors of those of us living today, and it belongs to all of us as humankind as well. As Anishinaabe poet-scholar and Idle No More activist Lesley Belleau says in "Nibi" (which means "Water"):

> Let us write a new script. Embed our own voices into pages not already written. Let us bring the petroglyphs as evidence of a naked moving of history. Let's not buy into settler words and their long papers that speak a rhetoric of immediacy. Let's submerge ourselves within our histories, bathe in ancestral swimsongs. . . . Nibi. You have released us to walking. And it is here where we are full-fleshed walking a guilty shoreline, the branches against our arms and face cross-stitched[,] and it is here we pray ourselves forward, giizis's [moon's] eyes writing our stories against the flattened sky. (17)

Eisegesis: The American Indian Science of Relatedness and Preventing "Earth's Outrage"

In the world of *Almanac,* meant to mirror our own contemporary reality as humans, there is perhaps no more exploited, dehumanized character than Seese. In this novel the characters have to learn to look past artificially imposed binaries such as race and gender and find commonality based on mutual oppression. Silko has said in an interview: "Seese is white and she is not evil, she is powerless and self-destructive" (Arnold, *Conversations* 130). As a nontribal female divorced from the network of her blood relations, Seese has been objectified and commoditized by those she turned to for love and protection. Even worse, so has her child. To the wealthy, warped males around them, both are nothing more than animated meat created for the amusement of others, the infant boy Monte brutally being slaughtered in a snuff film for entertainment. Quite obviously, in the world of *Almanac,* being relationless is the worst thing that can happen to a person, just as it is in traditional worldviews. *Almanac* urges a relatedness that seeks alliances, reaching out beyond tribal lines and the arbitrary borders of Westphalian nation-states and reaching out beyond illusory metaphysical borders to build the political, social, and spiritual capital necessary for decolonization. As Native literature professor Channette Romero says:

> [*Almanac*] attempts to overcome the limitations of the American Indian Movement by presenting readers with the model of "tribal internationalists," individuals who work with international alliances to reclaim their Indigenous land. In *Almanac,* Silko suggests that cross-cultural spiritual coalitions made up of "tribal internationalists" would

> provide a more powerful means of combating the social, political, and economic injustice faced by American Indians (and many oppressed peoples around the world) than secular politics based on ethnicity and race alone. ("Envisioning" 623)

Many of those whom *Almanac* seeks to draw into such alliances are Indigenous Americans separated by arbitrary borders and artificial colonizing categories, such as the ethnic label "Hispanic." According to the 2010 U.S. Census, Mexicans who identify as American Indians make up "the fourth largest tribal group in the country" (ICTMN staff). The U.S. Census Bureau adds, "In the 2010 U.S. Census, tribal groupings with 100,000 or more responses . . . were Cherokee (819,105), Navajo (332,129), Choctaw (195,764), Mexican American Indian (175,494), Chippewa (170,742), Sioux (170,110), Apache (111,810), and Blackfeet (105,304)." As Jose Barreiro, a Cuban-born writer and former professor of Native studies at Cornell University, has said, "'The mestizo is one less or one more Indian waiting to reemerge'" (qtd. in Rodríguez 106). Many people of American Indian descent have, however, acquired a different lens through which to view the other, both those whose descent is Indigenous to this hemisphere and those whose descent is not. Whereas American Indians north and south of U.S. borders used to view each other as part of a vast intertribal network of relationships,[15] today a good number of American Indians see Indian-descended Hispanics as citizens of other autonomous nation-states and/or as members of a distinct, separate "race."

This change, discussed more in the next two chapters, corresponds with a shift in worldview, with assimilation of virtually all Indigenous peoples into Western ways, the Western monetary system, and capitalism. As a result, these peoples, the planet, and all of Creation suffer physically, emotionally, spiritually, and mentally. This is the process of empire. The process of undoing empire, decolonization, must begin with our minds and with our words and our understandings of the words of others because it was on these fronts that the attack on us as Indigenous peoples began, from within and without. We are the frontier, the border between continued life on this planet and the destruction of Western ways, something that is becoming increasingly obvious not only to Indigenous people but to all of the disenfranchised and the oppressed. At the *27th Empowering Women of Color Conference: "A Holistic Approach: Justice, Access and Healing,"* held at Berkeley in 2012, African American feminist scholar, author, and activist Angela Davis and Chinese American author, human rights activist, and feminist Grace Lee Boggs engaged in a conversation about revolution. Davis, well known for her former association with the radically separatist Black Panther Party, said, "Revolutionary approaches require us to open up and make our ideas and our movements broader and more capacious so that what is revolutionary is not narrow and exclusive but rather broad and inclusive" (qtd. in Boggs and Davis). This is exactly the opposite of the way that the forces that run global corporate imperialism work. Davis suggests that our struggle as oppressed peoples is mutual now, that capitalism and empire affect Native people, other Indigenous people, other people of color, the poor in general, women, children, people who are LGBTQIA (lesbian, gay, bisexual, transgender, queer, intersex, and asexual), and the imprisoned. Boggs, then ninety-seven years old, had fought since the 1950s with her African American husband of forty years, James Boggs, to improve conditions for the people of Detroit. She presented her view of decolonization:

> We have colonized material, we have colonized people, we have colonized the earth. I mean, the abuse that we have done not only to each other, not only to people of color, but to ourselves, to people of humanity, is horrendous. And to recognize how horrendous that has been and therefore the need to create an alternative that is more human is the kind of revolution we need to make. And all the good that the Occupy Wall Street movement has done—I don't think their language, their ideas, are profound enough. They are against the corporations, rightly; they are against the greed and the avarice that corrupts our society. But [there is] the need to imagine an alternative in philosophical and human terms, the need to grow our souls, to say that proudly and unashamedly, to talk about the kind of tremendous human transformation we have to make. We must be courageous enough to think that way, and to talk that way and to relate that way.[16] (Qtd. in Boggs and Davis)

In the midst of struggling toward needed change, we as humans must become aware of how we speak, and we must equally be aware of how we are being spoken to and what the intent of those who are speaking is. Native people have long practiced ways of relatedness and respect that are crucial right now to humans beginning to deal with each other in balanced ways once again so that we might sustain life on Earth. As Joy Harjo expressed it in the title of one of her poems, "the real revolution is love." If we as Indigenous people recognize, reach out toward, and communicate with our relatives, our political capital becomes immense. American Indian studies scholar Robert Dale Parker points out that "millions of Indian people live in the United States, more than lived in the same area at the time of Columbus, and most of the people in the American hemisphere are Indians or descended from Indians" (3). The success of government-imposed notions about our own identity and of government-filtered information about the identity of those in the rest of our hemisphere is the essence of colonial power itself. The conquering of this hemisphere, the conquering of Native peoples, is *an illusion* that traps us in our own minds, that we *allow* to trap us. We are, in Harjo's words, "kept quiet in stalls of [our] own making" (*She Had Some Horses* 61). Undoing the imposition of colonial paradigms with Native paradigms, decolonizing our minds, empowers us in fighting the imperialism that oppresses us and threatens our survival in every sense of that word.

Sam Proctor, a Creek elder and the Hillis Heyya (medicine maker) for Tallahassee Wakokiye Creek (stomp dance) grounds and Hillabee Creek grounds, said to me one evening years ago, "My people, Creek people, we all carry a wound."[17] That, I think, we can say is true for all the tribes—though it manifested itself in various ways at various times with various tribal peoples, colonization has wounded us all. While we all have differences culturally as well as different life experiences, this sadly is a shared commonality. Being able to see our common woundedness and recognize it through the demonstration of pity—a positive virtue from Native perspectives—allows us to see things a bit more from one another's perspectives and find relatedness through common ground, while internally validating the integrity of culturally distinct individual tribes. My adopted Cheyenne relatives have "ways" (the Red English term for cultural practices) that are very different from Southeastern Indian ways, and I have taken on those Cheyenne ways through my relationships with them and participation in their culture. My relationship with my Comanche companion and his daughter, as well as his extended kin, has changed me and my daughters as well. All of this affects my scholarship in American Indian studies as much as my education does. My relationships and friendships with people from other tribes, whether Blackfoot or Cree, Navajo or Anishinaabe, change me because they make visible the similarity between their colonial *wounds* and my own and those of my peoples, as they also do the similarities between our cultures and our cultural strengths. My ancestry does not change, but *I* do, and therefore my thinking does as well.

In *Reasoning Together,* Tol Foster builds on an idea from Jace Weaver—that tribal worldviews are "polycentric" but tribally "privileged" (Acoose et al. 274). Maintaining tribal sovereignty while working together to preserve common ceremonial ways has been worked out well for quite a while. For instance, the stomp dance grounds at Stokes are polycentric. The fire that is at the center of the dance circle and is crucial in ceremonial terms does not change, but what it represents changes with the songs, alternating Cherokee discourse with Creek. That is, both Creek and Cherokee people use the grounds simultaneously, the calls distinguishing with a "Lucv!" or "Dv(ga)si!" whether the upcoming song will be Creek or Cherokee.

We must be inclusive as well as exclusive, look at similarities as well as differences. In *Reasoning Together,* Craig Womack and Janice Acoose argue for tribally specific studies as the baseline, so to speak, in American Indian studies. There is a balance to this; none of the members of the Native Critics Collective wanted to exclude the kind of study that allows us to see what we do have in common with each other and to share that with the academic world. That is what I define as Intertribalism. We were all, I think it is safe to say, opposed to the kind of study that imposes outside stereotypes upon us as though we are all the same—in other words, pan-Indianism. In this regard, what both Tol Foster and Phillip Carrol Morgan do in *Reasoning Together* is so important—grounding their work in specific tribal worldviews (Cherokee and Choctaw/Chickasaw) but also seeing connections in larger frameworks of literature, both in terms of areas of the "canon" and in terms of our own history as peoples of the Americas. Foster argues against separatism from American literary studies and for a relational regionalism as a critical frame. I agree and would suggest that just as much as "Indian Territory" constituted a region in the 1800s, "Indian Country" today is itself a region, one more empowering than the old "Indian Territory" because Indian Country is a region of our own creation, a region created of resistance, instead of what Foster calls "a subaltern space fashioned by those in power over [us]" (Acoose et al. 294). I agree with White Earth Anishinaabe literary critic and novelist Gerald Vizenor (*Manifest Manners* 68–69, 75, 77), Malea Powell ("Rhetorics" 399–400), and others that American Indians live in a paracolonial, not postcolonial, state. As Powell says, "It is difficult to describe American Indians as either 'postcolonial' or 'neocolonial' peoples" ("Rhetorics" 399). American Indian people and nations are clearly still colonized. However, I envision both the definition of the term "paracolonial" and the lived reality of American Indian people differently. First, I believe that Vizenor, as Chadwick Allen points out in *Blood Narrative,* never clearly defines "paracolonial" as a term. And though Vizenor may have been the first to use it in regard to American Indian *literary* study, he did not coin the term, as many scholars believe. In fact, Martiniquan Francophone scholar, poet, and politician Aimé Césaire used the term in 1956, saying that "all native cultures are to-day developing under the peculiar influence of the colonial, semi-colonial or para-colonial situation" (13). He uses the term two more times in the same speech.

Most scholars' definitions of "paracolonial" focus on colonial domination. This definition from the website *Beyond Greco-Roman Rhetorics* encapsulates the term as expressed in the literature:

> Paracolonial is a term used to define a political, cultural or economic domination by a colonial group that reaches beyond colonization. Paracolonial is a state in which the provincial or the local is reduced or silenced, and the history of the state is inverted or rewritten by the colonial power. If the colonizers continue to occupy the land long enough[,] then the history of the colonized becomes inseparable from the history of the colonizer. Paracolonial thus refers to the creation of this multidimensional history in which events beyond the scope of colonization are also included, so that the history that is created is not limited to or defined by society's reactions to, or resistance against[,] the colonial rule. In Vizenor's words it is colonialism beyond colonialism with the complications of neocolonialism and postcolonialism. (Driskill, "Paracolonial")

I, however, see paracolonialism as more related to Vizenor's term "survivance." American Indian cultures, though colonized, assimilated, and miscegenated, exist alongside settler colonial cultures, and they maintain cultural distinctiveness and integrity despite colonialism, precisely because of the syncretic nature of traditionalism.

Geographically, Indian Country encompasses the Americas, but more importantly, in terms of the intellectual sovereignty of American Indigenous people, it does so *imaginatively*. By stressing this, I am not suggesting that Indian Country, where many of us claim to live, is a paracolonial fantasy on the part of peoples of "conquered" nations, for I do not believe America's Indigenous peoples to be conquered. Rather, what I am suggesting is that Indian Country as a region of the mind is potentially a hugely empowering construct that is as grassroots as fry bread and corn soup—or as chicken and dumplings and cornbread in southeastern Oklahoma. Indian Country is not just where we live. It is where Custer got a new hairstyle, where Subcomandante Marcos called Leslie Silko after reading *Almanac of the Dead*, where AIM leaders stood up for Native people's human rights, where former U.S. assistant Interior secretary for Indian affairs Kevin Gover drafted an apology to all U.S. Indians. It is where Idle No More continues the battle not only for our survival but for the survival of all humanity as our relatives. Indian Country does not subsume tribal territory—either physically or in our minds, hearts, and spirits. Indian Country does not pretend that the United States and Canada do not exist—it can't. Indian Country is, however, the zone in which this book is happening right now for us as Indigenous writers and readers: it is where we come together and change happens.

Historically, we are in a time of change. We are in a time of revolution and resistance against oppression of Indigenous people around the world and in an age where many American Indians and First Nations peoples see commonality between today's U.S. imperialism and that which created this colonized state. To see commonality with other Indigenous peoples is key, I believe, to survival as sovereign tribal peoples. As we "decolonize" our minds, our theories, our methodologies, we also must decolonize our relationships with each other. As Morgan pointed out in the drafting process of *Reasoning Together*, "The so-called pre-contact North American civilizations did not exist in a vacuum." Many areas of study demonstrate commonality among tribes from all over the Western Hemisphere: studies of ancient roads of trade networks and the artifacts found there, revealing both physical commonalities, such as macaw feathers and shells found far inland in North America, and cultural ones, such as the sacred use of tobacco; studies of architectural commonalities; studies of origin stories and other aspects of oral histories; studies of confederacies; studies of the development and history of the Native American Church; studies of Plains Sign Language, Mayan glyphs, and petroglyphs mentioned earlier in this chapter.[18]

Though oral and visual "texts" differ from those in books, Powell suggests that we need to assert the validity of these other ways of encoding meaning ("Growing Our Discipline"). In line with this call, Lisa Brooks's work in *Reasoning Together* makes connections between the ways in which wampum belts acted rhetorically both to communicate meaning and to bond individuals and communities in alliance and how our writing as Indigenous Americans can do the same for us today. Likewise, Angela Haas's dissertation, *A Rhetoric of Alliance: What American Indians Can Tell Us about Digital and Visual Rhetoric*, shows how the hypertextuality of wampum belts, pictographs, and petroglyphs, which are read in conjunction with the oral tradition, is similar to the hypertextuality of contemporary blogs by Indigenous people. Haas also argues that hyperlinks between the writings of Indigenous people online connects our work in a way that parallels how technologies like wampum joined people together historically. As the work of Powell, Brooks, and Haas demonstrates, in material rhetorics as well as verbal discourse and written literatures, connections between specific tribal ways are both made *and* communicated. Healing relationships between tribes further strengthens individual tribal sovereignty, as sovereignty means nothing except in relation to other sovereign entities. That is, a nation/people/tribe with no relations to others would have no need for the concept to begin with. Both Idle No More, discussed further in chapter 4, and the United Nations Permanent Forum on Indigenous Issues are significant in their furthering of individual tribal sovereignty through making alliances.

I do not think tribal specificity has to be lost in order to reach out and find intertribal connections. My students from multiple tribal backgrounds do not lose their identities when they read texts from other tribal nations in American Indian literature classrooms; they find connections with the characters across time, place, and tribal lines. For tribes that do not have a lot of written literature such as the Comanche and Cheyenne and Arapaho Nations, intertribal readings become even more important. Simon J. Ortiz's *From Sand Creek*—a text that, from a narrow tribalist approach, would exclude the author from having the "right to write"—had a major impact on my Cheyenne and Arapaho students when I co-taught the first course for the Cheyenne and Arapaho Tribal College in 2002. This poetry text necessitates intertribal reading, as does a book like Silko's *Almanac of the Dead*. As we develop tribally specific approaches, we also need develop ways of reading in between cultures for commonality, carefully avoiding the dangers Womack (*Red on Red* 63–64) and others caution against—vague notions of "the Native perspective" or "the Native paradigm" that are not grounded in tribal specificity. As Foster says, "Anyone attempting general claims that fit all Native societies is bound to be wrong" (Acoose et al. 266). Keeping a balance between tribally specific references as evidence for our assertions and showing intertribal connections can prevent this.

The notion of race, like the notion of nationhood, obfuscates and obscures the lasting peoplehood that our ancestors knew and, hopefully, that our great-grandchildren will know. We must recognize that miscegenation and colonization have gone hand in hand in America. Infusions of white blood into Native American and African bloodlines facilitated the colonial enterprise despite laws forbidding intermarriage, which were mostly applied to liaisons between white women and men of color rather than vice versa, and which certainly did not prevent or deter the innumerable illicit relationships and rapes involving white men and Indian and black women. Although how persons of mixed descent have been labeled has varied given the particular needs of the government at any given time, in general it has been advantageous to the settler colonial enterprise for persons of mixed white and Native American descent to be considered white and for persons of African descent, mixed either with white, Native, or both, to be considered black. Simply put, this approach to defining race caused the Indian to "disappear," opened up their lands for settlement, and maintained blacks as a distinct population that could be exploited for labor. Today these distinctions serve to keep Native Americans and African Americans from finding that we often share even more than a common oppression.

The story of those with both Native American and European ancestry is complicated by two divergent attitudes toward them that existed side by side in America. Though the offspring of racially mixed unions were often ostracized, several prominent European American colonists, including Robert Beverley in his *The History and Present State of Virginia* (1705) and John Lawson in his *A New Voyage to Carolina* (1709), openly advocated white-Indian intermarriage for the purpose of "civilizing" the Indians and removing them as a possible threat to expansion (Hoover 62–63). Consider the words on Indian miscegenation written in 1728 by William Byrd, a wealthy Virginia planter about whom we will learn more in the next chapter. Byrd suggested, as an answer to the "Indian problem," that "a sprightly lover is the most prevailing missionary that can be sent amongst these, or any other infidels":

> The poor Indians would have had less reason to complain that the English took away their land, if they had received it by way of portion with their daughters. Had such affinities been contracted in the beginning, how much bloodshed had been prevented, and how populous would the country have been, and, consequently, how considerable? Nor would the shade of the skin have been any reproach at this day; for if a Moor may be washed white in three generations, surely an Indian might have been blanched in two.
>
> The French . . . have not been so squeamish in Canada, who upon trial find abundance of attraction in the Indians. Their late grand monarch thought it not below even the dignity of a Frenchman to become one flesh with this people, and therefore ordered 100 livres for any of his subjects, man or woman, that would intermarry with a native. (430–31)

Byrd's proposal was inspired by the French success in creating a Métis people, a mixed people who would not only strengthen the hold of colonial governments over the land but also act as go-betweens in trade and political relations. But his plan was also inspired by the immense success of the Spanish in the south. Along with disease, slavery, and outright slaughter, the building of the Spanish empire had been expedited by rape, sexual slavery, and forced prostitution. Michele de Cuneo, an Italian nobleman who accompanied Columbus on his second voyage, wrote:

> While I was in the boat I captured a very beautiful Carib woman, whom the said Lord Admiral gave to me, and with whom, having taken her into my cabin, she being naked according to their custom, I conceived desire to take pleasure. I wanted to put my desire into execution but she did not want it and treated me with her finger nails in such a manner that I wished I had never begun. But seeing that, . . . I took a rope and thrashed her well, for which she raised such unheard of screams that you would not have believed your ears. Finally we came to an agreement in such manner that I can tell you she seemed to have been brought up in a school of harlots. (Qtd. in Stannard 84)

The racial confusion and mixed loyalties that resulted from a little over three hundred years of such unions is evident in Simón Bolívar's Jamaica Letter of 1815, reflecting on the revolt against Spain. Spanish cultural/biological genocide had worked to Spain's advantage; the mestizo "Americanos" were "not prepared to secede from the mother country." Bolívar writes, "We were left orphans . . . uncertain of our destiny. . . . [We] scarcely retain a vestige of what once was; we are, moreover, neither Indian nor European, but an intermediate species between the legitimate owners of this country and the Spanish usurpers" (qtd. in Stannard 240).[19]

And, for a while at least, America followed the lead of France and Spain in this regard. In 1784 the legislature of the state of Virginia considered a bill offering payment to whites for marrying Indians and giving bonuses based on the number of offspring. Though the bill did not pass, by the time the United States had formed a nation, miscegenation was seen as a viable solution for "the Indian problem." On the frontier, "squawmen," their Indian wives, and half-breed children did, in fact, act as what Margaret Connell Szasz calls cultural brokers. They were translators when needed in both political and economic exchanges; they spread white cultural values to Natives far from the predominantly white settlements. Most importantly, their very existence symbolized a unified American future for both races. As Thomas Jefferson, speaking to a group of Delawares in 1808, said, "'Your blood will run in our veins and will spread with us over this great island'" (qtd. in Dippie 260).

Jefferson also felt that interbreeding of blacks and whites had a place in his plan for America; miscegenation offered a way for African slaves to be "improved." Proposing a plan for emancipation, Jefferson wrote in his *Notes on the State of Virginia*:

> Why not retain and incorporate the blacks into the state, and thus save the expense of supplying[,] by importations of white settlers, the vacancies they will leave? . . . Are not the fine mixtures . . . the expressions of every passion by greater or less suffusions of colour in the one, preferable to that eternal monotony, which reigns in the countenances, that immovable veil of black which covers all the emotions of the other race? Add to these, flowing hair, a more elegant symmetry of form. . . . The circumstance of superior beauty, is thought worthy attention in the propagation of our horses, dogs, and other domestic animals; why not in that of man? (144–45)

Of course, the calculated breeding of "more attractive" blacks was not the primary reason the offspring of black female slaves were often of mixed black and white descent; as in Cuneo's "India," black female slaves were subject to the sexual whims of white masters. Prices for young female slaves, black or Indian, reflected the widespread practice of concubinage. An article about Native slavery from a mid-nineteenth-century edition of a California newspaper, the *Marysville Appeal*, lists the price for "'likely young girl'" as roughly twice that for a boy, girls satisfying the master's needs for both "'labor and . . . lust'" (qtd. in Stannard 143).

Throughout this conjoined history of slavery and oppression, during which blacks and Indians were often in proximity to one another, sexual and marital relationships between blacks and Indians were also quite common. Jack D. Forbes, author of the landmark study *Black Africans and Native Americans: Color, Race and Caste in the Evolution of Red-Black Peoples*, observes,

> The ancestry of modern-day Americans, whether of "black" or "Indian" appearance, is often (or usually) quite complex indeed. It is sad that many such persons have been forced by racism into arbitrary categories which tend to render their ethnic heritage simple rather than complex. It is now one of the principal tasks of scholarship to replace the shallow one-dimensional images of non-whites with more accurate multi-dimensional portraits. (271)

Forbes shows repeatedly in his book that the meanings of various racial terms have never been static, that a term could mean different things at different times to different people. The terms "negro," "black," and "colored" have referred to those of African and Native American descent as well as to others of dark or "swarthy" complexions, whereas "mulatto," "mestizo," "half-blood," and "half-breed" have been applied to those of a number of racial mixtures. Moreover, Forbes demonstrates that laws that define race in the Americas have shifted back and forth over the years and that "the primary use of such terms in legislation was *to exclude* persons so categorized from the ordinary rights and privileges enjoyed by white subjects of the respective colonial powers" (269). The circumstances of people of mixed Cherokee and white descent offer a good example. Whereas from 1705 to 1866 in Virginia, parts of which were Cherokee lands, a person had to be one-eighth Indian to be defined as such by law (Forbes 195), during removal in 1838 anyone who identified primarily with the Cherokee Nation, whatever his or her racial composition, was forced on the Trail of Tears. On the other hand, until August 9, 1888, with the passage of 25 USC 182, "Rights of Indian Women Marrying White Men," Indian women who married white men lost all tribal rights. California, the state in which young Indian female slaves were bringing such a high price, provides another example. California passed a law in 1850 defining Indians as those of at least one-half Indian blood (Forbes 198). In practice, however, children too young to even explain their ancestry were routinely abducted into slavery, and all Indians were subject to legally condoned genocide. As the first governor of California, Peter Burnett, expressed it in his State of the State Address of January 6, 1851, "a war of extermination will continue to be waged between the races until the Indian race becomes extinct." Erasing the Indian heritage that many who are labeled as Hispanic, black, or white share with those who are enrolled citizens of tribal nations is one of the processes of genocide, the "paper genocide" Geary Hobson describes (see chapter 4). When we embrace our commonality, whether through shared Indigenous bloodlines or through shared experiences of oppression, we subvert colonization.

Conclusion

Transindigenism, which grows out of the nationalist paradigm upon which transnationalism is built, is problematized because of its nontribal origins. Thus, I favor the term "Intertribalism" over "Transindigenism." When Indigenous nations are dealing with other Indigenous nations, it is *still* Intertribalism, because the concept of nationhood from an Indigenous perspective is one of kinship, both blood kinship and "taken" (or "adoptive") kinship in a variety of ways. So when we deal with nations, we deal with groups of "my family" and "your family," which removes the objectifying element of the contemporary Western, Westphalian concept of nationhood. Objectification, learned from colonization, is what enables us to act in a destructive fashion towards other. Creation is a harmonious whole, all things working in balance with one another. When humans act out of accord with nature, the devastation affects all, ultimately coming back to haunt humankind. In Silko's *Ceremony*, this law of nature is depicted from a Laguna Pueblo perspective, with Spider Woman's creation being a web—fragile and resilient at the same time—that is attacked by "destroyers" or "witches" one strand at a time. The breach, alienation, is the first tool the destroyers utilize on non-Indigenous people:

Then they grow away from the earth
then they grow away from the sun
then they grow away from the plants and animals.
They see no life
When they look
they see only objects. . . .
They fear
They fear the world
They destroy what they fear.
They fear themselves. (135)

Alienation from the rest of creation, from the earth, from other people, from plants and animals, leads to objectification. Objectification of any part of creation leads to the abuse of it, which in turn leads to self-annihilation. Objectification, according to Silko, equals "witchcraft." In other words, objectification is bad medicine, and the only way to save the planet and to save humanity from the imperialism, capitalism, and materialism that has sucked us all in is to *stop objectifying each other*. The late, great Chicana theorist and writer Gloria Anzaldúa points out that objectification is what outside culture imposes on American Indigenous people: "White anthropologists claim that Indians have 'primitive' and therefore deficient minds, that we cannot think in the higher mode of consciousness—rationality. . . . [W]estern culture made 'objects' of things and people when it distanced itself from them, thereby losing 'touch' with them. This dichotomy is the root of all violence" (37). Instead of internalizing colonialism and enacting the lateral violence and racism it predicates, we must learn to recognize each other as relatives in our woundedness and go beyond both nationalist and racist paradigms to find holistic healing for the planet and us all.

THREE

The "Great Father's" Tongue Is Still "Forked"

The Fight for American Indian Resources and Red Rhetorical Strategies in Settler Colonial Politics

> My Father is with me, and there is no Great Father between me and the Great Spirit.
>
> —*Crazy Horse (qtd. in Neihardt 112)*

Throughout the history of settler colonial political discourse between non-Natives, from William Bradford's *Of Plymouth Plantation* to the present, Native peoples have always been "othered," have always been pushed to the "margin," seen as "extreme," while imperialism, Christianity, and capitalism have been "normalized" in the process of erasing colonial guilt. Simultaneously, in the process of placing Indians in a subaltern position, settler colonial leaders, including American presidents, have utilized Native rhetorical models in their speeches to America's First Peoples in an attempt to make violations of sovereignty and cultural and physical genocide "taste good," to put it in Cheyenne terms. Past presidents attempted to fit into American Indian rhetorical traditions as much as possible when they perceived themselves to be in Indian Country, but they excluded Indians not only from the conversation but also from the recognition of existence, as soon as they felt they were safely across "the frontier." Just as Native people learned English along with accompanying Anglo rhetorical structures in boarding schools, American leaders from colonial times to the present sometimes learned Indigenous languages or parts of languages and certainly learned Native rhetorical structures to use in their attempts to persuade Native peoples.[1]

Former president George W. Bush is no exception to this history. This chapter analyzes a few of his speeches and proclamations to and about Native

Americans, considering the historical context of presidential rhetoric in such speeches and unveiling the false promises he made, specifically in regard to sovereignty, American Indian education, economic development and the Energy Policy Act of 2005, and American Indians in military service. Bush posited himself as a "friend of the Indians," while his policies caused both American Indian people and the environment to suffer. This chapter suggests that Bush's smooth use of pseudotraditional oratorical devices in his speeches to American Indians allowed him to talk "in a good way" despite his later failure to keep his word in regard to policy. Moreover, the incorporation of American Indian rhetorics may have played a role in the collusion of several Native American politicians with lobbyist Jack Abramoff and Michael Scanlon, Republican press secretary to former U.S. representative Tom DeLay, a move that backfired for these Indian leaders and their people. This affair should serve as a reminder to us as American Indian studies scholars that Native rhetorics are valuable in reaching Indian Country with pragmatic contributions from our scholarly work, not because *any* rhetorical strategy can be a bearer of intrinsic truth. The chapter ends with my eisegesis exploring the idea of sovereignty in the context of these speeches and in current American Indian scholarship and concluding that the road to true self-determination might be found only with serious revision in tribal-governmental structures—with traditional forms of leadership replacing the federally molded "cookie cutter" constitutions and their subsequent revisions—and in intertribal and international alliances in the tradition of precontact confederacies.

Speaking to Indian Nations: A History of Rhetorical Appropriation

Throughout the history of the United States, its presidents have employed several of the rhetorical techniques I describe in previous chapters in their speeches to Indian people, in an evolving fashion. This strategy should not be surprising, as it is one of the basic understandings of the art of rhetoric today. As noted rhetorician Kenneth Burke asserts, "You persuade a man only insofar as you can talk his language by speech, gesture, tonality, order, image, attitude, idea, *identifying* your ways with his" (55). Though the scope of this chapter is too small to allow me to review and analyze that entire history here, at least a brief examination is necessary to demonstrate the context of Bush's speeches. If the body of presidential speeches to American Indians is examined, we again notice the dominance of repetition and recursivity and the technique of establishing kinship and identity, along with promise making or gift giving. Other devices that are sometimes seen are the inclusion of "insider" humor and allusions to Native values, beliefs, and cultural material in an attempt to suggest a commonality with the audience. An additional rhetorical mode used is the situating of listeners in a position of respect, often by noting the contributions the listeners have made to the speaker and by making self-deprecating remarks or declarations of humility that communications scholar Jason Black calls "self-mortification" ("Memories" 217; "Symbolic Suicide" 1–12, 14–15, 18, 20).

Records of early contact with Anglo settlers show that Native protocols of understanding relatedness were followed. But it seems that many settler colonial leaders forgot their obligations of relationship, especially when they gained power. A good example of one who forgot is John Smith, an English soldier who was among the leaders of the Jamestown colony. In *The Generall Historie of Virginia* (1624), he describes the relationship between himself and Wahunsenacawh, a seventeenth-century American Indian leader commonly known as Powhatan. Smith's famous depiction of his life being saved by Powhatan's daughter Pocahontas—"At the minute of my execution, she hazarded the beating out of her owne braines to saue mine" (121)[2]—is understood by some scholars to have been an adoption ceremony, a rebirth as a member of the community as Pocahontas's brother and Powhatan's son. Powhatan's words seem to confirm this:

> Captaine [Newport—Smith's commanding officer] you call father, and so you call me; but I see for all vs both you will doe what you list, and we must both seeke to content you. But if you intend so friendly as you say, send hence your armes, that I may beleeue you; for you see the loue I beare you, doth cause me thus nakedly to forget my selfe. (Qtd. in J. Smith 76)

Powhatan's speech gives evidence not only of an adoptive relationship but also of the betrayal of that relationship by Smith:

> Captaine Smith, you may vnderstand that I having seene the death of all my people thrice, and not any one liuing of these three generations but my selfe; I know the difference of Peace and Warre better then any in my

> Country. . . . [Y]ou are come to destroy my Country, so much affrighteth all my people as they dare not visit you. What will it availe you to take that by force you may quickly haue by loue, or to destroy them that provide you food. What can you get by warre, when we can hide our provisions and fly to the woods? . . . Thinke you I am so simple, not to know it is better to eate good meate, lye well, and sleepe quietly with my women and children, laugh and be merry with you, haue copper, hatchets, or what I want being your friend: then be forced to flie from all, to lie cold in the woods, feede vpon Acornes, rootes, and such trash; and be so hunted by you, that I can neither rest, eate, nor sleepe; but my tyred men must watch, and if a twig but breake, every one cryeth there commeth Captaine Smith. . . . Let this therefore assure you of our loues, and every yeere our friendly trade shall furnish you with Corne; and now also, if you would come in friendly manner to see vs, and not thus with your guns and swords as to invade your foes. (Qtd. in J. Smith 76)

Not only did Smith affirm his relationship with Powhatan and then fail to behave like a son—neglecting to care for his father Powhatan as well as Captain Newport had, by exchanging mutual gifts of love and respect—but he compounded the problem by demanding a corn tax by force, bringing along armed men on what should have been a family visit, and putting Powhatan and his people in fear for their lives on a regular basis.

This behavior pattern established by Smith and early settler colonials continued after 1790 and is evidenced in speeches of U.S. presidents. A few speech excerpts from the first U.S. president, George Washington, show that a greater understanding of American Indian terms of relationship developed quickly among U.S. government officials. In his speech to the chiefs of the Seneca Nation, given on December 29, 1790, Washington both establishes kinship and identity and promises good things for the people, saying: "The United States and the Six Nations should be truly brothers, promoting each other's prosperity by acts of mutual friendship and justice" (NHPRC, "From George Washington to the Seneca Chiefs"). However, Washington had been given the name "Town Destroyer" by the Iroquois people, though there is some scholarly debate as to the reason for this particular name. One theory is that it connected him with his great-grandfather John Washington, who was given this name by the Iroquois either because he had cheated them out of some land or because he had

had a role in the deaths of some Indians during Bacon's Rebellion. Others say that Tanacharison, a Seneca-adopted captive who grew up to become a chief and was extremely influential during the early part of the French and Indian War, gave Washington this name during an adoption ceremony to recognize his military efforts. Note the words of Seneca chief Cornplanter, who wrote to Washington in 1790 (the same year Washington made his claims to kinship): "When your army entered the Country of the Six Nations, we called you the Town-destroyer and to this day, when that name is heard, our women look behind them and turn pale, and our children cling close to the neck of their mothers. Our Councillors and warriors are men, and can not be afraid; but their hearts are grieved with the fears of our women & children, and desire, that it may be buried so deep, as to be heard no more" (NHPRC, "To George Washington from the Seneca Chiefs"). Eleven years earlier, Washington had sent orders to Major General John Sullivan in a letter dated May 31, 1779:

> The Expedition you are appointed to command is to be directed against the hostile tribes of the Six Nations of Indians, with their associates and adherents. The immediate objects are the total destruction and devastation of their settlements, and the capture of as many prisoners of every age and sex as possible. It will be essential to ruin their crops now in the ground and prevent their planting more[,] . . . that the country may not be merely overrun, but destroyed. . . . Our future security will be in their inability to injure us and in the terror with which the severity of the chastisement they receive will inspire them. (NHPRC, "From George Washington to Major General John Sullivan")

These attacks obliterated at least forty Iroquois communities. Washington's sincerity in claiming kinship with the Senecas is severely undermined by his orders for their destruction. Some Iroquois people still use the name "Town Destroyer" for any U.S. president, seeing all presidents as representatives of the same settler colonialism that has infringed upon their sovereignty and oppressed their people since 1790.

Cherokee people had similar experiences with Washington, with his seemingly sincere expressions of caring about Cherokee people in some of his speeches to Cherokees who were cooperative with the Americans and enabled their Revolution to succeed. In his "Talk to the Cherokee Nation," given in

Philadelphia on August 29, 1796, Washington utilizes repetition of his salutation, "Beloved Cherokees." For people familiar with Cherokee culture or history, an immediate connection is drawn between Washington's use of the word "beloved" and its connotations in Cherokee. "Beloved" women and "beloved" men were highly respected people of political power. In particular, "Beloved Women" or "War Woman"—"Ghigau"/ ᎩᎦᎤ or "Agigaue"/ ᎠᎩᎦᎤᎠᎡ—held a specific cultural role, having distinguished themselves either for greatly serving their community or for having gained honor in battle themselves. Washington intentionally uses this word, knowing its connotations for Cherokee people. Throughout the speech, he advocates assimilation in the interest of the future of the Cherokee people. He urges the Cherokee people to take up agriculture—which they had practiced even prior to European contact—to set a good example for other Indian peoples and nations. He points out that game had grown scarce—without taking responsibility for the settler colonial role in the decimation of it through the trade relationship between them and Cherokee people, particularly in regard to the high demand for deerskins. To Cherokees practicing agriculture, Washington promises the highly coveted Peace Medals, the visual rhetoric of which suggests a balanced future relationship between settler colonials and American Indian people. The Peace Medals depict Seneca leader Red Jacket at the edge of forested Indian Country, having just taken the pipe from Washington, who stands in the right foreground in front of a plowman and his oxen, his farmstead in the distance. It must be remembered that the main body of the Cherokee Nation were designated as "good Indians" because they sided with the Americans during the Revolutionary War, believing it to be in their best interest. A minority party of dissenters, among them Tsi'yugûnsi'ni (Dragging Canoe) and Inoli (Black Fox), fought against the Americans (discussed in more detail in chapter 4). But just as a great deal of assimilation, intermarriage with whites, and being at peace with the United States had not protected the "good Cherokees" in 1792 from unwonted attacks by American settlers (NHPRC, "Proclamation"), the further assimilation Washington urges and the agreement of peace he offers would do nothing to prevent further settler colonial encroachment, the deaths of great numbers of Cherokee people, and the loss of true Cherokee sovereignty.

In 1830, with the passage of the Indian Removal Act,[3] it *should have* become clear that trusting U.S. presidents—and the system of checks and balances intended to protect the people from a too-powerful president—was misguided. But even Andrew Jackson, the president most notorious to the "Five Civilized Tribes" because of this removal policy, could manage to "talk in a good way" to Indian people. Of course, there was a radical disconnect between his words and his actions. In his "First Inaugural Address," in March 1829, Jackson told his non-Indian audience, "It will be my sincere and constant desire to observe toward the Indian tribes within our limits a just and liberal policy, and to give that humane and considerate attention to their rights and their wants which is consistent with the habits of our Government and the feelings of our people." By December 1829, when he spoke to Congress, Jackson's true intentions were beginning to emerge, though they were couched in the language of sentiment:

> Our conduct toward these people is deeply interesting to our national character. Their present condition, contrasted with what they once were, makes a most powerful appeal to our sympathies. . . . Surrounded by the whites with their arts of civilization, which by destroying the resources of the savage doom him to weakness and decay, the fate of the Mohegan, the Narragansett, and the Delaware is fast overtaking the Choctaw, the Cherokee, and the Creek. That this fate surely awaits them if they remain within the limits of the States does not admit of a doubt. Humanity and national honor demand that every effort should be made to avert so great a calamity. ("First Annual Message")

In that speech, Jackson is promoting the idea of removal as the only means by which to save the remaining Southeastern tribes. In his second annual message to Congress, when he is announcing the Indian Removal Act, he still claims that the policy was instituted for the benefit of the Indians.[4] Ultimately, however, the Cherokee Nation and the other "Five Civilized Tribes" were dispossessed of their ancestral lands. Under Jacksonian policies, about 4,000 Cherokees and around 2,500 Choctaws died in the forced removal to Indian Territory, the region of the present state of Oklahoma, with many, many Chickasaws, Creeks, and Seminoles dying as well. Survivors suffered much individual misery because of detrimental conditions, disease, rapes, and other degradations. If removal was done in American Indian "best interest," it is truly frightening what this U.S. president found that best interest to be. As Friedrich Gerstaecker, an eyewitness, said of Creek removal:

> Many . . . died on the road from exhaustion, and the maladies engendered by their treatment; and their relations and friends could do nothing more for them than fold them in their blankets, and cover them with boughs and bushes, to keep off the vultures, which followed their route by thousands . . . ; for their drivers would not give them time to dig a grave and bury their dead. The wolves, which also followed at no great distance, soon tore away so frail a covering, and scattered the bones in all directions. (277)

Though I could certainly go into more detail with other U.S. presidents' speeches throughout history—Woodrow Wilson's attempt to get rid of the "Great White Father" appellation in a World War I speech is an interesting one—at least the bare bones of a historical framework for George Walker Bush's speeches to American Indians has been established by these few examples. Over the course of settler colonial history in these lands, as the relationship terms varied from "Father/Son" on the parts of Powhatan and Smith, respectively, to "Beloved" on the part of Washington, to "Great Father," so did the legal interpretation of the relationship between the tribes and the United States. From constitutional recognition of sovereignty, to dependent sovereign nation status under *Johnson v. M'Intosh, Cherokee Nation v. Georgia,* and *Worcester v. Georgia,*[5] to abrogation of treaties at the whim of Congress under *Lone Wolf v. Hitchcock,* American Indian nations have their relationships with the federal government interpreted and reinterpreted—what Scott Lyons terms "the rewriting of Indian sovereignty . . . over time" ("Rhetorical Sovereignty" 452). The shift in the terms used for relatedness over the course of the colonial and paracolonial era seen above is disturbing enough—American Indian people go from "my father" to "my red brothers" to "my red children." Jason Black builds on the work of U.S. Indian policy historian Francis Paul Prucha regarding how this paternalism disempowered American Indian people and nations (Black, "Native Resistive Rhetoric" 77–78).[6] Paternalism and a corresponding infantilizing is followed by an even more disturbing shift *from relatedness*—a fundamental aspect of tribal worldviews—*to nationhood,* definitely a Western paradigm. After all, although American Indian nationhood is first recognized in U.S. law in the Commerce Clause of article 1, section 8, of the U.S. Constitution, the language actually utilized in that section reads: "To regulate Commerce with foreign *Nations,* and among the several States, and with the Indian *Tribes*" (my italics). While Lyons asserts in *X-Marks: Native Signatures of Assent* that American Indian leaders committed to nation-state status when they placed their X-marks on treaties (location 172) and that "nation" is a word often used to denote the tribes in those documents, what is signified by that word slips over time. The idea of a dependent sovereign nation was born of the Marshall Trilogy.[7] This may seem like a slight change in rhetoric—going from using terms of relatedness and the ideas of groups of related people (tribes) for addressing American Indians to using terms of subaltern nationhood (domestic dependent nations)—and a change of medium, from the oral negotiations of intertribal diplomacy accompanied often by visual and material rhetorics to written treaties. However, these subtle differences mark a shift from American Indian perspectives of peoplehood to a Western concept of nationhood that corresponds with a loss of power and a decline in sovereignty for American Indian peoples. While things have improved on the international scene with the passage of the UN Declaration on the Rights of Indigenous Peoples (UNDRIP), the United States, because of its rhetoric of force and because of lopsided alliances between Indian leaders and those in power, still holds much sway over the destinies of American Indian people.

The U.S. Census Bureau reported that in the United States in 2010 there were over five million Alaskan Natives and American Indian people along with mixed-blood people who claim American Indian ancestry, a 39 percent increase since the 2000 census (Norris et al.). While some people discount this number as inflated by unenrolled mixed-bloods, significant increases in federally recognized tribal populations exist. In fact, American Indians, since the turn of the twenty-first century, have been having a measurable impact on elections in the United States for the first time ever. Ron DePasquale, a veteran reporter and news producer at the Associated Press's Nerve Center in New York, claims that American Indian votes began making a deciding difference in elections as early as 2002. Politicians running at the federal level in both parties recognize that the American Indian vote can make a difference in states such as Oklahoma, South Dakota, Arizona, New Mexico, and Washington because of the large number of Native citizens. Republican campaign brochures have even been printed in Navajo. According to *Politico* managing editor Carrie Budoff Brown, Shannon County, South Dakota, which encompasses the Pine Ridge Indian Reservation within its bounds and helped secure the state's Democratic Senate seat in 2002, was also influential in 2004 and 2006 elections: "Shannon County delivered 85 percent of the vote to Democratic presidential nominee John Kerry, making it his top county in the nation [in 2004]. The Native American vote was also considered key in Montana's 2006 Senate race when Democrat Jon Tester defeated Republican incumbent Conrad Burns." John Tahsuda (Kiowa), who served as a Romney adviser on American Indian issues during the 2012 campaign, believes the Indian vote had a significant impact on the presidential campaign itself as early as 2008. Moreover, tribes donated over $2.5 million to Obama's reelection campaign in 2012 and at least $750,000 to Romney (Capriccioso). Mark Trahant (Shoshone-Bannock), the Charles R. Johnson Endowed Chair of Journalism at the University of North Dakota, has observed that because of shrinking numbers of white voters, American Indians, particularly in Democratic coalitions with other people of color and white allies, can now have an effect on elections in states like Nevada, Alaska, Arizona, Wisconsin, and perhaps even staunchly Republican Oklahoma ("Confused"). Today, speaking directly to American Indian people is more important to politicians than ever. If several other factors are added to the mix—the amount of American Indian–held natural resources, the ever-growing and diversified economic development in Indian Country, the changes in international law regarding Indigenous people and tribal nations, and the power of movements like Idle No More to find connection through indigeneity, oppression, and the common need for survival throughout the hemisphere, with its millions of people of Indigenous ancestry, awakened and educated—Indigenous people could be a mightily powerful political force.

George W. Bush's successor, Barack Obama, made significant changes in government-government relations with the tribes, at least in terms of communication. Prior to his election, Obama focused on gaining the American Indian vote by meeting repeatedly with tribal leaders on the campaign trail (starting, ironically, with the Eastern Cherokees, whose ancestors we see in the next chapter on the forefront of Indian-Anglo diplomatic relations in 1730), holding a conference call with more than one hundred tribal leaders, and being formally adopted by members of the Crow Nation when he made the historic move of holding a televised campaign speech on the rez. Throughout his two terms in office he made good on campaign promises, holding an annual White House Tribal Nations Conference to meet with the leaders of all the sovereign tribal nations, holding a Cabinet Native Youth Listening Tour to improve education and other outcomes for tribal young people, and in general having strong Indian policies and strong relationships in Indian Country. Obama made history again in 2014 when he was only the sixth sitting U.S. president to visit Indian Country,[8] specifically the Standing Rock Indian Reservation in North Dakota, attending a powwow and other activities. Obama even believes that the Washington, D.C., football team should change its racist mascot. As the first president of color, Obama's notably lessened use of American Indian rhetoric and greatly improved relationship with American Indian people leave much to be explored for future scholars.

George W. Bush's history with American Indians and rhetoric is markedly different. An article in the August 26, 2000, issue of *Economist*, "Over to You, George," reveals he promised in his first campaign to "improve schools for Native Americans." Here, Bush makes what American Indians would traditionally view as an obligation in order to win them over as allies. He posits himself as a "friend." American Indian people should reasonably have been able to expect Bush to back up that promise with the necessary money once he became president, but of course that never happened. Bush's next noticeable mention of American Indians is in his 2001 National American Indian Heritage proclamation. Speaking soon after the September 11 terrorist attacks, Bush thanks American Indian people for their contributions to the United States, focusing on armed forces service, appealing to "warrior-culture" values and inspiring pride in much the same way that Native rhetors often do in community discourse such as powwows and soldier dances: "Almost half of America's Native American tribal leaders have served in the United States Armed Forces, following in the footsteps of their forebears who distinguished themselves during the World Wars and the conflicts in Korea, Vietnam, and the Persian Gulf. Their patriotism again appeared after the September 11 attacks, as American Indian law enforcement officers volunteered to serve in air marshal programs." Somewhat ironically, Bush asks Americans to learn about American Indian history, but in the sentences just before and after, he shows his *own* (and his speech writers') lack of knowledge. He sees the more than 560 sovereign nations as culturally homogenous: "We will work with the American Indians and Alaska Natives to preserve their freedoms, as they practice *their religion and culture*. . . . Such actions [studying Native history and heritage] reaffirm our appreciation and respect for *their traditions and way of life* and can help to preserve an important part of our culture for generations yet to come" (my italics). While Bush recognizes multiple practices ("traditions"), he fails to see that there are multiple cultures with multiple *bodies* of practice (the use of the singular in "way of life" and "their religion and culture"). His speech also shows that despite Native contributions, a dichotomy still exists between mainstream U.S. culture and that of American Indian peoples, that no matter how "patriotic" American Indian people are (as measured by service in the U.S. military), there is still an "us versus them" mentality. Not only does the group of "all Americans" he calls on to learn more about Native culture obviously exclude Native people, his statement that "*their* unique spiritual, artistic, and literary contributions, together with their vibrant customs and celebrations, enliven and enrich *our* land" completely negates his earlier reference to the U.S. motto "E pluribus unum," meaning "out of many, one." Although this division, in reinforcing some notions of sovereignty, might be desirable from American Indian perspectives, here it reinforces the paradigm of American Indian people as conquered, dispossessed tribes rather than sovereign nations with historical land bases and treaties with the government Bush represents. Bush simply continues the rhetorical tradition of "othering" American Indian peoples found throughout settler colonialism. He also makes several promises: "My Administration will continue to work with tribal governments on a sovereign to sovereign basis to provide Native Americans with new economic and educational opportunities. Indian education programs will remain a priority, so that no American child, including no Native American child, is left behind. We will protect and honor tribal sovereignty and help to stimulate economic development in reservation communities" ("Heritage Month" [2001]). These promises are discussed below.

Sovereignty

One clear element of American Indian rhetoric that George Walker Bush employs is embodied in his use (and misuse) of the word "sovereignty." "Sovereignty" is a shared value among American Indian peoples and is likely the most referenced term in contemporary American Indian political discourse, a term that has a unifying effect when drawn upon as a rhetorical strategy. Scholar Joanne Barker (Lenape/Delaware Tribe of Indians) says in her *Sovereignty Matters*:

> Following World War II, sovereignty emerged not as a new but as a particularly valued term within indigenous discourses to signify a multiplicity of legal and social rights to political, economic, and cultural self-determination. It was a term around which social movements formed and political agendas for decolonization and social justice were articulated. It has come to mark the complexities of global indigenous efforts to reverse ongoing experiences of colonialism as well as to signify local efforts at the reclamation of specific territories, resources, governments, and cultural knowledge and practices. (1)

Likewise, Lyons calls sovereignty "the guiding story in our pursuit of self-determination, the general strategy by which we aim to best recover our losses from the ravages of colonization: our lands, our languages, our cultures, our self-respect" ("Rhetorical Sovereignty" 449).

Lyons also points out that both within communities and in their discourse with outside entities, Indians are continually articulating "new rhetorics of sovereignty" ("Rhetorical Sovereignty" 456). Amanda J. Cobb says that the weight of this term shouldn't be underestimated and that sovereignty can have multiple meanings. She references a comment Vine Deloria made in an interview with me (published in *Paradoxa* in 2001) about the current generation of Native scholars: "They keep themselves in a little intellectual ghetto and throw around big words like 'sovereignty' and think they are doing something." Cobb then cautions, "Our understanding of sovereignty must be flexible and negotiable but not so flexible that the term can mean anything. If we are to heed Deloria's words, if our work is to be worthwhile to Native nations and not merely *about* them, then our concept of sovereignty must at least have some identifiable characteristics, some locatable meanings. Tribal sovereignty is too powerful a concept to diminish through frequent but diffuse conversation" ("Understanding Tribal Sovereignty" 115–16). In *Peace, Power, and Righteousness: An Indigenous Manifesto,* noted Mohawk scholar Taiaiake Alfred takes this one step further and interrogates whether or not this Western term coming out of very different hierarchical religious and political contexts is even appropriate for American Indian nations.

Whatever we as scholars have said, the U.S. government clearly defines sovereignty as something "bestowed upon" American Indian nations—as Native American historian Dina Gilio-Whitaker (Colville) of the Center for

World Indigenous Studies puts it—that allows for varying degrees of self-determination and government, and American Indian grassroots people often understand sovereignty as the "the state of political independence that existed prior to colonization," something inherent in tribal identity that predates colonization, definitely not a gift from later established settler colonial governments ("Indian Self-Determination"). Reflecting this contention over its definition, American Indian sovereignty as enacted in the Western legal, political, and economic realm has been increasingly challenged by various groups, including members of the religious Right, elected representatives, lobbyists, and gaming industry executives, since the passage of the Indian Gaming Regulatory Act in 1988 (Barker, "Recognition" 133). Moreover, Barker asserts that these groups contest sovereignty by means of what they deem reverse racism, claiming that "treaty and federal Indian law provide Native peoples with unfair economic opportunities, means and access to lands, and tax loopholes solely on the basis of race" ("Recognition" 133). The irony here is that though this argument is couched in legal, ethical, and religious language—similar to that of William Bradford's *Of Plymouth Plantation*—it is both racist and assimilationist, purporting to vie for fairness through "equal protection under the law," while ignoring a history of genocide, oppression, and violation of international law in U.S.-Indian relations. It also ignores the reality that American prosperity has been built with Indian land and Indian resources and with the spilling of much Indian blood.

Much attention was drawn to this conflicting notion of sovereignty when at a press conference with ethnic journalists in 2004, Bush called "sovereignty" something "given" to Natives by the U.S. Congress. Navajo Nation president Joe Shirley Jr. complained about Bush's "lack of understanding," which "makes your blood boil" (qtd. in DePasquale 12). Almost immediately the Bush administration began cleanup efforts. A "Memorandum on Government-to-Government Relationship with Tribal Governments," signed by Bush and issued on September 23, 2004, says, "My Administration is committed to continuing to work with federally recognized tribal governments on a government-to-government basis and strongly supports and respects tribal sovereignty and self-determination for tribal governments in the United States." Not wanting to be bound by his own words, Bush adds a disclaimer at the end: "This memorandum is intended only to improve the internal management of the executive branch and is not intended to, and does not, create any right, benefit, or trust responsibility, substantive or procedural, enforceable at law or in equity, by a party against the United States, its agencies, entities, or instrumentalities, its officers or employees, or any other person." But the definition of "sovereign" that Bush delivered later that same day, laboring further to rectify his earlier insult, sharply conflicts with the tone of this disclaimer as it adopts American Indian rhetorical forms: "Long before others came to the land called America, the story of this land was yours alone. Indians on this continent had their own languages and customs, just as you have today. They had jurisdiction over their lands and territories, just as you have today. And these sovereign tribal nations had their own systems of self-governance, just as you have today" ("Remarks"). I would like to take Bush at his word here because he speaks "in a good way," even utilizing repetition to reinforce the point that he understands that American Indian sovereignty is inherent and not given. Unfortunately, I cannot. Not only is it clear from the original September verbal blunder that this U.S. president served an entire term without understanding the principle of American Indian national sovereignty, but also his tendency to use doublespeak ought to make us call into question the veracity of his promises.

Good oratory built on lies has never been an American Indian tradition. Honesty, confirmed by the witness of others, is key to the warrior tradition of speaking (Masich et al.). In fact, there is a philosophical schism between Native and European cultures regarding honesty:

> The European and the Native American might disapprove of lying but adopt differing attitudes toward prevaricators. For the European, lying was a violation of Scripture and of "the Truth" referred to in the Christian New Testament. For the Native, "lying" might signify insanity: one who did not speak truth surely must not know what it is and therefore must have lost touch with reality. Thus cultural attitudes would differ: the white man who lied was devious, deceitful and not to be trusted by his fellows; however, within some tribes, the Native who lied was simply to be pitied, if not to be treated for his mind disease. (Cooper 104)

As people of Indigenous ancestry, we ought to hold our government officials up to the same standard we traditionally upheld for ourselves, whether those officials are federal, state, local, or tribal. Perhaps if we had looked at Bush's rhetoric from traditional perspectives, American Indians would have been forced to question Bush's sanity and, therefore, his authority or ability to negotiate with them on behalf of his people.

Indian Education

Let's begin by examining Bush's first promise: he would improve Native American education. American Indian education, with its history of coerced child removal from homes and with its attempts to "kill the Indian to save the man," has never matched the promises the United States made in the 120 treaties that included specific obligations for education. The creation of the boarding and residential school systems for the purposes assimilation is, rather, a genocidal act under the UN Convention on the Prevention and Punishment of the Crime of Genocide, because it "forcibly transfer[s] the children of the group to another group." In a paper commissioned by the U.S. Department of Education's Indian Nations at Risk Task Force in 1992, education scholar Jon Reyhner reports that at that time three out of ten Native American and Alaskan Native students dropped out of high school, about twice the national average. Reyhner attributes some of this to being "pushed out" and not respecting the students' cultures:

> Too often in schools today teachers are not reinforcing what Native parents show and tell their children[,] producing cultural discontinuity between home and school and forcing Native children to choose between their Native heritage and school success with disastrous results. Many of the problems faced by students such as drug and alcohol abuse are symptoms of the poor self concepts of Native students who have unresolved internal conflicts resulting from educators asking students to give up their Native culture. Teaching methods and school curriculum need to be changed to reduce cultural conflict between home and school. ("Plans")

The dropout rate for American Indian students has only grown in the intervening years since Reyhner's paper. According to an article in *U.S. News and World Report*, nationally, only 51 percent of American Indian and Alaskan Native students get their high school diplomas. Oklahoma fares a little better than the national average, with 63 percent of the students graduating high school (Sheehy). Correcting this failure of the educational system is supposed to fall under the province of two federal programs: Johnson-O'Malley and Title VII.[9] Tribes can use funds from the Johnson-O'Malley program to improve education and funds from Title VII to support their cultures. As per Bush's budget requests, these programs experienced larger than proportionate cuts in bad funding years for education and smaller than proportionate increases in good budget years, forming what the National Indian Education Association identified as an observable pattern ("NIEA Appropriations Priorities"). Clearly, the Bush administration did not live up to the president's promises of improving educational opportunities for American Indians. An American Federation of Teachers press release dated May 23, 2003, shows that Bush and the Bureau of Indian Affairs (BIA) even had plans to privatize Indian schools. Only staunch opposition by American Indian teachers and tribes to this plan halted what would have clearly been yet another trust violation (American Federation of Teachers). Furthermore, had these teachers and tribes not succeeded, and if the privatization of Indian schools had been anything comparable to the privatization of prisons, the results on the human level would have been disastrous, but the profits for investors would have been great.

Under Bush, education all over the United States increasingly moved to a model compatible with business, one in which learning can be measured and commodified, where students are objectified as either successful (i.e., have product consistency) or failed (i.e., are irregular, factory rejects). Bush's educational policy of No Child Left Behind (NCLB) directly conflicts with traditional American Indian pedagogy and cultural ways. Bobby Ann Starnes, president of the National Center for Collaborative Teaching and Learning, says in "Same Story, Different Century":

> NCLB will leave long-lasting casualties. . . . Learning will be more fragmented. . . . [M]ost NCLB programs use the methods and materials that are the exact opposite of those known to be effective with Native American children. . . . And as in the boarding school days, these programs reduce opportunities for children to build identities. They include no cultural connections and no concern for Native values, customs, or experiences. If they are effective, these programs will force more assimilation. (331)

The basis for NCLB is linked to similar programs in Texas during Bush's governorship of that state, policies that grew out of late 1980s school reform. Texas's claims during that time to have "narrow[ed] racial achievement gaps" seemed true only because "more of the lowest-scoring students dropped out" (Rubin 1). Bush's Program Assessment Rating Tool (PART)—an assessment policy based on the same testing principles as NCLB—led to a $225 million funding cut for Even Start literacy programs on twenty reservations and closed eleven Even Start centers in Indian Country at least temporarily because funding was directly tied to assessment results (Reynolds). Thus, programs designed to help preschoolers start their educations on a more equal footing have been subjected to educational theory that made them fail. NCLB and PART were not in the best interest of American Indian students.

Bush's assertions about education and Native Americans extend beyond his promises regarding Indian education itself, to the education of mainstream Americans about American Indian cultures and contributions to the United States. In doing so, he appeals to American Indian core values of protecting both traditional ways and knowledge of Native history in the same ways that American Indian rhetors uphold these as values in the communities. For instance, in November 2006, Bush utilized the occasion of Native American Heritage Month to sign H.R. 3085, the Trail of Tears Study Act, allowing researchers to more accurately establish the several Trail of Tears routes that were previously overlooked and revealing more accurately the location of the original Cherokee towns. Similarly, during Bush's administration, the Smithsonian's new National Museum of the American Indian opened in Washington, D.C., after moving most of its collection from its original New York City location, which was eerily close to the 9/11 Ground Zero site. Bush's speech on this occasion is given "in a good way," the way he typically structures his discourse when speaking to Indian people in order to persuade American Indian nations and constituents.

During his remarks at the opening of the new museum, Bush suggests that the museum would "introduce generations of visitors to a strong and living tradition." Throughout the speech Bush attempts to relate to his audience by stressing American Indian values of cultural vitality, honor, humor, and military service. But when he recognizes and renews relationships with American Indian historical figures, he chooses Sacagawea. The American Indian rhetorical strategies Bush draws on are incongruent with the binary oppositions of colonial discourse that necessitate the othering of American Indian people, at best as noble savages or Indian princesses. Bush situates Sacagawea in the paradigm of a "good Indian" because she helped the U.S. government during the Lewis and Clark Expedition. Of course, Sacagawea as a human being was a fully dimensional person, not a "tool" for white explorers, and of course the Native people mentioned during the speech have *not* dedicated their lives to being helpful to Bush or the federal government. Instead, they construct their own identities as integrated members of families, communities, and sovereign nations and as citizens of the United States, among other discourse groups. But it is Bush's construction of them as tropes rather than human beings that is troubling—just as his forefathers did to Squanto,[10] Pocahontas, and Sacagawea, as Hollywood has done to both the fictional Tonto and the real-life Code Talkers of World War II. George Bush can no more have a relationship with a stereotype than American Indian people can with the metaphorical entity Bush represents that "presents" presidential speeches.[11] Relationships are made human being to human being. The education that mainstream Americans need regarding American Indian cultures and American Indian contributions to America must begin with seeing Indians as human.

Economic Well-being and the Energy Policy Act of 2005

George W. Bush implied in his National American Indian Heritage Month proclamation of 2001 that he cared about the economic well-being of American Indian people and would help stimulate economic development on reservations. In his National American Indian Heritage Month proclamation of 2005, Bush touted the Energy Policy Act of 2005 as a solution to American Indian economic development: "To enhance energy opportunities and strengthen tribal economies, my administration is working to ease the regulatory barriers associated with tribal energy development[,] . . . allocating $2 billion in the form of grants, loans, and loan guarantees for exploration, development, and production of energy." Aside from concerns that this sort of development might not be in the best interests of Indian people, nations, or the land, Bush's financial concerns regarding Native lands did not seem to focus on Native people being the ones who profited. A few days after Bush's speech, *Indian Country Today* reported that under H.R. 4241, a budget reconciliation act called the Deficit Reduction Act of 2005, Congress had plans to sell federal lands, some of them still under claim by the Western Shoshones, in order to reduce the federal deficit (Melmer, "Federal Sale"). Unlike in the past, this land, under the supervision of the Bureau of Land Management, could be sold without proof of mineral value for other development purposes, such as ski resorts and condominiums, despite what Democratic congressman Nick Rahall of West Virginia called "America's commitment to protect these lands." Hunting, fishing, and gathering rights, as well as access to sacred sites, would have been affected by such sales. The Indigenous Environmental Network suggested this would have been "the final blow to Indigenous nations and communities attempting to re-establish title or use of what is rightfully theirs" (Melmer, "Federal Sale"). Bush, in his official response to the bill a couple of weeks later, objected only to the sale of lands in the District of Columbia, mentioning neither the western lands up for sale nor the drilling proposed in the Arctic National Wildlife Refuge ("Statement of Administration Policy"). Fortunately, by the time the bill actually passed, Shoshone lands were off the table, as was drilling in the Arctic National Wildlife Refuge. The next year, the United Nations Committee on the Elimination of Racial Discrimination (CERD), in a "historic and strongly worded decision," sided with the Shoshones as efforts by conservative political groups involved with large multinational corporations kept pushing for land and resource acquisition. CERD stated that the United States should immediately move to "respect and protect" the Shoshones' human rights; engage in open dialogue to negotiate a plan that the Shoshones could accept and that respected those rights; immediately cease negotiations to sell their "ancestral lands . . . to multinational extractive industries and energy developers"; and end all activities on those lands in the meantime, including the collection of "grazing fees, livestock impoundments, hunting, fishing and gathering restrictions." The Shoshone delegation to the United Nations testified to a number of abuses. Western Shoshone spokesperson Joe Kennedy pointed out that one major issue involved government and corporate plans to use Yucca Mountain, a Shoshone sacred site, for underground nuclear waste storage. Other tribal members complained that the air and water were being contaminated by resource extraction and contended that there was interference with sacred site use and burial sites (Western Shoshone Defense Project).

The Shoshone situation is, unfortunately, not unique. Other tribes also experienced negative consequences to their health and environment in the name of "economic progress" during the Bush regime and indeed still continue to do so. Though that history is too long to detail here, a few examples can demonstrate just how great this impact can be. Brad Miller, in a 2002 article entitled "Draining the Life from the Land: Mining and Indigenous People," suggested that "with the Bush/Cheney Energy Plan's emphasis on fossil fuel extraction, Native communities . . . are facing new threats to their water supplies and environmental integrity by the coal industry." Miller noted, "[The] Peabody Western Coal Co. pumps three million gallons of pure drinking water a day from beneath Black Mesa. Hopi and Diné (Navajo) residents are watching the ancient springs and washes that have sustained their way of life for centuries dry up." Miller also reported that the Salt River Project of Phoenix wanted to exploit the Zuni Salt Lake—a sacred site utilized for thousands of years by the Zuni, Laguna, Acoma, Dine, Apache, and other tribes—for coal mining, thereby not only contaminating the environment but also interfering with these tribal peoples' rights to religious practices. In *Indian Country Today*'s coverage of the Protect Endangered Peoples, Protect Endangered Species: Honor the Earth Tour in 1995, the late, highly respected American Indian journalist E. K. (Kim) Caldwell pointed out:

> [Because] Native peoples retain approximately 4 percent of their original land base and are second only to the federal government as land holders, it is no surprise that crucial environmental battles center on Indian land. In the US alone approximately two-thirds of the nation's uranium deposits, significant deposits of oil and natural gas, and over 15 million acres of prime forest are all on Indian held land. According to the World Watch Institute, almost all 317 reservations in the US are threatened by environmental hazards.

In addition to the Shoshone Yucca Mountain nuclear dump site, Caldwell lists coal leases on Northern Cheyenne land; "80 million acres of Alaskan offshore oil leases . . . in water surrounding Native coastal villages"; a metallic sulfide mine threatening land adjacent to that of the Sokaogon Chippewas at their Mole Lake reservation in Wisconsin; the dumping of toxic sewer sludge on the lands of small California tribes; and gold mining in the Sweet Grass Mountains of Montana.[12]

Besides the situations listed above, the Mescalero Apache, the Hopi, the Skull Valley Goshute, and the Navajo tribes, among others, have suffered from effects of the mining of radioactive material on their lands and the dumping of nuclear waste. Other tribes have seen their lands deforested. What the U.S. government refers to as "economic progress" has come at a high cost in terms of American Indian health and the well-being of the environment. Idle No More, the activist movement mentioned briefly in chapters 1 and 2, has brought a greater awareness to "ecocide," or environmental genocide—that is, damage to the land base of a people group that affects the members' well-being. Attorney and scholar Andrea Smith's *Conquest: Sexual Violence and American Indian Genocide* does an excellent job of clearly demonstrating how the interrelated health of the people and health of the land have been repeatedly affected by corporate imperialism. American Indian people and their Indigenous relatives worldwide continue to suffer from ecocide just as they did in the land boom era, but they are now seeking and recognizing relationships with each other and speaking out.

Bush and the Warrior Tradition

During his war-ridden presidency, George W. Bush made much of the American Indian warrior tradition, strategically voicing appreciation of Native military service in an era of soldier shortages. In his 2005 National American Indian Heritage Month proclamation, Bush pointed out, "Since the earliest days of our Republic, Native Americans have played a vital role in our country's freedom and security. . . . Today, that proud tradition continues, with Native Americans bravely defending our country in Operations Enduring Freedom and Iraqi Freedom and helping to spread liberty around the world." The text of this speech was accompanied by a photo of Laura Bush, wrapped in a shawl while attending an American Indian dance demonstration in Arizona earlier in the year. The image's symbolism alludes to the tradition of American Indian women proudly supporting American Indian war heroes. Bush has never demonstrated bravery in combat, so this imagery is both misleading and culturally offensive.

But Indians have demonstrated bravery in a war Bush began on "terror." Just as with every war since the American Revolution, American Indians have served in greater numbers per capita than any other group. Additionally, American Indian servicepeople and their families have made great sacrifices in support of the United States. According to a Congressional Research

Service report entitled "American War and Military Operations Casualties: Lists and Statistics," 26 Native Hawaiians or Pacific Islanders and 73 American Indians or Alaskan Natives had died in Operation Enduring Freedom, Operation Iraqi Freedom, and Operation New Dawn up to January 2, 2015 (DeBruyne and Leland). During that same time span, 135 Native Hawaiians or Pacific Islanders and 532 American Indians or Alaskan Natives were wounded in those operations (DeBruyne and Leland).

Throughout Indian Country, American Indian and First Nations people who have served in the U.S. or Canadian military recount their stories of coups,[13] kills, and evasion of the enemy to survive. Just as their warrior ancestors did, they offer these narratives to their people by making a personal contribution—a story that is an offering, if you will—in larger ceremonies that appeal to God for blessings and continued life for the people or that maintain and reinforce community structures. These tales are necessary for ceremonies such as the Cheyenne Sundance, Blackfoot appointments of chiefs, and even the Blackfoot Beaver Bundle opening mentioned earlier in this book. However, rarely does U.S. warfare live up to American Indian warrior traditions, which have at their core honor and respect, qualities military recruiters appeal to in their messages directed at American Indians. One of the most insightful statements on American Indian involvement in the war in Iraq is an open letter to Indigenous people that circulated through Native communities in the United States and Canada in 2006, entitled "Why Are Indigenous (American Indian) Soldiers Serving in Iraq?" by Michael Yellow Bird, professor of Sociology and director of Indigenous tribal studies at North Dakota State University. Yellow Bird questions why sovereign American Indian nations that understand the impact of war and that have a history of careful consideration and much council prior to engaging in war, have allowed the United States to make decisions regarding their participation in warfare. Particularly after it was proven that Bush lied both when he initiated the Second Persian Gulf War and after horrible atrocities were committed in the name of the United States, Yellow Bird suggests that American Indians should have questioned whether military service was in their best interest and the interest of their people. When U.S. motives for warfare do not align with Indigenous values of honor, American Indians who wish to continue warrior tradition in service to their people and families are placed in an extremely difficult position emotionally, mentally, and spiritually while they risk their physical lives.

Eisegesis: A Lack of Accountability and the Settler Colonial Governance Model

Tribal politicians, as well as U.S. politicians, must be held accountable to their constituencies regarding their relationships with outside interests and their duty to represent their peoples' needs. Certainly, there were questionable dealings in this vein during the George W. Bush administration. A 2002 *Business Week* article entitled "Campaign Reform Loophole" disclosed that, under campaign finance reform, Indian nations were not subject to the same rules as other entities. While others, such as political action committees, must limit candidate donations to $25,000 a year, there is no limit on the amount a sovereign nation can contribute. Also, unlike other groups, tribes are not bound to reveal the origin of their funds (Dunham and Bernstein 51). Using this loophole, convicted former lobbyist Jack Abramoff, who was sentenced to six years in prison for fraud and conspiracy, laundered money through tribes to finance politicians without accountability or limit. According to *U.S. News and World Report*, Abramoff testified that he "defraud[ed] four clients, Indian tribes that owned casinos." Abramoff and the four tribes donated $4.4 million in campaign moneys "to more than 300 lawmakers, federal candidates, and political committees" over a six-year period (Pound), a little less than a dollar for every person who claimed Native ancestry in the 2010 U.S. Census.

According to the *Washington Post*, Abramoff and Michael Scanlon, former press secretary to Republican congressman Tom DeLay, negotiated to "corruptly offer and provide things of value, including money, meals, trips and entertainment, to federal public officials in return for agreements to perform official acts" ("Unraveling Abramoff"). While this legal but unethical move for the tribes in question might have seemed like a good idea at the time to the tribal officials who made these decisions, the "favors" owed to tribal nations never materialized. From traditional perspectives, unethical choices yield bad outcomes. For instance, Ralph Reed, the first executive director of the Christian Coalition in the early 1990s and a onetime Republican candidate for lieutenant governor of Georgia, took money from Abramoff to "lobby against Indian casino gambling . . . at the same time that Abramoff was being paid to promote Indian casino gambling." The *Washington Post* also claims that Abramoff used a shady connection between former Interior secretary Gale Norton and Italia Federici, president of the Council of Republicans for Environmental Advocacy, to have tribes contribute more than $500,000 over three years to "obtain inside information affecting his tribal clients" from the Department of the Interior. Apparently, Abramoff referred to Federici's organization as "our access to Norton" ("Unraveling Abramoff").

Obviously, lobbying and contributing to political campaigns, the tools used by other segments of American society to gain political power, sometimes fail to advance tribal interests with the U.S. government. Cuts in funding to tribes and American Indian social services were rampant during the two George W. Bush administrations. An article entitled "Senators, Tribal Leaders Bash Bush's Latest Budget" lists a $2 million cut from the National American Indian Housing Council for 2007; a $33 million proposed cut from urban Indian health programs; a loss of $50 million for repair and building of BIA schools; and a loss of $16 million needed for the Johnson-O'Malley programs. Participating in dubious politics with federal officials and with lobbyists who work for other entities has not been proven beneficial to American Indians.

One problem is that American Indian tribes and people in oxymoronic legal relationships with the United States are stuck somewhere between having true sovereign-to-sovereign diplomatic relations and true representative democracy. Moreover, while Joanne Barker provides an excellent history of how this problematic legal relationship between the federally recognized tribes and the United States developed, she also points out that laws regarding tribal recognition have been unevenly applied, that laws regarding enrollment in federally recognized tribes have been unevenly applied, and that status means everything in terms of what rights American Indian people(s) do have ("Recognition" 134–36). But even for tribes with federal recognition, the cookie-cutter constitutions that so many have had for years, despite nominal revisions, are not based on Indigenous concepts of nationhood, governance, and law. As peoples, American Indian tribes should have the right both to determine citizenship on their own terms and to utilize their own Indigenous structures of decision making. Taiaiake Alfred says, "There has been a total theoretical exclusion and extinguishing of indigenous nationhood, leading to what a recent United Nations Human Rights Commission study labeled the unjust 'domestication' of indigenous nationhood" ("Sovereignty," *Sovereignty Matters* 36). Alfred challenges American Indigenous people to a "profound reorientation of indigenous politics and a recovery of indigenous political traditions in contemporary society" (38). American Indian nations should have the right to create their own governmental structures and laws and the right to enforce those laws by traditional means in their jurisdictions, as long as those laws and means are in accordance with international human rights.

Though some constitutions, such as that of the Cheyenne and Arapaho Tribes of Oklahoma, have been rewritten, they still are based on Western models; in this case, two *sovereign* nations are still forced to operate as one, and the governmental structure is traditional for neither. Anthropologist Loretta Fowler points out that the traditional Cheyenne and Arapaho structures are very different from today's governmental structures and that this inconsistency causes dysfunction within these tribal nations. Fowler suggests that the quagmire that is Cheyenne and Arapaho tribal politics today arises from the genocidal incident of Sand Creek, the tribes' subsequent removal to the reservation, their interactions with the federal government and the legal documents and policies that have guided those interactions, and a long history of racism and discrimination by non-Natives in western Oklahoma. However, tribal members often perceive their economic problems to be due to internal corruption in tribal government rather than to external factors. They accuse officials of graft and continually ask for recalls and new elections, hoping to ease their struggles but in actuality causing a breakdown in tribal governance. Fowler argues that despite this dysfunction, the tribes, particularly the Cheyenne, maintain traditional social order and successfully promote communal values in their continuance of social dances, powwows, giveaways, and ceremonies, proving that they are capable of success when working within an Indigenous political system.

Fowler's analysis holds true for many other tribal nations as well, because of the impact of similar political and economic circumstances created by colonization. I see the answer as lying in a needed restructuring of the governments to bring them into alignment with the traditional norms of each tribe. Much of the criticism levied in communities centers around sometimes perceived and sometimes actual favoritism extended to family members by those in office. As respected Cherokee scholar, attorney, and former judge Steve Russell says in *Sequoyah Rising: Problems in Post-Colonial Tribal Governance*, "Within tribal communities, too often nobody even bothers to pretend that power could come from anything but a blood relationship to the powerful" (161). In Western ways of governing, such favoritism is considered nepotism. Indigenous governance models, however, are built on family, on relationship. In traditional ways, what is viewed today as nepotism is simply "the clan system." In other words, the action of helping one's family is not morally wrong; the *system* is simply not designed for the culture. Were tribal nations to reorganize along their traditional guidelines, which would differ from tribe to tribe, governmental structures would be grounded in relationship. Extended family groups—clans, bands, or townships, for instance—would elect someone to represent their interests and speak on their behalf. That representative would be accountable to his or her own family members and represent them as they saw fit, or he or she would shortly be removed from office. Families would be forced to reconcile their differences and learn to work together again, or they would lack representation at the tribal level. Both of the major reasons for corruption in tribal governance would be alleviated; nepotism would end because the system would shift back to being based in relatedness, and individualistic graft would end as familial repercussions against a member who acted selfishly rather than seeking their common good would be even more punitive than the legal repercussions are now. The Absentee Shawnee Constitutional Revision Committee needs to be commended for the changes its members proposed to their people in this regard, recommending that the legislative districts be changed to represent the two historical bands—the White Turkey and Big Jim Bands—rather than geographical areas. Former committee member Paulette Blanchard says,

> There are pieces that we did get passed by vote at General council meetings. I spent about two years on the committee, and the process is beyond painfully slow. There are multiple ideas of what should be considered "traditional" and how that needs to look in modern political structures and within our own community. There are great ideas, but to create change too quickly is met with rejection as with anything misunderstood. The entire document is still in revision and continues to attract AST [Absentee Shawnee Tribe] citizens toward finding ways to blend our past with our present towards a future . . . [but] it will have to be approached in increments.

While this measure has yet to be approved in its entirety, I believe these sorts of revised structures have much potential to improve governance in Indian communities in years to come. To my knowledge, the only tribal nation in the United States operating under its traditional structure is the Onondaga Nation, which is still led by its Council of Chiefs and guided by its Clan Mothers.

Scholarship is greatly needed that examines tradition political structures for each tribe and how traditional structures and processes could be used in and *between* tribal governments today. This scholarship must be written from tribally specific perspectives by those knowledgeable in tribal history and ways, as well as in U.S.-Indian and international law. For example, Russell in *Sequoyah Rising* details Cherokee history in regard to economic systems and governmental structures—"a confederation of towns" (15)—and the history of changes that have occurred because of colonization and shifts in both economic systems and values. He rightly points out, however, that true freedom for "domestic, dependent nations" can be had only by sacrificing economic dependence on the United States, something many tribes are not truly prepared to do at this point (39–40, 45). Russell nevertheless demonstrates legal possibilities that the practice of arbitration could afford tribal nations, empowering them greatly in negotiating with corporations (49–62). He admits, though, that "economic integration" is still controversial among more traditional Indian people (66). Traditional people simply do not have the same value system as mainstream society. American Indian governments, on the other hand, are structured as businesses, as multi-enterprise corporations often dedicated to the Western notion of progress.

Given the kind of *intratribal* conflict seen in some current situations, such as that among the nations of the Blackfoot Confederacy regarding oil exploration at Chief Mountain, utilizing economics to achieve true sovereignty might seem impossible to many. Moreover, some critics point to the social issues brought about by colonization—suicide, homicide, alcoholism[14]—and suggest that these hinder both sovereignty and economic development. To the contrary, Russell notes: "The empirical results of the Harvard Project on American Indian Economic Development . . . draw a much more complex picture. While Indians have serious social problems that impede economic activity, and some of those problems might be considered cultural, 'the evidence is clear that as sovereignty rises, so do the chances of economic development'" (*Sequoyah* 69; internal quotation from Cornell and Kalt 8). However, there must be "a fit between the culture of the community and the structure and power of its governing institutions." Russell adds, "[Otherwise] those institutions may be seen as illegitimate, their ability to regulate and organize the development process will be undermined, and development will be blocked. Without a match between culture and governing institutions, tribal government cannot consistently do its basic job: creating and sustaining the 'rules of the game' that development in any society requires" (*Sequoyah* 69–70). Ultimately, however, Russell finds that survival as culturally distinct peoples will be guaranteed, not through economic development, but through the creation of the tribally based structures themselves, echoing Fowler's ideas explored above. Still, the Oneida Indian Nation in Wisconsin and the Chickasaw Nation in Oklahoma are two examples of tribes whose economic development actually enables and supports cultural resurgence, proving that those processes are not mutually exclusive. The Chickasaw Nation, for instance, used profits from various tribal enterprises to create both a world-class cultural center and the first tribally owned press, while the Oneidas use their profits to fund language classes and other forms of cultural revitalization.

Tribal attempts have been made to better deal with social issues through the venue of the justice system. To some people, this process marks a beginning in changing dominant-culture structures, through the emergence of restorative justice talking circles in a few First Nations in Canada and the development of the Navajo Peacemaker Court. They see this as the start of sovereign control over criminal justice (Barker, *Sovereignty Matters* 22). However, Barker points out:

> Translating indigenous epistemologies about law, governance, and culture through the discursive rubric of sovereignty was and is problematic. Sovereignty as a discourse is unable to capture fully the indigenous meanings, perspectives, and identities about law, governance, and culture, and thus over time it impacts how those epistemologies and perspectives are represented and understood. (19)

Alfred claims that "so long as sovereignty remains the goal of indigenous politics . . . Native communities will occupy a dependent and reactionary position relative to the state" (*Peace* 59), that "a paradigm bounded by the vocabulary, logic, and institutions of 'sovereignty' will be blind to the reality of a persistent intent to maintain colonial oppression of indigenous nations" ("Sovereignty," *Companion* 466). Russell reminds us that even current tribal laws regarding citizenship are grounded in a "'derivative discourse'" of race, a non-Native construct ("Racial Paradox" 163). Finding truly Indigenous perspectives about nationhood, governance, and law will take a great deal of cooperative effort between American Indian people, especially elders, tribal officials, and Native studies scholars. Federally recognized tribes of the United States and other peoples of American Indian descent must think outside of paracolonial boxes, finding Indigenous ways of working together to further the interests of Indigenous peoples and of humanity as a whole. In fact, the Constitution of Bolivia, as revised in 2009, offers an Indigenous take on the Westphalian nation-state that could be as beneficial to tribal constitution revision committees as the proposed Sequoyah Constitution of 1905, which Russell explores. Both of these constitutions offer a view of human rights that is far more in line with traditional ways in many tribal nations than the U.S. Constitution, the various state constitutions, or any tribal constitution of which I am aware, with the exception of that of the Onondaga Nation.

In the meantime, legally pursuing the best interests of Indian peoples is complicated by the fact that tribes were denied the right to diplomatic representation in dealings with the United States for years and are still denied the right to deal on a sovereign-to-sovereign basis with other nations. American Indian nations also lack representation in the U.S. Congress (but have tax-exempt status). Congress is, however, along with the Department of the Interior, in control of the tribes' destinies under U.S. law. Lobbying therefore became the only avenue for tribal representation. But for lobbying to be effective, more tribes need to hire their own lobbyists whose sole duty is representing their interests. American Indian nations should check the records of the lobby firms thoroughly and have tribal individuals keeping track of the lobbyists' work. Better yet, tribal members need to become educated to do the lobbying work for the tribes themselves, increasing accountability. The Navajo Nation, for example, is now employing its own tribal lobbyists in Washington. Tribes could also work together under the paradigm of precontact confederacies, joining their lobbying efforts together when common interests arise. In either case, American Indian people should be hired both tribally and intertribally to carry out this work *on behalf of* their people(s). Individual American Indians have worked as lobbyists in Washington for nontribal entities, but the level of corruption in the lobbying industry parallels that found in tribal governments across North America. Such corruption largely exists because Western governance structures are incongruent with tribal values.

Despite many obstacles, tribal diplomatic representation has changed at the national and international levels. In 1990, Chickasaw Nation governor Bill

Anoatubby appointed Charles W. Blackwell as a delegate to the United States. Anoatubby then named Blackwell as the Chickasaw ambassador to the United States in 1995, making him the first ambassador to the United States from an American Indian nation. Blackwell served as ambassador until his death in 2013 (the position has remained vacant since that time). The opening of an Embassy of Tribal Nations in Washington, D.C., in 2009 by the National Congress of American Indians (NCAI) is a further step in this direction, but currently the embassy simply provides permanent space on "Embassy Row" in D.C., functioning as a center for visiting tribal officials and intending to create more respect for tribal sovereignty. At this time, the name is still a misnomer. How can one have an embassy without having an ambassador (in this case, 566 ambassadors)? A good number of tribal officials serve in the NCAI as well as hold elected office in their tribes, such as Chickasaw lieutenant governor Jefferson Keel, who is the president of NCAI. However, their capacity in NCAI differs from both that of an ambassador and that of a congressperson, for NCAI itself has no actual legal authority under the domestic dependent nation paradigm—it is not a representative, legislative body.[15] In short, the embassy nominally grants tribal nations the dignity afforded to other sovereign nations, but it does not have the power to further sovereignty. Therefore, sending ambassadors from tribal nations to the United Nations would be an even more significant step. Sovereignty exists only in relation to other sovereigns. As we Native Americans try to conceive Indigenous political structures, sovereignty, and peoplehood, we come back to the concept of relatedness so clearly delineated in the nation-to-nation discourse analyzed above. Kinship organization that accounted for both the rights of the individual and the reality of mutual dependency for survival and balance formed the paradigm for inter-, intra-, and extratribal relations between individuals and groups. Alfred points out, "Even 'traditional' indigenous nationhood is commonly defined relationally, in contrast to the dominant formulation of the state: there is no absolute authority, no coercive enforcement of decisions, no hierarchy, and no separate ruling entity. . . . True indigenous formulations are nonintrusive and build frameworks of respectful coexistence by acknowledging the integrity and autonomy of the various constituent elements of the relationship" ("Sovereignty," *Sovereignty Matters* 42, 46).

A more traditional form of confederacy would better serve Native needs. In many ways, Idle No More is a grassroots expression of kinship extended across tribal lines, across borders, and even across ethnicity; this movement places the needs of humanity and the health of the planet and its creatures as a whole above the interests of capitalism and development. Idle No More is supported by some bands in Canada—such as the Attawapiskat First Nation, led by Chief Theresa Spence, whose six-week hunger strike was a major catalyst in drawing widespread solidarity for the movement—but has enjoyed only nominal support from U.S. tribal nations. In fact, there are a good number of grassroots Indigenous people in the movement who feel that the interests of their tribal leaders do not coincide with the interests of the people, particularly in regard to environmental health for future generations. As we try to bridge the gap between tribal nations, ceremonial elders, and grassroots activists, we need to explore both traditional and legal means of confederation in order to build more powerful solidarity. In examining the legal powers that could be utilized in forming confederations, Russell lists the power of taxation, used only in a limited way by tribes (*Sequoyah* 147). He also points out other legal avenues open to tribes, such as intertribal compact making; the issuance of "tax-exempt bonds"; the creation of tribally owned corporations and the ability to trade stocks issued from those; and the protection of "tribal intellectual property with trademarks, copyrights, and patents" (148). Russell holds up the State of Sequoyah[16] as "a paradigm for intertribal cooperation that is legally possible but lacking in practice" among tribes "linked by history, by geography, or simply by the exigencies of maintaining self-government in a postcolonial era" (146, 148).[17] He proposes that this sort of intertribal alliance could manifest itself in shared tribal courts, economic enterprises, and educational resources at all levels, including tribal colleges. It could also make possible tribally produced electricity, tribal think tanks, technology incubators, or an intertribal stock market for trading shares of Indigenous tribal enterprises. He suggests that increased adoption of the practice of alliances could make a new Sequoyah-like alliance possible:

> Sequoyah could rise again as the all-tribal union that eluded Pontiac, Dragging Canoe, and Tecumseh, a unified vision that might someday force a U.S. president to recognize that Congress *had no* constitutional authority to end treaty-making, a quintessentially executive function. *None* of this can happen while we cling to our historical role as victims, accurate as that memory may be. . . . [I]f we are still the people with

> peaceful trading patterns that spanned the entire continent before Europeans set foot on it, then the future belongs to us. (148–49; my italics)

The United Indian Nations of Oklahoma, Kansas, and Texas—a coalition that grew out of NCAI—is a good example of how such a paradigm can be put into action today. We, as individual people of Indigenous American descent, need to remember that we are not each other's enemies, even if our tribes were so traditionally, and that everyone's needs are furthered when we work together as related beings and entities. This was an underlying principle of all Indigenous American cultures. American Indian tribal representatives should promote their collective interests and be held accountable to that task.

And as nations, tribes need to interact as sovereigns with other Indigenous nations throughout this hemisphere and around the globe when interests are common. Tribal officials should educate themselves about international Indigenous issues and make decisions that are in the best interests of their nations. As people with ancestors who were here thirty thousand, maybe even seventy thousand years ago, we must look past artificial borders. Economic joint ventures, such as the programs that late former Venezuelan president Hugo Chávez and Citgo engaged in with the Micmacs and the Penobscots that provided the tribes with discounts on heating oil, offer tribes potential alliances that respect our ancestors and benefit both current and future generations as well as Mother Earth (Galvin). Tribal officials should know about the reformation of the Bolivian parliament by its president, Juan Evo Morales (Quechua), along Native models and about Bolivia's revised constitution, mentioned above. A number of tribal political and traditional leaders should be commended, such as Sid Hill, Tadodaho of the Haudenosaunee; Oren Lyons, Onondaga; and Alex White Plume, tribal chairman of the Oglala Sioux Nation, who met with Morales prior to a UN meeting to work together with him and First Nations leaders from Canada on passing UNDRIP (UCTP Taino News). Tribal officials should know about U.S. tax money being used for "dispossessing the Indigenous peoples of Peru, Ecuador and Colombia" (Reynolds). Sovereign nations should judge the behaviors of other sovereign nations for themselves. Michael Yellow Bird says that tribes have "outsourced" their "thinking" to the United States with respect to war. In truth, the federal-Indian relationship has forced tribes to outsource thinking on many issues to the United States.

Indigenous nations in the United States need to continually question the U.S. definition of Native sovereignty. Barker proposes that the Marshall Trilogy, upon which the entire notion of "domestic dependent nations" rests, is inherently flawed, as shown by use of the term "aboriginal title" to imply that Indians held only a limited title to their lands:

> Marshall's "aboriginal title" was directly at odds with the treaty-making efforts of the United States at the time. The treaty most certainly did recognize a title in the land that could be negotiated as well as the authority of the signatories to function as representatives of their governments. Under the precepts of international law, the 371 treaties ratified between the United States and indigenous peoples between 1778 and 1871 provided for the clear recognition of indigenous peoples as nations who could enter into treaties and, therefore, as nations who possessed jurisdiction and territorial rights. (*Sovereignty Matters* 9)

Furthermore, Barker points out that the people of the Cherokee Nation, as the party involved in the cases, had engaged in agriculture and had "established rights of property in the soil," that Cherokees did not have the kind of nomadic, sustenance-level culture that "aboriginal title" suggests (12). Barker suggests that American Indian tribes utilized the concept of sovereignty in relations with colonists and European nations as early as the 1600s (18). However, she also asks whether "sovereignty" as a concept has "ideological origins [that] might predispose a distortion or negation of indigenous epistemologies of law and governance" (21). In short, Native nations might find that their own concepts of nationhood, governance, and law do not fit within the Western paradigm at all. However, despite this incongruity and despite the lack of legal weight of UNDRIP, that document asserts that Indigenous peoples still have the right to their own traditional ways of understanding nationhood, law, and governance. With court decisions like *Mabo v. Queensland* in Australia in 1992 and *Delgamuukw v. British Columbia* in Canada in 1997, Indigenous concepts have been recognized in the courts of some settler nations as being firm legal grounding for "aboriginal title" that predates colonization (23). With American Indian studies scholarship that is conducted in cooperation with tribal people and governments and intentionally investigates Indigenous concepts of who we are as groups of related people, and with the results of that scholarship communicated to tribal people in clear, culturally appropriate ways, we can have hope that American Indian concepts of who and what their nations are will postdate colonization as well.

Conclusion

One crucial element of Native American rhetorics is missing in George W. Bush's presidential speeches and other speeches by settler colonial representatives to Native people, one that should make us think. To really explain anything *well* in Native communities, one must tell a story, one must give the audience a narrative context for how the subject at hand relates to us all. When one does not include a story, the speech must either be not very important or not very well thought out. If that is the case, then why should we listen? In terms of these specific speeches, however, it suggests that the context is masked, intentionally or not. Every speech act is inherently part of a bigger story, and those stories are part of the story of us as peoples, and those are part of the larger story of our existence as humans and as humans within the cosmos. We owe it to ourselves to get educated about diplomatic histories of U.S.-Indian relations if we wish to create better futures for our children and grandchildren.

Tribal governance and business should be conducted from an informed historical perspective. Ideally, institutes for tribal governance should be created in New Mexico, Washington, Oklahoma, California, and Alaska,[18] as these states have large numbers of tribal nations within their borders: 21, 29, 39, 102, and 229, respectively. State flagship institutions, such as state universities, would be ideal locations, and tribal nations should be stakeholders that both contribute funding and share in power regarding curriculum, scholarship, and outreach. Courses for current and future tribal leaders based in history, governance, law, natural resource management, and business should be offered in order to prepare them to lead their nations in economic development that benefits the states as well as tribal nations and their citizens. Moreover, the institutes should act as centers for pragmatic research needed by tribal nations as they make decisions regarding a rapidly changing political, environmental, and economic future. Tribal politicians owe it to their constituents to *interact* with U.S. government officials and interpret their statements to Indian people with as much knowledge as possible about both history and the current global political situation. Tribal officials must research the truth, about both the past and the present, *for themselves,* in order to best represent and protect their people.

That is what American Indian intellectuals and leaders have done traditionally. Good leaders have been aware, listened, and spoken out. With his usually astute analysis, a Cherokee intellectual whom I greatly respect, Will Rogers, once said of a dam dedication speech by President Calvin Coolidge to a group of Apaches whose land was covered by the resulting new reservoir:

> Here was the old warlike Apaches that fought to hold all they had, and most of them wound up in jail, but there was a Washington that fought for his tribe against invaders and wound up with a flock of Statues and a title Father of his Country. And yet I expect . . . the old Apache Chiefs went through more and fought harder for their Country than George did. But George won, that's the whole answer to history, it's not what did you do, but what did you get away with at the finish. . . . [W]e were out there on Indian land dedicating a Dam to get water for white people to come out and use and gradually take more Indian land away. There is going to be nothing different. . . . The more so-called civilized we get the more we kill and take. But I bet many an old Indian got many a quiet laugh out the speeches of "good fellowship" there that day, that were meant to be serious. (Smallwood and Gragert 125–26)

There are certainly times that it seems little has changed, really, except perhaps the last name of the George in question. From the early archives of U.S. history to the present, readers and listeners ought to be highly skeptical regarding presidential speeches to or about Indian nations and people. Furthermore, we as humans need to work toward developing mutual understandings of relatedness in the interest of our common survival of the Anthropocene era. As the Lakotas say, "*Mitakuye oyasin*—We are all related." However, relatives have obligations toward one another and should engage in respect and reciprocity. There used to be solutions for those who violated the rules of kinship. They found themselves in the worst condition possible—alone.

Even when we know we are dealing with those who violate the rules of kinship, who lie to us, perhaps we are scared to speak out. After surviving the era of the Homeland Security Act, of the Patriot Acts I and II, of the U.S. military prison at Guantánamo Bay Naval Base, of federal budget cuts that severely affected tribal programs, and of relatives serving overseas in the U.S. military, perhaps there is a good reason for this fear. But in closing, I would like to quote another American Indian intellectual, Vine Deloria, the one who encouraged us to speak out, to be activists. In "It Is a Good Day to Die," Deloria wrote:

> Living cannot be postponed. . . . [A]nything that has an identity calls men and societies to it. "It is a good day to die," Crazy Horse used to call as he rode out into battle. People accepted his challenge and followed him. . . . If vocation is to exist in today's world it must certainly involve a heady willingness to struggle for both long and short term goals and at times simply for the joy of getting one's nose bloodied while blackening the other guy's eye. . . . [V]ocation . . . is the solitary acknowledgement that the question of man's life and identity is to let the bastards know you've been there and that it is always a good day to die. We are therefore able to live. (*For This Land* 81, 94)

Our actions today will affect our descendants seven generations into the future. Leaders of all sorts throughout Indian Country—elders and traditional leaders, tribal officials and employees, scholars and educators—all of us must stand up for what is right. Whatever our roles, we must not allow ourselves to be deceived. We must open our own eyes through education and then share that knowledge with others. We must become warriors for the futures of our children and grandchildren. We must become warriors for ourselves and each other. Too much is at stake. Whatever our role in life, we need to fulfill that vocation for what it is, a calling. We need to live up to our own promises to our peoples, our ancestors, our children, as the great Vine Deloria suggested. It is always a good day to give our all for our Indigenous peoples.

FOUR

"That Little Savage Was Insolent to Me Today"

Ada-gal'kala, Idle No More, and the Perennial Problem of "Our Mad Young Men"

> Blood Quantum or any other form of pedigree for pets will result in statistical genocide. They will have mathematically phased us out. Quit with that fullblooded this and that[;] get with the language, ceremony and values, defend mother earth, grow your families proper.
>
> —*Lastrealindians*

Cold sweat covered White Owl's handsome brow, blanched as it was by this bad air and odd weather. His heart beat in his chest rapidly like a drum. His windpipe rattled, a redheaded woodpecker in a cypress. He felt uncomfortable and greatly overdressed in the fancy clothing made of stiff fabrics that they had given him, though he loved the colors and ribbons and knew that despite his small stature, they set off his fine features. He might be an oddity and a "wild man" to these people, but even their women were intrigued by his good looks. These people and their town, though, smelled of so many strange and unpleasant things. At first, that had been the worst. Their places to go to water were unused by most of them and filthy in their own right. And the noises, so many, a cacophony of words, rocks, and metal, along with the sounds of captive animals and unhappy children, all living in their own filth in buildings that were never renewed, but remained standing for untold generations, if their stories were true. But there was so much to see . . . so despite their heaps of animal dung

Portions of chapter 4 were previously published in "Who Is Cherokee? Federal Recognition, Culture, and Rhetorical Sovereignty," by Kimberly G. Wieser, in *A Listening Wind: Native Literature from the Southeast*, ed. Marcia Haag (Lincoln: University of Nebraska Press, 2016).

in the streets and homes and nightmare houses where they tortured those born touched by spirits, despite the false creeks full of sewage and pits of their dead lying uncovered at crossroads around London, despite even their burning water that overcame his senses and left him sick, he was going to try to understand these people and their ways. As Moytoy and the others had encouraged him back home, he would learn a lot from this journey. Though trained for peace, he was a warrior of the Ani-Wayah, Wolf Clan. He wasn't going to let his fear rule him. These people, as different and rude as they were, were human beings as well. And now the Ani-Kituwah had become relatives with this nation, adopted by their Father, King George. Surely these Ani-Gilisi could be reasoned with. He would go home to Taskigi soon enough. He'd stand here and let that yoneg make black marks like a didanawisgi on the thin wood to keep his likeness. It was probably just for the women anyway, who couldn't bear for him to leave. But he wasn't putting down his gourd or his knife. The yoneg could draw him just like that, whether he thought they matched his fancy clothes or not. As far as he himself could tell, there were only two things that could really hurt him in London, and he wasn't leaving himself vulnerable to either one.

Called Oukaneka at birth (variously spelled as Oucounacou, Okoonaka, Ukwaneequ, and Onacona and translated as "White Owl"), Ada-gal'kala (also spelled as Attacullaculla and Attakullakulla[1] and translated as "Little Carpenter" or "Leaning Wood") may have been born on Sevier's Island in Tennessee, sometime between 1700 and 1712, by best estimates (Kelly 3). He may have been full-blood Cherokee, born to the sister of Old Hop, as whites called Standing Turkey, and his father a minor chief. He seems to have been related to Amaedohi (or Moytoy), who would be named "emperor" of the Cherokees on April 3, 1730, by Sir Alexander Cumming.[2] Alternatively, he may have been an Algonquian-Nipissing Indian from Canada, captured as an infant adopted by Old Hop's sister. One of Ada-gal'kala's sons, Turtle at Home, is reported to have claimed this. Either way, Ada-gal'kala was a Cherokee of the Wolf Clan, and Old Hop would have been, as a maternal uncle, among the men responsible for carrying out what contemporary mainstream Americans would see as a father's role in relation to young Oukaneka.

Oukaneka was naturally intelligent and reared by Cherokee men whose family had been leaders for multiple generations. They likely educated him and his kin through traditional pedagogies that inculcated Indigenous men's knowledge about warfare, hunting, and governance. He would have been taught to be acutely aware of his surroundings at all times, ever alert to notice nuances, changes, and anything out of the ordinary. Oukaneka's oratorical skills were probably honed by hearing and reciting from memory great speeches, rich with cultural rhetorics. He and his peers would have been taught to utilize judgment based on the experiences of their ancestors and people, hearing and reciting oral traditions as well. He would have engaged in ceremonial and cultural practices that taught self-restraint and discipline and required perfect replication of ritual acts that sometimes included many minute and subtle details. All of this would have contributed to extremely strong memorization skills, giving him an additional advantage as a leader and a negotiator. Most of all, he had great men to observe in action as he became old enough to accompany his uncles in council and in diplomatic and trade encounters, seeing how they applied all of their knowledge and rhetorical practices to persuade others and look out for their people's interests.

However, there were some situations in the changing times in which Oukaneka was born for which his traditional education could not prepare him. One was the full entry of the Cherokee Nation into Transatlantic international relations, with his trip to London in 1730 to visit King George II as part of the first group of Cherokees on European soil—all young men from leading families like his own.[3] During this historic encounter, Oukaneka's lack of knowledge of the English language was used to deceive him, along with his companions. But the Cherokee young men discovered from the translator, Mr. Wiggan, that the "Articles of Friendship and Commerce" to which they had been tricked into having their names "appended" declared that George II had dominion over Carolina. At first the Cherokee party proposed to repudiate the claims and to kill both Wiggan, whom they had known most or all of their lives as the first trader among the Overhill Cherokees, and Oukayuda, their eldest companion and chosen spokesman.[4] However, in the end they decided to wait until they returned home from England, when they would let those older men of the nation who held actual authority straighten it out (Kelly 4).

Oukaneka had not wanted to go on this trip. He had been wary when Sir Cumming asked him to accompany him back to England to cement relations between their nations. But Wiggan talked him into it. Six other Cherokee men who knew Oukaneka was reluctant to go alone and feared that crossing the ocean would take too long volunteered to accompany him. So on May 4, 1730, they boarded the man-of-war *Fox* in Charleston and set sail, landing at Dover on June 5. After arriving in London, the party lived first above the Mermaid Tavern and then in the Covent Garden district in a King Street basement below an undertaker. Neither circumstance would have been culturally acceptable for multiple reasons. They were carted about as curiosities, at first in their Cherokee attire—complete with what seems to have been thonglike loincloths, with aprons in the front and horsetails in the rear, and face and body paint in red, blue, and green dots—and then in British attire, minus wigs and white powder. They were taken to Canterbury Cathedral, to court, to plays, to pubs, and to the lunatic asylum. They sat for a portrait, saw the Crown Jewels in the Tower of London, went to a spa, and attended fairs replete with jousting, acrobats, and miracle plays. *The Court Magazine* recalled some thirty years later: "[Adagal'kala] was shy of being stared at, and therefore always chose to go incognito to any publick place. 'They are welcome,' said he once to his interpreter, 'to look upon me as a strange creature. They see but one, and in return they give me an opportunity to look upon thousands'" (qtd. in Kelly 3–4). With the preparation he had for becoming a diplomat, from the time he was old enough to be away from his mother's side and follow about his uncles, it was wasn't long before Oukaneka began learning English himself: "He had so far advanced himself in learning . . . English . . . that at his embarking, he took . . . the last person's hand that met his, which happened to be an old Fisher Woman's; wringing it hard, with tears in his eyes, he repeated . . . [,] 'I tank you, I tank you, I tank you all'"[5] (qtd. in Kelly 4).

Cherokee people have always realized that knowledge, writing, and language are power. In telling the ancient oral migration stories, well-known Cherokee author and storyteller Sequoyah Guess, a descendant of the Sequoyah who is credited with inventing the Cherokee syllabary, emphasizes the importance of language:

> As this time went along, . . .
> the original language was lost.
> And the writing that we had back then was lost, too.
> And the only ones that remembered anything about it was the
> Unanti.[6]
> And that was one of the reasons why they thought
> they held such great power over the people. (C. Teuton et al. 75)

Ada-gal'kala, who rose in prominence to become the nation's Peace Chief—second to his maternal uncle Old Hop, the principal War Chief of the nation—is mentioned repeatedly over the course of his lifetime in the settler colonial record and has several transcribed speeches and a dictated letter attributed to him, along with fragments of discourse that are in longer multispeaker dialogues. A non-Indian contemporary, physician George Milligan, says that Ada-gal'kala was "accounted the most sensible Man" among the Cherokees (81). Many historians also hold Ada-gal'kala to be one the greatest orators and diplomats of his era, the preeminent Cherokee of his time. For instance, late nineteenth-century South Carolina attorney, theologian, and state representative Edward McCrady, in *The History of South Carolina under the Royal Government, 1719–1776,* calls Ada-gal'kala "eloquent, sagacious, and brave" (305). Even historian Albert V. Goodpasture, a contemporary of McCrady's who presents generally racist depictions of Cherokees in his 1918 article in *Tennessee Historical Magazine,* casts Ada-gal'kala's diplomatic and rhetorical skills in a positive light:

> For fifty years he stood out between the contending races, a sublime and, often, a solitary figure, ever pleading, conciliating, pacifying. He was the grandest and most amiable leader developed by his race; and I doubt whether a nobler character, of any race, could have been found on the border.
>
> Though he came of a race of large men, Attakullakulla was remarkably small, and of slender and delicate frame; but he was endowed with superior abilities. He did little to distinguish himself in war, but his policy and address were such as to win for him the confidence and admiration of his people. He was the leading diplomat of his nation, and conducted some of the most delicate missions with singular tact and sagacity. (Issue 4.1, p. 5)

Ada-gal'kala was the chief negotiator for the Cherokee Nation in an extremely volatile and continually shifting diplomatic environment. The British and French had, despite the practice of royal intermarriages, been at war with one another off and on over hundreds of years for territory and for economic and political power. Religion became a factor—or at least was used as a factor to justify warfare to the masses who actually fought—after the Protestant Reformation in the sixteenth century. That struggle was imported to

American soil and was actually a good portion of the impetus for colonization—the Americas offered natural resources that could be exploited to fuel European power. Spain was also a player in this domination game. For American Indian people, the pull to be involved came from a variety of directions. European trade goods—cloth, knives, guns, ammunition, pots and pans, and alcohol—were introduced as incentives to draw them into trade and military alliances with European factions. Colin G. Calloway, the John Kimball Jr. 1943 Professor of History and Professor of Native American Studies at Dartmouth University, writes:

> After the English established Charles Town, South Carolina, in 1670, traders funneled new goods, new values, and alcohol into Cherokee communities, and Cherokee hunters furnished thousands of deerskins for insatiable European markets. Traditional hunting practices that involved observing important rituals to establish and preserve reciprocal obligations between hunters and prey became strained under the pressure of new economic forces. Subsistence practices and settlement patterns began to change. ("Declaring" 186)

Having had a system of warfare that had more to do with maintaining dominance over hunting areas and gaining both masculine spiritual and cultural capital and an influx of captives who provided genetic diversity, American Indians had long had their own systems of alliances and confederacies. As in Europe, alliances were not entirely stable but shifted with changing needs. Europeans utilized this system of American Indian alliance making to facilitate their own aims, causing a need for better access to European guns and ammunition for the tribes to protect themselves from each other. The French had attempted to stabilize trade by building forts throughout Indian Country to provide both protection for their Indian allies and a steady supply of goods. The Ohio and Mississippi Rivers were the high-speed interstate freeways of the trade and warfare network already utilized by Indians in the Americas—Indian "paths" were its smaller highways and backroads. Goodpasture observes that the building of Fort Toulouse in 1714 by the French, along the Coosa River near what is now the site of Montgomery, Alabama, strengthened their influence in the south, causing Francis Nicholson, then the royal governor of South Carolina, to begin treating with Cherokees for trade and friendship in 1721.

Cumming's visit in 1730 was a follow-up to this (Goodpasture, issue 4.1, p. 4). The subsequent London visit by the Cherokee delegation was part of a series of diplomatic meetings in Europe between Indian representatives and the British crown (Pratt 135). The outbreak of hostilities in 1753 that would become the French and Indian War, otherwise known as the Seven Years' War, was instigated by Virginia governor Robert Dinwiddie when he sent twenty-one-year-old George Washington to the Ohio River Valley with written orders for the French to vacate, which, of course, they refused. In 1754, Lieutenant Colonel Washington returned, backed by hundreds of soldiers, and led his first military engagement. In retrospect, Winston Churchill called this war the "First World War"—this battle for dominance was Transatlantic, including armed conflict not only from Haudenosaunee country to Cherokee and Creek country but also in Europe, Africa, India, and the Caribbean. At times, the British were Cherokee allies. At times, the two nations fought each other bitterly. And during the American Revolution, the greater portion of the Cherokee Nation fought against the Tories on behalf of those British who were becoming Americans. This was the fifty years through which Ada-gal'kala led negotiations and battles on behalf of the Cherokee Nation. Ada-gal'kala was the "chief Indian spokesman" at the discussions with South Carolina governor James Glen on July 4, 1753 (McCrady 305). Two years later, the friendship and trade agreement were renegotiated: "Old Hop appointed Attacullaculla to speak for the Nation. . . . The Little Carpenter's speech is a model of Cherokee oratory, forceful, eloquent, and dramatic. So well did he acquit himself that he was thereafter considered the Speaker for the Nation in dealings with the white men" (J. Brown, "Eastern Cherokee Chiefs" 7). In September 1761, Ada-gal'kala was responsible for negotiating peace between the British and the Cherokees with Colonel James Grant and ultimately with Governor William Bull, also of South Carolina. His negotiations were not always successful. At various times, Ada-gal'kala had disagreements with others both within and without the Cherokee Nation, including a disagreement with his son Tsi'yugûnsi'ni (Dragging Canoe) and son-in-law Inoli (Black Fox)[7] that split their nation regarding with whom they should ally during the American Revolution. Despite this, Ada-gal'kala stands among the greatest Cherokee leaders of all times, primarily because he had the foresight to know that the white people he had taken as relatives were not going anywhere; he did his best to lead Cherokee people through a treacherous political environment that threatened their very survival. Ultimately, it was not merely the infamous "guns, germs, and steel"—as chronicled in the eponymously titled book by environmental historian and University of California at Los Angeles geology professor Jared Diamond—that caused the loss of most of the Cherokee Nation's lands and led to removal. The rhetorical situation was complicated by even more unsavory factors: the loss of the food sovereignty[8] and the use of alcohol, as well as lies and betrayal.

This chapter uses the lens of Intertribalism[9] to better situate Ada-gal'kala and fellow rhetors, such as Tsi'yugûnsi'ni and Inoli, so that we as scholars might approach American Indian studies from a lens of relatedness, here utilizing a Cherokee-centric explanation of this notion for our specific purposes. That is, it views relatedness from a Cherokee center looking outward in a nonbinary dualistic notion of identity that acknowledges kin from degrees of what I call "Cherokicity"[10] in an attempt to offer a model that transcends static notions of time and rather examines beings in space in interaction with other beings.[11] The chapter offers a reading of the rhetoric utilized by Ada-gal'kala as well as the settler colonial figures around him, much of which deals with kinship, and to a lesser extent that of Tsi'yugûnsi'ni and Inoli. Tsi'yugûnsi'ni's speech can be seen, in this context, as rebellion against a culturally specific form of what Scott Lyons calls rhetorical imperialism ("Rhetorical Sovereignty"). This rule of polite discourse within the Cherokee Nation relegated both Tsi'yugûnsi'ni and Inoli to the position of "mad young men" who had much less auctoritas when speaking on behalf of their people according to Cherokee ways. The division among Cherokee people that began over the American Revolution ultimately was a result of differences in viewing relationships taken with outsiders and how those outsiders behaved in relation to Cherokee people, compounded by a disagreement over who had the right to speak for the people. Though these relationships with outsiders themselves were problematic, I argue that the issue was not ultimately taking relationships with outsiders but teaching outsiders to see the world through an Indigenous view of kinship, because only people with a lens of relatedness have the foresight to create a sustainable future. The chapter ends with my eisegesis examining Idle No More (INM), the international Indigenous movement mentioned in previous chapters that models the type of intertribal relatedness put forth in this chapter, and the two rhetorical strains that have emerged within the movement, focusing on an intergenerational disagreement and on a rhetorical imperialism similar to that discussed in the first portion of the chapter. In a world where American

Indian natural resources are in high demand by outsiders and where planetary health is increasingly threatened by an unsustainable system, American Indian leaders can no longer afford to be illiterate signers of treaties lavished with goods by outsiders taken as kin. While Lyons is right that "treaty signers committed themselves to nation status" (*X-Marks*, location 2581), historically, X-marks have been problematic in terms of how well things worked out for Indian peoples on the whole. So have ill-founded adoptions in some relationships taken with outsiders. American Indian leaders must make sure that those with whom they ally understand just how related we humans and all of our destinies truly are.

Intertribalism: Cherokicity, Indianicity, and the Spectrum of Kin

Examining the context of speeches made by Ada-gal'kala, Tsi'yugûnsi'ni, and Inoli means thinking about the nature of kinship, not only what it means to be "Cherokee," but also what a "good Cherokee" owes to his or her kin. Three great Cherokee thinkers—Daniel Heath Justice, Tom Holm, and Robert K. Thomas—have written and published materials about what constitutes a tribal nation that offer much to this discussion. Thomas points out that "kin relations are the content of tribal experience and the key to its psychology and ecology" (Cooter and Thomas 98). His Peoplehood Matrix Theory—best known from a 2003 article written by Holm, along with J. Diane Pearson and Ben Chavis—defines a people as sharing four key characteristics: "language, sacred history, religion, and land" (12). Justice's Kinship Criticism builds on the peoplehood model as it "puts kinship principles in practice" and examines "the interpretive significance of the relationship between kinship, peoplehood, and decolonization" ("'Go Away'" 148). Justice notes,

> Early in my studies of the Cherokee literary tradition, I realized that my initial supposition that there was a single, unitary idea of "Cherokeeness" was both naïve and, ultimately, impossible, especially given the long and tangled realities of Cherokee social history. Yet I also came to realize that though there are many different ways of understanding what it is to be Cherokee—some more suited to the preservation of Cherokee nationhood, communitism, and decolonization than others—each way is still an attempt to give shape to an idea of what it is to be, think, and

> live Cherokee. Thus, easy assertions of a unitary definition break down, and the complicated living realities of the Cherokee people are revealed. The definitions might differ, but all the definitions still speak to the idea of Cherokeeness. The fires of Cherokee nationhood still burn: around the kitchen table, in the council house, in the churches, in the ceremonial grounds, and in the classroom. (153)

Cherokee people are "people of one fire." Since the pivotal moment of Water Spider bringing fire to the people in her basket, Cherokee people have shared fire with one another. Traditionally, in the annual ceremonial cycle, a new sacred fire was started, and the fire in each Cherokee home was put out, replaced with the new fire shared throughout the nation. In articulating his Kinship Criticism, Justice urges that "we have to give voice to Fire, even if it means our tongues will burn" (148).

This is my giving voice to Fire . . .

In linguist Marcia Haag's edited volume, *A Listening Wind: Native Literature from the Southeast*, Cherokee language professor, elder, and artist Harry Oosahwee (Adawi) asks what may appear to be an easy question: "Who is Cherokee?" The answer is not as obvious as it seems. Although Oosahwee never answers that question directly, the answer is implied. Oosahwee firmly believes in his answer to this question, but he wants to be as polite as possible about staking his claim. For Oosahwee, to be "Cherokee" is to be a full-blood Cherokee speaker immersed in Cherokee family, community, lifeways, and culture. He speaks of the years of his upbringing in the 1950s:

> We were pretty isolated from the mainstream society during this time. Therefore, we were able to maintain close relations to our extended families and maintain a large part of our culture as well as our language. I believe this isolation was by choice: we did not want to be bothered by the white people or the mixed bloods. We wanted to live the life of a Cherokee community: what we had for substance came from the land, creeks, and wild game. We also raised our own hogs, chickens, and cows. Although we did go into town every now and then. We mostly stayed around our communities. On occasion we would visit other communities

> when there was something going on like a stomp dance, gospel singing or a birthday celebration and there was always a big hog fry during these occasions. (Haag 247)

This answer—that to be truly Cherokee, one must be a full-blood Cherokee speaker immersed in Cherokee family, community, lifeways, and culture—might not sit so well with a lot of people. For instance, many of the citizens of the three federally recognized Cherokee nations—the Cherokee Nation of Oklahoma (CNO), the United Keetoowah Band of Cherokee Indians (UKB), and the Eastern Band of Cherokee Indians (EBCI)—fall outside Oosahwee's definition. While all citizens of these nations descend from ancestors whose lands at the time of contact were in North Carolina, northern South Carolina, Georgia, Tennessee, Virginia, and Alabama, blood quantum requirements for citizenship varies. CNO, in fact, has no blood quantum requirement. All that is required for citizenship is that one has an ancestor listed on the 1903 Dawes Roll. UKB and EBCI require one-quarter Cherokee ancestry. Fluent Cherokee speakers are few and far between. Moreover, the diaspora caused by Andrew Jackson's removal of many Cherokees to Indian Territory on the Trail of Tears, and further diaspora caused by urbanization and the relocation era of the mid-twentieth century, spread Cherokee citizens all over the country. Not all citizens grew up in or live in Cherokee communities. Today Cherokee citizens have diverse lifestyles and reside in many locales. Although Thomas and Holm's Peoplehood Matrix no longer fits so clearly, they remain Cherokee, otherwise known as Tsalagi, Aniyunwiya, or Anikituwah—the People of Kituwah, the People of the Place That God Made, according to Cherokee scholar Tom Belt.

Certainly, all of those thousands and thousands of folks who are of Cherokee descent, who claim a long-ago mythical Cherokee "princess" as grandmother, or who are members of non-federally recognized groups—some of which are more social clubs or hobbyist associations, and many of which have no connection to traditional Cherokee culture or communities—would fall outside of what Oosahwee defines as Cherokee. While some of these people have documentable Cherokee ancestors, some are victims of what Geary Hobson (Cherokee/Quapaw descendant) calls paper genocide:[12] they may have Cherokee ancestry, but no proof of that is found in official records (Hobson et al. 1). They are not legally Cherokee—that is, citizens of one of the three federally recognized tribes. Others claiming to be "Cherokee" may actually have ancestry from other tribes that is lost in the oral history of their families and has been handed down falsely as "Cherokee." In the introduction to *The People Who Stayed: Southeastern Indian Writing after the Removal,* Hobson writes of these people, detribalized by the Southern Diaspora, who are tribal descendants of mostly white or mostly black heritage and culture or who were "paper victims" of genocide, a practice Hobson shows to have been widespread: "Genocide by administrative or clerical fiat occurred through . . . such methods used by government officials and, later, sometimes, by anthropologists and linguists as well." Hobson asks, "What other agents and agencies of disappearance still exist in the Southeast, and are still at work denying identity and sovereignty to indigenous peoples and their descendants?" (Hobson et al. 1). But there are also people out there claiming to be Cherokee who may have no American Indian ancestry at all, causing quite a bit of consternation for those clearly as identifiable as Cherokee. Mark Edwin Miller explores this subject thoroughly in *Claiming Tribal Identity: The Five Tribes and the Politics of Federal Acknowledgment.* While this may seem confusing or unimportant to non-Cherokees, for a number of years CNO and EBCI have considered this to be a serious problem. Some people claiming to be Cherokee have misrepresented to the outside world not only themselves but also what it means to be Cherokee or of Cherokee descent. Some incidents of this have been so offensive that CNO and EBCI issued "Resolution #08-08": "BE IT FURTHER RESOLVED that any individual who is not a member of a federally recognized Cherokee tribe, in academia or otherwise, is hereby discouraged from claiming to speak as a Cherokee, or on behalf of Cherokee citizens, or using claims of Cherokee heritage to advance his or her career or credentials."[13]

As a person reared with familial knowledge of distant Cherokee ancestry, I have searched for twenty years for documentation. If some genealogies are to be believed, I have documentable Cherokee ancestors, but only ones who predate the 1903 Dawes Roll—Ada-gal'kala and his wife; their daughter, along with her husband, Inoli; and Martha Sherill, born in Cherokee, North, in 1766, on my mother's father's side of the family. There are others, also on my mother's father's side, whom I suspect are of Cherokee heritage—Rainwaters, Davises, Proctors, Smiths, and Hollands. On my father's mother's side of the family, I likewise suspect Reeds, Bryants, Littlefields, and Nances of having Cherokee ancestry.

This chapter is my x-mark, and I come to it through an x-mark . . .

Scott Lyons tells me:

> *Making an x-mark means more than just embracing new or foreign ideas as your own; it means consciously connecting those ideas to certain values, interests, and political objectives, and making the best call you can under conditions not of your making. So, the next time some Indian identity controversy rears up and someone asks you for an answer to the perennial question, consider what's at stake and make the best x-mark you can. (Locations 1549–52)*

This chapter is my x-mark, and I come to it through an x-mark . . .

Here are what the records say of my family.

Dr. William Alexander Davis (b. 1790), my great-great-great-great-grandmother Rhoda Davis's brother, put his x-mark on behalf of the Cherokee Nation beside the name "Young Davis," after the signature of Charles Hicks and before Souanooka's x-mark, on the Treaty of 1817. Maybe he was illiterate at that time. Perhaps someone seeking signatures thought he was. He had taken over as headman for a group of Cherokees in what is today Jackson County, Alabama, after the passing of Chief Arthur Burns in 1816. In 1819 that group had a 64-acre plot of land set aside for them there as "the Heirs of Arthur Burns." Many claim that Davis took over because he was Burns's son-in-law. However, although Young Davis married Burns's daughter, Mary (b. 1804), the earliest reference I have found to their marriage lists it as occurring in 1820, and their first child, Cynthia Pack Davis, wasn't born until 1830, so they may have married even later. It is unlikely that Young Davis and Mary Burns were already married when he became headman, particularly as she was only twelve years old. Even in earlier times, Cherokee women had typically waited until around the age of sixteen or so to enter their first marriage.

Young Davis was also part of the delegation listed in the Treaty of New Echota, "composed of John Ridge, Elias Boudinot, Archilla Smith, S. W. Bell, John West, Wm. A. Davis, and Ezekiel West, who represented that portion of the nation in favor of emigration to the Cherokee country west of the Mississippi" and who "entered into propositions for a treaty with John F. Schermerhorn, commissioner on the part of the United States," though neither his signature nor his x-mark is anywhere to be found on the bottom of the document. He is listed as "Davis, William Dr." on the 1835 Henderson Roll in the Cherokee Nation East

Census, Alabama, right before Deer Head. David Cornsilk, a Cherokee genealogist involved in a number of controversial cases, including the controversy regarding Andrea Smith's identity as Cherokee, told me that William Alexander Davis was the only member of the Treaty Party to avoid assassination.[14] *In fact, his son William Henry Davis reports in a biography that Young Davis became a medical doctor sometime between 1817 and 1835 and attended in that capacity to Ridge's widow during and after her husband's assassination.*

The name "Young Davis" was part of the Cherokee tradition of the time, "Old" and "Young" utilized much as we use "Junior" and "Senior" today. The names "Old Tassel," "Young Tassel," and "Old Hop" are other examples of this common practice. Young Davis's name implies that his father, William Davis, was called Old Davis. I believe that Old Davis was white but well known enough to Cherokee people to be referred to this way. John Sevier, who was governor of Tennessee from 1803 to 1809 and died in 1815, a year before Young Davis took over for Arthur Burns, reportedly called Davis "an important Chickamauga Chief." Moreover, Chiefs Black Fox, Sour Mush, Davis, Chulio, Big Half-breed, Quatueskee, Tholuntuskee, Will Shorwy, John Lowery, and Toochalle met with Agent Return Johnathan Meigs on August 25, 1807, to receive late annuity money when Young Davis was only seventeen years old. Allowing men that young to speak on behalf of or represent the people would have been an extremely unusual practice for Cherokees. All of this supports the idea that the Davis referred to by Sevier was Old Davis, and it makes sense if Old Davis's wife, Mary, was the daughter of Black Fox and Ada-gal'kala's daughter, as many of the genealogies widely available online through sites like Ancestry and Geni claim. Some claim that Old Davis could not have been married to a Cherokee woman, because he fought against Cherokees in the American Revolution. However, not only were the Cherokee Nation and Cherokee families divided at times during that war, but there are also many instances of white men married to Cherokee women during the colonial and revolutionary eras who fought against Cherokees in battle. Some of those white men were even captured by Cherokees and released by Cherokees sympathetic to them because of their marital ties, such as Captain John Stuart, known to Cherokees as Bushyhead. All of this suggests to me that further research is necessary to obtain a clearer picture of Old Davis's exact relationship with the Cherokee people.

Cornsilk does not believe, however, that the genealogy widely published online for the elder Mary Davis is accurate, because of two documents that seem to contradict it. William Henry Davis, the son of Young Davis mentioned above, lists his paternal grandparents on an Eastern Band document (figure 7) as white, and his 1896 Dawes application lists him as only one-quarter Cherokee when applying for his and his sisters' allotments on his mother's (Mary Burns's) part. On the other hand, William Henry Davis has the Indian name "Enorly" or "Inoli" on the Eastern Band document, even though he is supposedly not the great-grandson of Black Fox. However, William Henry Davis's reference on the third page to a Supreme Court decision that would allow him to file on behalf of his father as well as his mother seems to support his claim that his grandmother—and thus his father—was white, for it seems to be a reference to the Cherokee Intermarriage Cases decided by the court on November 5, 1906.

Much time has passed, and it's hard for anyone to determine what the truth is. The fact of the matter is that there is no clear evidence as to who Mary Black Davis was or was not. As Daniel Justice said to me, "Our families are complicated things, Kim, and there's a lot we don't know and will never know."

No matter what I don't know, I do know that Dr. William Alexander Davis enacted the Cherokee identity of the Alabama Cherokee headman Young Davis, an identity that endowed him with signatory authority on the 1817 treaty. I know that, as a Cherokee leader, he joined Ridge and others in negotiating the Treaty of New Echota. This treaty required him to walk the Trail of Tears with his wife and children, a consequence that he could have easily escaped for himself and his loved ones if he had enacted a white male identity, a choice—like that of all x-mark makers, according to Lyons—that shows agency at least in that it was some choice, though it wasn't true "liberty": "An x-mark is a sign of consent in a context of coercion; it is the agreement one makes when there seems to be little choice in the matter" (locations 151–52).

In the same way that Young Davis made a choice with his x-mark, I am consciously choosing to write with respect about my alleged ancestors and to treat them as I would blood relatives, just as I do with my adopted relatives throughout Indian Country, just as Indian people always have.

This chapter is my x-mark, and I come to it through an x-mark . . .

Despite suppositions one way or the other about my genealogical quandaries, I *do not* want to mislead readers about my degree of Cherokicity and must add a disclaimer to this chapter. I hardly speak any Cherokee. Though I attend and participate in stomp dances and other ceremonies, both Southeastern and intertribal, I am not a member of a Cherokee ceremonial ground.

Commissioner of Indian Affairs,
Washington, D. C.

SIR:

I hereby make application for such share as may be due me of the fund appropriated by the Act of Congress approved June 30, 1906, in accordance with the decrees of the Court of Claims of May 18, 1905, and May 28, 1906, in favor of the Eastern Cherokees. The evidence of identity is herewith subjoined.

1. State full name—
   English name: William Henry Davis,
   Indian name: Enorly.
2. Residence: Stilwell,
3. Town and post office: Stilwell,
4. County: Cherokee Nation,
5. State: Indian Territory.
6. Date and place of birth: April 8, 1838 in Flint District.
7. By what right do you claim to share? If you claim through more than one relative living in 1851, set forth each claim separately: For my own share. My mother: Mary Davis, My brother and sister: Laura Cornelia and George Washington Davis. My uncles: Hammer and George Burns.
8. Are you married? Yes.
9. Name and age of wife or husband: Eliza Davis, Age 60 years.
10. Give names of your father and mother, and your mother's name before marriage.
    Father—English name: William A. Davis,
    Indian name: Not known.
    Mother—English name: Mary Davis,
    Indian Name: Not known.
    Maiden name: Mary Burns,
11. Where were they born?
    Father: In Virginia
    Mother: In Cherokee Nation, east.
12. Where did they reside in 1851, if living at that time?
    Father: In Flint District.
    Mother: In Flint District.
13. Date of death of your father and mother—
    Father: Oct. 1862 Mother: May 2, 1852.

6—624

Figure 7. Eastern Cherokee claim of William Henry Davis, page 1.

14. Were they ever enrolled for annuities, land, or other benefits? If so, state when and where:
Mother on Emigrant Cherokee Pay roll of 1851 in Flint District.

15. Name all your brothers and sisters, giving ages, and if not living, the date of death:

	Name	Born	Died
(1)	Cynthia P. Mayes, dead.		
(2)	Laura Cornelia Davis, died without escent.		
(3)	~~Susan Ophelia Mayes, dead.~~		
(4)	John Lowrey Davis, dead.		
(5)	George Washington Davis, died without descent.		
(6)	Mary Elizabeth Fulsom, Stilwell, I.T.		

16. State English and Indian names of your grandparents on both father's and mother's side, if possible:

Father's Side	Mother's Side
They were Whites.	Arthur and Aky Burns, nee Lowrey.

17. Where were they born? Maternal grandmother in Cherokee Nation, east.

18. Where did they reside in 1851, if living at that time?
Maternal grandmother died before 1851.

19. Give names of all their children, and residence, if living; if not living, give dates of deaths:

(1) English name: Hammer or Ah-ha-mer, died without descent.
Indian name: Elizabeth Hufacre, dead.
Residence: George Burns, died without descent.

(2) English name:
Indian name:
Residence:

(3) English name:
Indian name:
Residence:

(4) English name:
Indian name:
Residence:

(5) English name:
Indian name:
Residence:

20. Have you ever been enrolled for annuities, land, or other benefits? If so, state when and where: On Emigrant Cherokee Pay roll of 1851 in Flint District.
On Cherokee Authenticated roll of 1880 and am a Cherokee Allottee.

6—624

Figure 7. Eastern Cherokee claim of William Henry Davis, page 2.

21. To expedite identification, claimants should give the full English and Indian names, if possible, of their paternal and maternal ancestors back to 1835:

My maternal grandfather, Arthur Burns, lived in Cherokee Nation, east in 1835.

REMARKS.

(Under this head the applicant may give any additional information that he believes will assist in proving his claims.)

During The Civil War our family was scattered, and some died, but our family Record was destroyed, therefore births and deaths can be told only approximately.
Under the decision of the Supreme Court, will I not be allowed to draw for my father W. A. Davis? He was a Delegate and assisted in making Treaty of 1835

NOTE—Answers should be brief but explicit; the words "Yes," "No," "Unknown," etc., may be used in cases where applicable. Read the questions carefully.

I solemnly swear that the foregoing statements made by me are true to the best of my knowledge and belief.

(Signature.) William H Davis

Subscribed and sworn to before me this 10th day of December, 1906.

My commission expires June 5, 1910, 190

Robert C Trenske
Notary Public.

AFFIDAVIT.

(The following affidavit must be sworn to by two or more witnesses who are well acquainted with the applicant.)

Personally appeared before me Johnson Riley and W L Cowart, who, being duly sworn, on oath depose and say that they are well acquainted with William Henry Davis, who makes the foregoing application and statements, and have known him for 20 years and 5 years, respectively, and know him to be the identical person he represents himself to be, and that the statements made by him are true, to the best of their knowledge and belief, and they have no interest whatever in his claim.

Witnesses to mark. Signatures of witnesses.

Johnson Riley
W L Cowart

Subscribed and sworn to before me this 10th day of December, 1906.

My commission expires June 5, 1910, 190

Robert C Trenske
Notary Public.

NOTE—Affidavits should be made, whenever practicable, before a notary public, clerk of the court, or before a person having a seal. If sworn to before an Indian agent or disbursing agent of the Indian service, it need not be executed before a notary, etc.

6—624

Figure 7. Eastern Cherokee claim of William Henry Davis, page 3.

Though my grandfather Leo Frank Daniels and his brother Jimmy taught me that we were Chickamauga, and though that side of my family continued the practice of polygamy until their generation, I did not grow up in a traditional Cherokee community. Though I grew up in a matriarchal household led by my "Mammy"—my dad's mother, whom I mentioned in the introduction to this book—and her sisters and learned to cook traditional Southeastern American Indian foods like chicken and dumplings and cornbread and learned to pick berries, muscadine grapes, poke salad, and such, I did not grow up with any oral traditions other than those belonging to my immediate family for just a few generations back. My words here are not based on knowledge I gained growing up. My knowledge has been gained mostly through study and scholarship. I hope here that I speak in a good way that does not offend people who are fully grounded in their Cherokee identity in all respects.

As I broach a theory of relatedness, I realize that "theory," in general, can be contentious in Indian Country. As Bryan McKinley Jones Brayboy, a Lumbee scholar of Native education, puts it, "Locating theory as something absent from stories and practices is problematic in many Indigenous communities" (426). He continues:

> For some Indigenous scholars (and others), theory is not simply an abstract thought or idea that explains overarching structures of societies and communities; theories, through stories and other media, are roadmaps for our communities and reminders of our individual responsibilities to the survival of our communities. These notions of theory, however, conflict with what many in the "academy" consider "good theory." At the heart of this conflict are different epistemologies and ontologies. . . . I want to make connections between different forms of knowledge. (427)

LeAnne Howe's tribalography offers some solution for Native studies scholars who want to connect different forms of knowledge. It takes into account how American Indian writers bring together multiple genres, modes, and voices, layering meaning the way meaning is layered in place for Indigenous people over the course of what most mainstream thinkers call "time."[15] As I develop both the theoretical section of this chapter and the chapter as a whole, I draw on Howe's approach in order to bring together disparate notions regarding Cherokee identity over time as they inform both Ada-gal'kala's and

Tsi'yugûnsi'ni's ideas about kinship and their own respective positionality in regard to other Cherokees, the British, and the colonists during the American Revolution. In doing so, I also problematize my own positionality and realign it within this framework as I examine the words of those who are possibly my blood kin, undeniably Cherokee, yet marginalized from their own Cherokicity in different ways. For this reason, an intertribal critical mixed-race theory is an appropriate underpinning for this particular scholarly act.

Trying to find connections between European and Euro-American theoretical constructs and Native perspectives is the approach many of us as Native studies scholars have attempted to use in constructing Native theory, and as I suggested in chapter 1, when that theory can be clearly explicable from American Indian perspectives, this approach is justifiable. Anishinaabe (Chippewa) theorist and writer Gerald Vizenor is probably the best known of Native theorists in regard to approaches grounded in mixed race; he draws heavily on European philosophers Bakhtin, Derrida, Barthes, Lyotard, and Foucault in the construction of his theory of Trickster discourse. Vizenor highlights Native literature's paracolonial aspect and fights formulaic, static identity as either white/mainstream or Indian/traditional by proposing that mixed-bloods appropriate the Native American figure of the Trickster and call themselves crossbloods, purposefully subverting the racial categories imposed by colonization, slipping back and forth across and between identities. He writes: "Crossbloods are a postmodern tribal bloodline, an encounter with racialism, colonial duplicities, sentimental monogenism, and generic cultures. . . . Crossbloods are communal, and their stories are splendid considerations of survivance" (*Crossbloods* vii–viii).

Vizenor claims the Trickster as a "semiotic sign" (*Narrative Chance* 188), in a poststructuralist sense of the word, enabling the crossblood to continually shapeshift rather than being defined by others. However, I find Vizenor's approach generally unsuitable for many of my relatives who are tribally enrolled. While his approach is formulated on an intertribally common concept and used as a framework for both survival and resistance as Indian people, enrolled or not, Vizenor's focus on the Trickster camouflages issues of sovereignty and citizenship. More importantly, like the Francophone theorists on whose work he builds, Vizenor uses language that is inaccessible to many of our community members. But in articulating sociotribal constructs in America, I still find that a poststructuralist approach becomes extremely important when one takes into account the history of those of mixed race. Approaches such as Critical Mixed Race Theory in Native literary studies can offer new frameworks in Intertribalism for viewing how texts—oral, written, material, visual, embodied, and kinesthetic—speak back to power and confront genocide and erasure due to miscegenation in ways that also support sovereignty. I find Brayboy's Tribal Critical Race Theory (TribalCrit) an extremely useful framework upon which to build, as it posits that "colonization"—in addition to the racism noted by more mainstream forms of Critical Race Theory)—"is endemic to society" (429). Brayboy's work meets the demand of being grounded in intertribally common philosophical tenets, while recognizing tribally specific differences. In other words, Brayboy makes room for Justice's "many different ways of understanding what it is to be Cherokee." All works that fall under the larger rubric of American Indian, First Nations, and Indigenous texts, by nature, speak out to the power structures of settler colonialism and imperialism from a paracolonial state, and they also can and do speak out to internalized colonialism and internalized racism within paracolonial nations and communities.

While this idea has application across Native studies and specifically to the rhetorical situations I analyze in the next section of this chapter, I will first use contemporary American Indian literature as an example of how this idea could be applied to help me explain the poststructuralist aspects. If written or drawn texts are a series of symbols designed to stand for something, then when we call a work an example of American Indian, First Nations, or Indigenous literature or a piece of tribally specific literature, that work has to be made of a series of symbols that stand for Indians or Indians from a specific tribe. This is even further complicated in genres of literature that are Western, such as the novel, and intend to *represent* rather than *express* culture. Culture itself cannot stand on a piece of paper; paper can only bear symbols of simulations of culture. Here I must acknowledge the insight of Anishinaabe scholar David Treuer in his *Native American Fiction: A User's Manual*, that the "elements" used to construct some fiction, "even though they might look Indian or seem cultural, . . . do not come from 'the culture'" (197). Indeed, modern and contemporary American Indian fiction differs substantively from oratory, letters, oral traditions, ritual expressions, and precontact visual and material genres because fiction is a mediated simulation, not unmediated cultural expression. One does not "tell" a novel. Even if one reads one's own novel aloud to an audience, the genre itself is a mediation.[16] Treuer says that "style"—the way in which authors as artists utilize words/symbols as tools to craft literature—"creates the convincing semblance of culture on the page" (5). A work purporting to be a Cherokee novel, then, or one that someone claims is a Cherokee novel, is made of a series of symbols that act as "Cherokeeisms" to evoke a sense of Cherokicity, what Justice calls Cherokeeness. A novel that simply purports to be a Native novel might then put forth a set of "Indianisms" to evoke a sense of "Indianicity." Within this hermeneutic framework, an immediate and significant difference becomes apparent between tribally specific and intertribally common depictions.

This representative quality does not make modern and contemporary American Indian literature any less significant, however, or less powerful than more traditional forms that are more expressive than representational. Although modern and contemporary literature is art rather than artifact, art and culture are intertwined within it in such a way that each affects the other. Moreover, from many traditional American Indian perspectives, the power of the word to change reality is not lessened merely because the word is a symbol in a work of art. More importantly for the purposes of this chapter, from the perspective of Western symbiotic studies, the symbols in American Indian literature mirror a reality in which people who are grouped together as "Indian" identify in more or less tribally specific ways because they more or less enact their own symbols or markers of "Indianicity" or "tribalicity" in their behaviors and cultural expressions based on their heritage, their environments, and their experiences. Most texts that we as academics consider Native literature have a balance of these two kinds of markers, as do contemporary American Indian behaviors and cultural expressions. An implication of this, with major legal significance, is that in life, only specific tribalisms are markers that help maintain cultural distinctiveness, a portion of what the U.S. government requires in title 25, part 83 ("Procedures for Establishing That an American Indian Group Exists as an Indian Tribe"), section 7, of the federal code. In *American Indian Politics and the American Political System*, David Eugene Wilkins and Heidi Kiiwetinepinesiik Stark observe, "As tribes have learned, their legal and political status as sovereigns will be and has been terminated or seriously diminished when they have been perceived to have 'lost' their cultural uniqueness in the eyes of Euro-America" (49). Philip Deloria similarly points out in "The Era of Indian Self-Determination: An Overview":

> Indian governments are thus subjected to a different status than other governments. There are not constant reviews of the demographic status of all the little countries in Europe that are frequently compared in size and population with Indian tribes. No one asks whether Monaco and Liechtenstein are sufficiently culturally distinct from neighboring countries to justify their continued existence. Unlike that of Indian tribes, their political status is taken for granted. (193)

The ways in which tribal cultures are symbolized and the ways in which Indian identity is represented are *both* key to sovereignty for Indian people who are citizens of federally recognized tribes, in that culture is both reflected and affected by fictional depictions.

Because tribalisms and Indianisms are more or less at play in the behaviors of all Indian-identified peoples, a nonbinary dualism is created that subverts *by its very nature* the binaries used to separate and control American Indigenous peoples, making an intertribal Indianicity a cardinal balance of tribal specificity, in that both are shades of the same thing, like Light and Dark, Good and Not Good, Male and Female, Fire and Water, Sky and Earth. This nonbinary dualism allows us to view each other—from full-blood, enrolled citizens of sovereign tribal nations, to the most culturally removed mixed-bloods of whatever ancestry plus some tribal descendancy, to the adopted or married-in non-Indians ("captives")—within a traditional framework of relatedness by blood, by social kinship, by captivity, by confederacy, and by alliance. Recognizing relationships is far more respectful both of sovereignty and of each other as human relatives, and it can open doors for reciprocity and renewal for a mutually beneficial relatedness in the future. Justice himself says in *Reasoning Together*:

> Indigenous nationhood is more than simple political independence or the exercise of a distinctive cultural identity; it's also an understanding of a common social interdependence within the community, the tribal web of kinship rights and responsibilities that link the People, the land, and the cosmos together in an ongoing and dynamic system of mutually affecting relationships. It isn't predicated on essentialist notions of unchangeability; indeed, such notions are rooted in primitivist Eurowestern discourses that locate indigenous peoples outside the flow and influences of time. ("'Go Away'" 151)

Also in *Reasoning Together*, Tol Foster asserts in an essay that "relations are the primary axis through which we can understand ourselves and each other" (Acoose et al. 277). This approach is more conducive to a better future for all of us as humans than a radically separatist or nationalist approach, and it creates a massive collective force of relatedness, a confederacy to speak out for change to create more balanced, healthier existences for all living beings in the face of global-corporate hegemony. But it also considers those who oppose Indigenous people and those who have historically oppressed us or our ancestors and relatives to be part of that spectrum of relatedness and takes into account that the fates of all of us humans are ultimately intertwined.

This framework would "recapture" into relatedness those Hobson writes of in the introduction to *The People Who Stayed* (Hobson et al.). In the post-1839 years, some of Hobson's ancestors, like some of my own, eventually ended up in Chicot County, Arkansas, a dumping ground for mixed-bloods (the county's name comes from the term used by early French settlers that compared mixed-bloods' skin to the color of a Caucasian person's unclean posterior). Still disenfranchised and oppressed, despite a lack of recognition, some of us mixed-bloods see our alliance with our more tribally grounded relatives as mutually beneficial. Viewing relatedness from a traditional perspective of kinship, captivity, confederacy, and alliance speaks back to government-imposed notions of identity based on Jeffersonian politics of assimilation through miscegenation, notions that threaten tribal national sovereignty with extinction by numbers and give up for lost those already victimized by historic and present government-imposed definitions of Indian identity. Otherwise, when sovereignty based on federal recognition ceases to exist—as it inevitably will according to current definitions of legal Indian identity based on citizenship in tribal nations and blood quantum requirements in many tribes yet unrevised, as it inevitably will if the trust fund "settlement" results in another broken government promise and massive loss of land base, or as it could at any time because termination is *always* possible under U.S. law—what will replace it as a source of power for the descendants of even enrolled full-bloods today, if not traditional ways of seeing identity as part of a network of relatedness? Conversely, what will happen to those with federal recognition today if the composition of the Supreme Court changes in such a way, during the Donald Trump administration or subsequently, that Justice Clarence Thomas's "critique of the Court's Indian Commerce Clause jurisprudence" becomes majority opinion and there is a "wholesale reshaping of the law that has governed Indian affairs for the past century and a half" that causes, in the Court's own words, "'an entire Title of the United States Code (25 U.S.C.) . . . [to] be effectively erased and the solemn commitment of the Government toward the Indians . . . [to] be jeopardized'" (Ablavsky)? If the current nation-to-nation bases of power are no longer and/or if the federal-Indian relationship is radically revised, the descendants of today's tribal citizens will need two things: (1) other ways of continuing Indian identity that will surely continue culturally and genetically despite the loss of legal Indianicity; and (2) the power of an expanded network of relatedness in order to survive against an imperialism still threatening to eradicate Indian people as Indian people one way or another. Current constructs of tribal sovereignty based on the trust relationship between the federal government and its "domestic dependent nations" do not replicate the representative tribalist decision-making and decision-articulating collectives embodied by the people of ancestral groups. As I mentioned in chapter 3, Taiaiake Alfred and others have suggested that we who identify as scholars need to think about what nationhood is from specific tribal perspectives as we explore and seek to strengthen sovereignty in a globalizing world. Relatedness *is* a traditional framework for doing so. Besides helping us see our common ground, this framework as I have adapted it works particularly well, I think, for demonstrating kinship as a spectrum and for acknowledging limitations related to positionality. My own perspective on Ada-gal'kala, Tsi'yugûnsi'ni, and Inoli as rhetors is necessarily limited because of my low degree of Cherokicity. I grew up with Indianisms, more than Cherokeeisms. I am not enrolled. I do not speak fluent Cherokee. I did not grow up with a specifically Cherokee worldview. I do not, most importantly, have a clan. Although I was told by various relatives that I was of Cherokee, Choctaw, and Creek descent, I did not know Ada-gal'kala as my seventh great-grandfather. Despite the possibility that he is my genetic ancestor, he himself would likely consider me, from a Cherokee perspective, a nonrelative—his wife's great-great-grandson's wife's son's wife's grandson's wife's granddaughter, because only matrilineal heritage counted traditionally. Likewise with his wife's son Tsi'yugûnsi'ni and his wife's son-in-law Inoli. Nevertheless, I am consciously *choosing* to treat them as relatives, and I hope here to honor them and do them justice.

Red Rhetorics in the Revolutionary Era: Ada-gal'kala, Tsi'yugûnsi'ni, and Intergenerational Disagreement

Of the rhetorical devices mentioned in the previous chapters, two are probably the most obviously and commonly used in Indian oratory, often in conjunction with one another: (1) repetition and recursivity; and (2) the technique of establishing kinship and identity. When this first device is used with the second device, the relationship between the speaker and the audience is being emphasized in hopes of renewing or strengthening that relationship in regard to the context of the speech. Often accompanying this is the promise or offering of gifts, evidence of the reciprocity inherent in Native kinship. Leroy Little Bear's Native Paradigm, which teaches relationship, renewal, respect, and reciprocity (Cajete ix–xii), guides my reading of the rhetoric of speeches in both inter- and extratribal exchanges as well as my reading of the rhetoric of speeches in tribal-governmental exchanges. Sometimes this device of establishing and renewing kinship is manifested by merely mentioning the names of some or all of those present as a way of recognizing or renewing the relationship between the speaker and the listener(s). This device is commonly used in speeches in Native American Church ceremonies, for instance, and in the social interactions that happen before and after the ceremony itself. American Indian ideas of relatedness need a bit more explanation for clarity. Relatedness is not dependent on shared ancestry. For instance, Leroy Little Bear once told me, "When white people came here [Southern Alberta], we expected them to become part of us, not the other way around. They surprised us." When Blackfoot people came into contact with Europeans—which happened relatively late in settler colonial expansion because of geographic and climatic barriers—they simply and naturally expected that Europeans, if they were staying, would become part of the family, would take on Blackfoot ways of living with this land. This had been the practice with those coming into the group and the land before contact with non-Natives. According to Laverne First Rider—wife of Rodney First Rider, the leader of the most prestigious Blackfoot ceremonial society[17]—women captured on raids among Plains tribes often chose to stay and become part of the band. Traditionally, Native peoples have had a long history of "making kinship" with outsiders, of understanding who someone is in relation to themselves by taking relationships with that person. War captives, both Native and non-Native, both male and female, both pre- and postcontact, are one example of this, with many, if not the majority, of them taking kinship relations and becoming part of the particular group they were with. French traders and trappers understood this concept of kinship early on in colonization, and many of them took wives in the Indian way, or *le fashion du pays*, because they realized it was the quickest way to establish good business relations, or, from Native perspectives, to engage in mutual gifting.

Lee Hester, the Choctaw scholar mentioned in chapter 1 and an American Indian studies professor at the University of Science and Arts of Oklahoma, once shared a story with me that illustrates a traditional concept of identity and relatedness. When Sam Proctor, the late Creek elder and Hillis Heyya mentioned in chapter 2, was a guest speaker in Hester's Native identity class, a student asked this respected figure what Hester calls both the most obvious and the most difficult of all questions: "What makes you Creek?" Proctor replied, "If you come out to the stomp dance grounds for four years, take the medicines, and dance, *you will become Creek*." Identity in traditional cultures not only is of paramount importance but also, despite the seeming paradox, is malleable. As Foster notes in *Reasoning Together*, "In tribal communities, one is not just born a tribal person, but instead becomes one through practices and behavior that serve the community, which then recognizes the individual as a member" (Acoose et al. 288). I would go so far as to say that this recognition, which happens in speech, behaviors, and material goods—many of which can be read as texts—is *performative*. Relationships are realized and manifested in words and texts, just as Kiowa author N. Scott Momaday suggests personal identity is in "The Man Made of Words." Identity in Indian Country is grounded primarily in relationship, and relationships are manifested in action and language.

The rhetoric of relatedness is perhaps the dominant characteristic of traditional American Indian discourse because the idea of relatedness governed all American Indian ways of dealing with one another intertribally; eventually this model would expand extratribally. Allies were conceived of in terms of familial relationships. Daniel Justice points out that the occasion of the 1730 visit of the Cherokee delegation to England is indicative of a Cherokee propensity for transnationalism and that "indigeneity . . . is, in many ways, inextricable from definitions of the transnational" ("'To Look Upon Thousands'" 170–71). The particular transnational lens through which Ada-gal'kala viewed these exchanges would have been grounded in Cherokee notions of relatedness. Thus, to him, the only difference between diplomatic relations with the

English and the intertribal relations for which he had been trained would be that the Ani-Gilisi lived across the ocean and that they had customs that must have seemed bizarre to their Cherokee visitors. As allies, the English and the Cherokees became relatives from a Cherokee perspective. When the "Honorable Richard Winn Esquire, Superintendent for the Southern Department," recorded the speech of Little Turkey in 1788 at Ustinali, he was so aware of the dominance of the rhetoric of relatedness in Cherokee discourse that he emphasized its significance in structure by aligning the repetitive refrains "Friend and Brother" and "Brother" at the left margin of the page and indenting the rest of the speech's text (figure 8). This repetition of relatedness was and is common practice across Indian Country. Tecumseh's speech at Machekethie in the spring of 1812 has him addressing the Hurons as "Father and Brother Hurons"; he refers to the Potawatamis as "our Younger Brothers" and designates his own "Shawanoes," along with the "Kikapoos and Winibiegoes," as younger brothers of the Hurons. Tecumseh shows respect to his listeners as older relatives by thanking the Hurons for pitying them and their women and children, thereby putting himself in an appropriately deferential relationship to his listeners. The use of the rhetoric of relatedness forms a repetitive refrain, each of the "paragraphs" beginning with the salutation of relatedness, "Brothers," both emphasizing the importance of the relationship and creating aesthetic appeal. This is not an isolated phenomenon in only one of Tecumseh's speeches but a regularized structural pattern, as the same device can be seen in his speech to the Osage people in the winter of 1811–12, and the same sort of structural pattern is seen elsewhere in American Indian oratory.

These traditions of brotherhood extend beyond the intertribal collective to the personal level, both intra- and intertribally as well as extratribally. The *hatsi* relationship in Comanche culture and the *kola* relationship in Lakota culture demonstrate how seriously adoptive brotherhood is regarded among many Native people. To commit to an allegiance that contradicts the needs of one's fellow tribal citizens is, in effect, placing the relationship with one's "brothers" above that of other relatives to whom one also has an existing obligation; it is opting for benefiting the self and those with whom one is involved in an *exclusive* relationship rather than making decisions based on the needs of the collective in a manner congruent with traditional Native structures and ways. Indeed, here, as I examine the rhetoric used by Ada-gal'kala, I have to keep in mind the relationships he had with others that seem problematic to me.

(A true Copy.)

A [struck] Talk from the Head ~~Warriors~~ Men [inserted] Warriors of the Cherokey Nation at a meeting held at Ustinare the beloved town 20th November 1788. Addressed to the Honorable Richard Winn Esquire Superintendant for the Southern Department in answer to a talk sent by him dated the 12th Octr 1788.

Friend & Brother

We Received your talk likewise the resolves of Congress Dated 1st September 1788 likewise a Copy of a Letter from the Govenor of North Carolina to you and the Proclamation from Congress all which affords us much satisfaction that we may have in you a Real friend who tells us the truth and endeavours to do us Justice; it Likewise gives us much satisfaction to hear from Congress and Virgina

(Brother)

You have opened our Eyes and Likewise our hearts the talk we received from you pleases us much that Congress is ~~combin~~ Determained to have our hunting grounds Open so that our Young men may hunt and Kill Deer to purchase goods of our traders to Cloath our selves and familys Our hunting Grounds was very small, now it gives us the greatest satisfaction that it will be soon enlarged as appears by the Proclamation from Congress, it Likewise gives us much Satisfaction that we have a View of returning from the woods where we have been drove & once more again setling in our old towns which we propose to do when we are certain that the white people have Quitted our hunting Ground

(Brother)

It affords us much Satisfaction that a friendly talk will soon take place; you Inform us you have wrote to the Governor of North Carolina to fix a time and place for that purpose at that time we will talk over all Matters and smoke the pipe of Friendship.

The Head men and Warriors from the middle Settlements was on their way to Ustinare but being informed that it was ~~likewise~~ good talks and that white beads and tobacco was sent from Ustinare to all the towns in the Nation they went back fearing that same young Men might go out again and do Mischeife the head men

determined [in margin] were ~~determined~~ to put a stop to all Hostilities and for the time to come live like Brothers and friends as long as the sun shines and the waters runs

Ayer N.A. ms 157

Despite his suspected consorting with Indian allies of the French subsequent to his captivity with the Ottawa Indians, he was reported by Ludovic Grant, a Carolina trader, to "everywhere profess . . . the English to be his Brothers and the French his Enemies" (Kelly 7). This should be expected, as he had for all intents and purposes formed this relationship with them with his trip to England in 1730. He had also taken very specific, personal brotherhood relationships with both William Byrd III and John Stuart; they each owed Ada-gal'kala their lives, for he had saved them from death after capture by Cherokees, Byrd in 1755 and Stuart in 1761.[18] Ada-gal'kala went to great trouble to free these men he had taken as brothers, especially Stuart, with whom he was particularly close. James C. Kelly states that "Attakullakulla gave his gun, his blanket, and everything he had with him except his breechclout as a ransom for Stuart" (20). Ada-gal'kala's ability to save the two men, despite British atrocities, shows how his diplomatic skills as a Peace Chief saved lives on both sides.

As his elders had suggested to him when he was a young man about to embark on a historic journey, the things Ada-gal'kala learned from his trip to England helped prepare him for a future where speaking and negotiating in English to effect and enact relatedness, the American Indian paradigm for alliance, would be absolutely necessary. He learned early that working through a translator would leave the Cherokee people too vulnerable to imperial ambition. Utilizing English for trade and democracy, however, also opened Cherokees up to potential double-dealing. Sequoyah Guess notes that people cannot "use innuendo" to lie in Cherokee through misdirection as can be done in English—"you can't manipulate the Cherokee language that way." In Cherokee, something either happened or it didn't; it will, or it won't. There is no maybe (C. Teuton et al. 101–2). Making misleading claims or promises is possible in English through verbal sleight of hand, as Cherokees learned. Moreover, dishonesty in business dealings seemed to be an exception to Christianity's prohibition on lying, particularly when settler colonial figures significantly

Opposite: Figure 8. Transcription of a speech from Little Turkey (Cherokee chief) to Richard Winn on Nov. 20, 1788: "A talk from the head warriers of the Cherokey Nation at a meeting held at Ustinare . . . : addressed to the Honorable Richard Winn Esquire, Superintendent for the Southern Department in answer to a talk sent by him dated the 12th Oct. 1788." Photo courtesy of The Newberry Library, Chicago. Call number Ayer MS 157.

othered and objectified those with whom they were dealing. Traders who married Native women had obligations as relatives to the rest of the community and thus engaged in reciprocal relationships, as did soldiers and officers such as John Stuart. They became "real" relatives to Cherokee people in the sense that Little Bear describes above. They would rank fairly high on a scale of Cherokicity. They might not have been born Cherokee, but they adopted Cherokee ways of being in relation to Cherokee people. "Excerpt from Governor Glen's Talks with Little Carpenter [Ada-gal'kala], Skiagunsta, and Others on July 5, 1753" reveals that problems with other traders, both those who lived within the Cherokee Nation and those who lived in colonies adjoining it, caused diplomatic entanglements (Rozema, locations 308–474). Glen distrusted Ada-gal'kala, who had been held captive by French allies, the Ottawas, for four years. Through the captive system, Ada-gal'kala had been adopted into a high-ranking Ottawa family, leading Glen to accuse him of being a French sympathizer. Glen had a point—Ada-gal'kala, skilled in intertribal diplomacy, had to have done a good job of becoming Ottawa in order to become kin with the family he did—but the very fact that identity is malleable in Indian Country means that Ada-gal'kala had no difficulty returning to full Cherokicity when he was freed. In his own right, Ada-gal'kala was discontent, not only because of the "lies" he was called to defend himself against, but also because he had been deceived into signing a treaty in 1730 that guaranteed trade, and South Carolina under Governor Glen was not making good on that promise (Kelly 7). Having come to Charleston with six of his headmen to discuss this, Ada-gal'kala told Glen:

> It was on account of the trade that we went to Virginia. When I was in England I was told that I might go any way for goods when I could get them the cheapest. The price of shirting is dearer now than formerly. . . . The traders are very cross with us Indians. We dare not speak to them. If we do, they take our skins, and throw them on the ground, and deny us goods. If we do not give them their prices we must go without any. . . . Do what we can, the white people will cheat us in our weights and measures, and make them less. What is it a trader can not do? They cheat us in the measure of our powder. Some of the white men borrowed my yeard [yard][19] and cut it, and then gave it back for which I was blamed. (Qtd. in Rozema, locations 335–49)

Ada-gal'kala wanted to go to England to deal directly with the king because of what he considered violations of their agreements as representatives of nations and as honorable relatives. Glen, however, made it clear that he did not respect Cherokee sovereignty to the extent that he would treat Ada-gal'kala with the dignity he would afford a representative of an equivalent office in a European government, and his responses to Ada-gal'kala were dismissive and evasive.

In addition to the linguistic trickery that English made possible by its very nature, settler colonial figures were dishonest and reinforced their lies by engaging in the American Indian kinesthetic and visual rhetorics of gifting, smoking pipes, and exchanging wampum. These they had learned from Indians, along with verbal means of persuasion. For instance, Cherokees used a kinesthetic rhetoric that performatively expressed their new relationship with Virginia royal governor Henry Timberlake and the other settler colonials he represented. Barbara Duncan, education director of the Museum of the Cherokee Indian in Cherokee, North Carolina, tells me that the Cherokees of Citico and Chilhowee welcomed Timberlake with the War Dance, the men's bodies painted red as they danced, accoutered with their weapons of war. They then engaged in the Peace Pipe Dance, their bodies now painted white, dancing with "eagle wands." According to Duncan, "Ostenaco and his interpreter assured Timberlake this was to give him 'a hearty welcome' as an emissary of Britain and to 'make reparations' for the role of those towns [Citico and Chilhowee] in the recent war, so these were conscious overtures"[20] (Duncan e-mail). A number of white men—among them Timberlake, William Byrd III, and Governor Glen—professed relatedness and a sense of fidelity to Cherokee people through multimodal discourse. Behind the backs of Cherokee people, however, they and others spoke quite rudely when expressing their true feelings. Although it is unsurprising that letters between these settler colonial figures and others were liberally sprinkled with generally racist terms like "savages" and "squaws," there are plenty of more specific insults in the record as well that are multimodal in nature. Timberlake makes it clear that only with great personal discomfort does he engage in Cherokee customs of kinesthetic rhetoric to renew relationships, as he finds physical proximity to Cherokee people repulsive. After being invited into the home of Ostenaco and his wife—whom Timberlake insists on labeling as Ostenaco's "consort," in the pejorative sense of the word—and then joining him and the other Cherokee men in the council house, Timberlake later writes in his memoirs: "Smoaking was always very disagreeable to me; but as it was a token of their amity, and they might be offended if I did not comply, I put on the best face I was able, though I dared not even wipe the end of the pipe that came out of their mouths; which, considering their paint and dirtiness, are not of the most ragoutant [tasty], as the French term it" (Rozema, locations 547–50). Clearly, Timberlake thinks of Cherokees as "unclean." While smoking tobacco is a deeply spiritual act from traditional Native perspectives—and can be, in fact, seen as a physical manifestation of a prayer, the exhaled smoke carrying one's thoughts up to God and out to the spirited universe—sharing a pipe is also a kinesthetic rhetoric that becomes embodied, performatively bonding people in relatedness to one another through the intimacy of sharing breath/smoke. Because of this, many tribes have cultural proscriptions against smoking with just anyone. These British men, however, were considered "brothers," and in addition to smoking with their Indian brethren, they introduced their own brotherly practice of drinking together. The practice of using alcohol to ease the conquest of people almost completely unfamiliar with it goes all the way back to Julius Caesar's conquest of the Germanic tribes. Ada-gal'kala himself is documented as being drunk and needing to be carted back to his lodgings in London during the 1730 trip and is reported to have imbibed on other occasions. While alcohol brought a whole host of ongoing issues to Indian Country and continues to plague communities, the British brothers consistently utilized alcohol to their advantage in both trade and peace negotiations. Alcohol, in effect, became a rhetorical weapon. Captain Raymond Demere, for instance, while waiting for Governor Glen at Fort Prince George on the way to build Fort Loudon, reported that "[Ada-gal'kala's] conduct aroused his suspicions, but was passed over upon the ground of intoxication, not however to the entire satisfaction of the captain, who regarded the Indian as deceitful when sober and an impertinent fellow at all times"[21] (McCrady 324). The practices of drinking and of smoking pipes together become an inequitable dialectic, of which the British were aware and which they celebrated in blatantly speaking of their Cherokee brothers as their inferiors. This is not the only time that Ada-gal'kala's "impertinence"—that is, his strong attachment to his personal sovereignty and that of his nation—led to insults and infantilizing behind his back. Byrd says of him in a letter to Governor William Henry Lyttelton three years after Demere's report, "That little savage was very insolent this morning" (qtd. in Tinling 651). Byrd clearly does not see Ada-gal'kala as an equal or a brother. Byrd fails at embodying brotherhood, even though he has taken rhetorical steps to bind himself to Cherokee people in their presence.

When Governor Glen met to negotiate a second treaty, the Treaty of Saluda, with the Cherokees in 1755, being that even the British did not consider the agreement wrought by trickery in London 1730 valid, he had suggested that Ada-gal'kala would be able to go with a delegation to London to discuss the new treaty with the king. When Glen reversed himself after the Cherokees agreed to the treaty terms, Ada-gal'kala had a small child brought to him and reinforced the relationship that Glen and the Cherokees were supposed to have—thus correcting Glen's dishonesty, which was behavior unbecoming of a good relative—through means of indirect discourse, saying:

> I am the only living Cherokee that went to England. . . . What I now speak the great King should hear. We are brothers to the people of Carolina, and one house covers us all. . . . We, our wives and children, are all children of the great King George. . . . I have brought this child, that when he grows up he may remember our agreement this day and tell it to the next generation that it may be forever known. . . . We freely surrender part of our possessions. The French want our Lands, but we will defend them while one of our Nation is alive. . . . These are the arms we have for our defense. We hope the Great King will pity his children the Cherokees and send us guns and ammunition. We fear not the French. Give us arms, and we will go to war against the enemies of the great King. My speech is at an end. . . . It is the voice of the Cherokee Nation. I hope that the Governor will send it to the great King that it may be kept forever. (Kelly 10–11)

He then turned to his people for agreement, and they gave forth acclaims of "Yo-hah" (Kelly 11).[22] Ada-gal'kala makes use of visual and kinesthetic rhetoric a number of times in this speech to reinforce his points. First, he uses the powerful visual pathos of the small child, a child being both innocent and honest as well as actually embodying the future; second, he pours out a small bag of dirt at Glen's feet when he mentions parting with a portion of their land; third, he holds a bow in one hand and a quiver of arrows in the other when he wants to emphasize that they will need weapons to fight the British war for their now formal allies; and finally, he seals the deal with the traditional contract written in wampum to be sent to the king. Ada-gal'kala utilizes this multimodal rhetoric to renew the Cherokee and British relationship.

Multimodal rhetorics had ritualized alliances and renewals of alliances between tribal nations for millennia, alliances negotiated by men who had been trained, in much the same way that Ada-gal'kala had as a young man, to be intertribal diplomats. Speaking in response to Governor Bull in 1761 after smoking a pipe with him, the kinesthetic and embodied rhetoric of which made it impossible for him to lie,[23] Ada-gal'kala says:

> When I came to Keowee, Colonel Grant sent me to you. You are on the water side, and are in the light. We are in darkness; but hope all will be clear. I have been constantly going about doing good; and though I am tired, yet I am come to see what can be done for my people, who are in great distress. As to what has happened, I believe it has been order by our Father above. We are of a different color from the white people. They are superior to us. But one God is father to us all, and we hope what is past will be forgotten. God Almighty made all people. There is not a day but that some are coming into, and others going out of the world. The great king told me the path should never be crooked, but open for every one to pass. As we all live in one land, I hope that we shall all live as one people. (Qtd. in Goodpasture, issue 4.1, p. 22)

A rhetorical element discussed in chapter 3, Jason Edward Black's "self-mortification," is perhaps the most glaring in Ada-gal'kala's remarks. Self-deprecating comments, however, convey humility, a virtue in Indian Country, and are meant to place the audience in a position of respect. But what is notable here is the shift in the way relatedness rhetoric is used. In the speech to Governor Glen the common "father" that makes the British and the Cherokees brothers is King George. Here, instead, that father is God. Moreover, the indirect discourse makes it clear that Ada-gal'kala expects justice under God that he cannot obtain from the king or settler colonial leaders, who are not his superiors despite what they believe.

A letter dated May 27, 1758, from Ada-gal'kala to Byrd[24] shows that the Cherokee leader truly believed in the brotherhood relationship they had taken and that he posited himself as Byrd's equal. While John Watts, to whom Ada-gal'kala dictated this letter, does not use the organic paragraphing of the

Ustinali speech transcription (figure 8), the text of the letter is organized by the same refrain of "Brother" that appears in the speech, making three sections of discourse. In the letter, Ada-gal'kala discusses the logistics of his getting to Winchester to meet up with Byrd and reinforces that he "remember[s] the talk of the grate King George our father, who desired us to help . . . and I am very willing for to help my brothers, and both to die together" (qtd. in Tinling 656). Ada-gal'kala sees himself and Byrd as mutually indebted to one another, even though he has gone so far as to save Byrd's life. He recalls, "I have recei[ve] d a grate maney preasants, from you, and you may depend that I shall give orders not to hurt our brothers the English" (656). His words let us know that he sees this relationship as inviolable—". . . for the grate King George when I was in England, and our head men, made the path between the English and our Nation of iron, never to be broken. Little Carpenter [X]" (657). Ada-gal'kala views the gifts he has received as part of diplomatic rhetoric from a Native perspective rather than from a materialistic, Western perspective. These gifts embody a rhetorical and spiritual currency that transforms even enemies into brothers and cannot be measured in money. Ideally, most if not all of these gifts would be redistributed throughout the kinship network—from traditional Native perspectives, strengthening ties even further. Certainly today, gifts that are "captured" out of the mainstream economic system to become an entirely different kind of capital in an Indian economy of relatedness are often regifted repeatedly. Shawls and Pendleton and Hudson's Bay Point blankets, often part of the formal giveaways at powwows and ceremonies throughout various parts of Indian County, are frequently regifted when the recipient finds himself or herself in a sociocultural situation where gifting is appropriate and almost mandatory if one does not wish to "look bad." In Blackfoot country, where the settler colonial footprint on Indian ways is less visible, this tradition of a gifting economy is still so strong that if someone indicates he or she likes something that someone else owns, it is considered very bad form for the person not to immediately give it to him or her.

The seriousness with which Ada-gal'kala took his relationship with the British is also evident in a speech he gave to Byrd, transcribed by "a serjeant" and included in a letter sent by Robert Stewart to George Washington on July 20, 1761 (figure 9). Stewart describes the transcription as "the substance of the Carpenter's talk, which [the transcriber] very incorrectly wrote" (qtd. in Tinling 745). Even at a cursory glance, this letter was obviously not written in Cherokee or even in Red English. Nevertheless, even the context of this speech, minus Ada-gal'kala's direct words, shows where his allegiances lie; he is revealing information from Cherokee discussions with "the headmen of the northern Nations," who were French allies:

> [They] gave us [Cherokees] to understand, they intend'd to strik the wite people again and were desirous that all the red people might unite, and as they look'd upon them to be nothing it would be easie to distroy them. They desir'd the Cherokees to be strong in the war and not by any means to listen to peace, that they would join them heartily, and had sent word to all the French down the river to lend their assistance.
>
> That they would soon fall upon all the forts which the white people had taken from the French, not to lurk about them, but to surprise and cut them off all at once, then they would fall upon the northern colonies, while the Cherokees should attack the Carolin's.
>
> That they had sent large belts of wampum to invite the Creek, Chekasaus, Choctaws &c. to ingage with them in falling upon the English. I do not tell this as a truth but only as news which I heard and this all I know from the northward. (Tinling 743)

Ada-gal'kala then gives further evidence in the form of news that had reached Cherokees through a man who had recently been to the Creek Nation and reported that the Creeks had killed all of the traders living among them. Ada-gal'kala also reports on his interactions with Colonel Grant, with whom he had met at Keowee at some trouble to himself because of the volatile environment. Grant requested that Ada-gal'kala ask the other Cherokee headmen to turn down the opportunity to join the intertribal alliance with the French and promised that if they did so, they would be safe. Otherwise, Grant threatened to "kill them all." Ada-gal'kala says he took this news to "Occonnerstota Otoseita[25] the Standing Turkey and all the head men who had been active in the war," who agreed that "the English had always spoke the truth to them, . . .

Opposite: Figure 9. Transcription of a speech from Attakullakulla (Cherokee chief), July 17, 1761, to William Byrd. George Washington Papers at the Library of Congress, 1741–99: Series 4; General Correspondence, 1697–1799. Library of Congress, Manuscript Division.

Mahaltkulla's Speach to Col. Byrd July 7th 1761

As I was Sent out by You a Messenger, to Deliver Your talk to the head-Men of our Nation, and to bring You in an exact acct. of the Disposition of The People in Regard to the present war, of all Their Transactions and News Stiring among them, I am now return'd for that Purpose and Shall be Very Open & Sincere in Telling You every thing I know. Two Days before I set out two of our People came in from the Northward, where having talk'd with the head men of the Northern Nations gave us to understand, they intended to Strike the white people again and were Desirous that all the Red people might unite, and as they Look'd upon them to be Nothing it would be easie to Destroy them. They Desir'd the Cherokees to be Strong in the War and Not by any Means to listen to Peace, that They would join them heartily, and had Sent word to all the French Down the River to Lend their assistance.

That they would soon fall upon all the Forts which the white People had taken from the French, Not to Lurk about them, but to Surprise and cut them off all at once, then they would fall upon the Northern Colonies, while the Cherokees should attack the Carolin's.

That they had sent Large belts of Wampum to Invite the Creek, Chickasaws, Choctaws &c. to Ingage with them in falling upon the English. — I do not tell this as a truth but only as News which I heard and this is all I know from the Northward.

A man who had been in the Creek Nation and Lately Return'd Inform'd me, that the People of that Nation had Lately kill'd all their Traders, & had taken up the Hatchett. N.B. afterwards he said he believ'd this to be true; but that two Towns Near est to Albaney remain'd Neuter, gave Shelter to the Traders that escaped, and Did this by the advice of the French who Dissuaded them from entering into a war, as they were Not able to Supply them with Necessaries.

when I heard that Col. Grant was coming with a Number of Warriors towards the Nation I went to Keowe to Meet him he was Not come up so far, and After I had staid as Long as I they should never ingage in a war against them, if they did they would loose all their trade [and] be naked for want of cloaths, and . . . they determined to stay at home & and leave the young warriors to themselves. Ada-gal'kala tries unsuccessfully to get the young warriors to accompany him to Colonel Grant and sets off alone to go to the Lower Towns.[26] Along the way, he meets a man who tells him his mission is fruitless, as the warriors had battled with "the white people" two days prior. Ada-gal'kala becomes "determined never to interfere in the publick affairs again, but leave every one to follow his own inclination" (Tinling 744). Ada-gal'kala has done all he can to remain true to Byrd as his brother and their mutual father King George II. In doing so, he acts directly against the powerful intertribal alliance as well as against a large portion of the Cherokee Nation who have chosen to go to war.

By July 7, 1761, the date of the letter containing Ada-gal'kala's speech to Byrd, British forces had completely devastated a number of towns. Governor Bull's South Carolina–led "Cherokee War" was horrifically brutal.[27] Ada-gal'kala says, "The people are so starv'd for provision that several have been found dead in the paths, & were reduc'd to kill their horses for subsistence." Here he points out to Byrd exactly what the British have been willing to do to the Cherokees, despite their alliance and relationship. Ada-gal'kala skillfully uses pathos to intensify his point and invoke in Byrd what would be a positive response from Native perspectives: "pity" for his relatives. Ada-gal'kala mentions another source of pity: "A northern Indian warrior with Col. Grant took me by the hand, said he esteem'd me as a friend & after some talk gave me a twist of tobacco saying All your people are sick. Give them this tobacco to smoak. It is good phisick, will soon make them well, bring them to their senses again, and will make them think of the English as I do" (Tinling 745). With this, Ada-gal'kala not only reinforces the notion that his people deserve mercy under the circumstances but also gives a Native explanation of their motivation—they were out of their minds. This shared tobacco, even without shared smoking of it, reestablishes an alliance between the Cherokees and the Indian allies of the British, and by extension the British as well. Ada-gal'kala's talk ultimately resulted in the Cherokees doing far better in peace negotiations than they would have otherwise. Moreover, he was able to persuade settler colonial authorities to name his brother John Stuart as the Indian superintendent in charge of the area.

Further disagreement between Cherokee generations regarding policy with settler colonials—leaders, traders, and otherwise—occurred over the next few years. Prices for deer hides dropped in response to Cherokee demand for trade goods. Cherokee people developed insurmountable debt at the hands of many unscrupulous traders who already had been infringing upon both the national sovereignty and the personal autonomy of Cherokees by threatening them with collection unless they complied with their desires regarding the acquisition of Cherokee-controlled territory. In response, Cherokee leadership began to part with lands, against even the advice of John Stuart, whom Ada-gal'kala highly esteemed. Tsi'yugûnsi'ni, who disagreed with this decision, emerges as a great orator himself at the negotiating of the Treaty of Sycamore Shoals. He responds to this series of transfers of Cherokee Nation lands:

> Where now are our grandfathers, the Delawares? . . . We had hoped the white man would not be willing to travel beyond the mountains. . . . They have passed the mountains, and have settled upon Cherokee land. They wish to have that usurpation sanctioned by treaty. . . . [T]he same encroaching spirit will lead them upon . . . the whole country, which the Cherokees and their fathers have so long occupied . . . and the remnant of the Ani-Yunwiya, "The Real People," once so great and formidable, will be compelled to seek refuge in some distant wilderness. . . . [T]he extinction of the whole race will be proclaimed. Should we not therefore run all risks . . . rather than submit to further laceration of our country? Such treaties may be all right for men who are too old to hunt or fight. As for me, I have my young warriors about me. We will have our lands. *A-waninski,* I have spoken. (J. Brown, *Old Frontiers* 10)

While historians such as John P. Brown have almost always concluded that this is the "general tenor" of Tsi'yugûnsi'ni's speech, not its exact words, Tsi'yugûnsi'ni's disagreement that day is noted throughout the historical record. What is important here for the purposes of my argument are two aspects of this speech: one that seems authentic, given what we know of Red Rhetorics; and another that is dependent only on the fact that he spoke out at all. The first aspect is that Tsi'yugûnsi'ni is still speaking from a traditional Cherokee ontology of relatedness. He refers to the Delawares as the grandfathers of the Cherokees, partially in recognition of their land tenure and partially in recognition of the alliance and friendship between the two tribal nations.

The other aspect is more complicated. Tsi'yugûnsi'ni speaks out of turn, given his age and social stature. Cherokee culture certainly had clear protocols that dictated that one must be of a certain age, experience level, and position to speak formally to or on behalf of the people. Tyler Boulware, in "'Our Mad Young Men': Authority and Violence in Cherokee Country," gives a good overview of Cherokee auctoritas on matters of trade, diplomacy, and war, detailing (1) gender—generally, the outside sphere was the proper domain of men, though more rarely women were occasionally active in one or more of these areas; (2) heredity; (3) the gaining of meritorious war titles, such as "Raven, Slavecatcher, Mankiller, and Skiagusta"; (3) and advancement in age. Boulware reports that "a British officer in 1756 found that village leaders were usually 'old or middle-aged People who know how to give a talk'" (83). In fact, the reason Oukayuda was chosen as spokesman on the trip to London was due to Ada-gal'kala's young age at the time. Ada-gal'kala says in his own words: "Tho I was the first person who had agreed to go, yet as I was the youngest of the company it would not be right that I should be the Speaker, and therefore Oukayuda was appointed" (Kelly 4). This basis for auctoritas was so strongly ingrained that it was an articulated device at times. The Raven of Hiwassee, for instance, gives weight to his own speech by saying, "This my talk is not to be looked upon as Nothing. I am not a young man." The Skiagusta of Keowee stressed his authority by saying, "There were many head Men here, who are but Boys to me" (Boulware 83). Though likely already the headman of Mialoquo at that time, Tsi'yugûnsi'ni was probably in his late thirties to early forties and Ada-gal'kala was approximately in his mid- to late sixties when the Treaty of Sycamore Shoals was negotiated. Still today, it would seem exceedingly rude for a man of Tsi'yugûnsi'ni's age to disagree so publicly with someone of Ada-gal'kala's age and station. Individual autonomy was also valued, however, and this indeed is what led to Tsi'yugûnsi'ni and others to form the Chickamauga Confederacy and to ally with even those who had been traditional enemies of the Cherokee Nation, such as the Muscogee Creeks. This process redefined notions of Cherokicity as new relationships were formed. Nevertheless, Tsi'yugûnsi'ni's speaking out violated the rules of good kinship, despite how astute and seemingly prophetic his words were regarding American hunger for land. While in some respects, this restriction could be seen as a form of what Lyons terms "rhetorical imperialism," or "the ability of dominant powers to assert control of others by setting the terms of debate" ("Rhetorical Sovereignty" 452), this practice stood the test of time in regard to experiential wisdom and to what preserved the Cherokee Nation as a whole. As Ada-gal'kala himself says, "Some of the warriours of my Nation . . . upon hearing Storys true or false, are immediately in a flame, but that is not my way—I love calmness and moderation" (qtd. in Kelly 29). Maturity gives people a greater propensity for that sort of deliberation.

Certainly, however, the entire intergenerational and familial conflict was further complicated, from a Cherokee perspective, by the American Revolution. Emmet Starr notes:

> For fifteen years peace reigned in the Cherokee nation, but on May 9, 1776, circular letters were sent out by the British Superintendent, Stuart, to the Cherokees and Tories asking them to fall on and destroy the western American settlers. The Cherokees at first demurred but finally acceded to the wishes of King George, as they understood that he was the head of the English. It was hard for them to understand how one part of any people could fight others of their own nationality. But at last many of the young warriors listened to the persuasive Stuart. (31)

Initially, the Cherokee Nation as a whole supported the British, as might be expected given their respect for the relationships they had taken. Moreover, supporting the Tory cause arose from another alliance, the intertribal resistance led from by the Haudenosaunees[28] and Shawnees in the north. Delegates from this alliance had arrived in May, asking for alliance both with words and with material rhetoric. The Mohawk delegate urged, "Better to die like men than diminish away by inches" (qtd. in Calloway, "Declaring" 190). Then he offered the Cherokees "a War Belt about 9 feet long and six inches wide of purple Whampum strewed over with vermilion." Despite the hesitancy of Ada-gal'kala, Oconostota, and other older chiefs to involve their people in war again, Tsi'yugûnsi'ni accepted the belt (Calloway, "Declaring" 190). Starr says that eventually the Cherokees committed to bringing seven hundred warriors into the British cause, planning a three-pronged, coordinated attack on the Americans on July 21, 1776, with Tsi'yugûnsi'ni's force attacking the Holston settlements; Abraham of Chilhowee's force, the Watuga settlements; and Raven (Colonah), Carters Valley. However, Ghigau / ᎩᎦᎤ / Beloved Woman[29] Nancy Ward intervened by sending advance warning to the American forces. The majority of the Cherokee Nation made peace with the Americans in two treaties—one on May 20, 1777, with South Carolina and Georgia; the other on July 20, 1777, with Virginia and North Carolina—that stipulated the loss of 5,264,000 acres of Cherokee land, breaking the nearly fifty-year alliance and—more importantly—*relationship* with Great Britain as family, just as the Americans had done. Many of the "mad young men" such as Tsi'yugûnsi'ni and Inoli, along with older leaders Outacita and Young Tassel, did not attend the treaty talks and instead left, forming the Chickamauga towns. Ultimately, as settlers who had come to America under British rule divided their loyalties, Cherokee relationships with others who were ethnically Scotsmen, as Stuart was, proved to be some of the closest in many ways. The Chickamaugas sided with Stuart over the Americans after the revolution and continued the British cause (Starr 32–34). Tsi'yugûnsi'ni himself had taken as a brother Alexander Cameron, who married a Cherokee woman and had Cherokee children. Other Scotsmen who married into the tribe chose to align with the Chickamaugas as the Cherokee Nation split (Calloway, *White People* 153). However, even after the British concluded peace with the United States in 1783, the Chickamaugas, with the support of the viceroy of Spain, continued their war with the Americans. The Chickamaugas grew ever more intertribally and transnationally related to others, while the larger group of Cherokees became increasingly isolated as a domestic dependent nation-state, divided eventually by removal from each other into three distinct legal entities. As Gary B. Nash points out, Tsi'yugûnsi'ni was one of "the exemplars of pan-Indian resistance after the peace without peace" (440).

When Tsi'yugûnsi'ni passed away, Inoli spoke in memory of him at the Great Cherokee Council held at Estanaula on June 26–30, 1792: "The Dragging Canoe has left the world. He was a man of consequence in his country. He was a friend both to his own and the white people" (Goodpasture, issue 4.3, p. 171). In the end, it is Tsi'yugûnsi'ni's loyalty to his allies and to what he saw as the best interests of people that Inoli commemorates him for, as well as the stature his skills in warfare and leadership gave him. Inoli, his brother-in-law, appreciates Tsi'yugûnsi'ni's true devotion to fraternal values and alliances.

Idle No More: Educated Grandmas and Our Mad Young Men

The authoritative elders and the "mad young men" in the Cherokee Nation from the French and Indian War through the American Revolution and eventually on to removal had competing but complementary rhetorics, despite the cultural prohibitions against young men's speaking. The two competing but complementary strains of rhetoric in Idle No More, an intertribal resistance movement of today, mirror in a number of ways the intertribal diplomatic discourse of that earlier era and its responses to settler colonialism. Today the mainstream, official branch of the movement is more affiliated with Western legal and political structures, having had support from many band and tribal governments—one leader even hunger-striking for the cause—and has connections with the United Nations Permanent Forum on Indigenous Peoples. Its name is not trademarked, as many have believed; the group began the process to do so in Canada on January 10, 2013, but abandoned it on April 29, 2014. The other branch of the movement is more aligned with those "mad young men" of the past, has its roots in ancient prophecies of revolution and change, and is based more closely on historical alliances that took up "the war belt," that are, in other words, more militant. Both branches ask for paradigmatic shifts on the part of humanity as a whole.

Idle No More began in Alberta, Canada, in November 2012, in response to Bill C-45 and other legislative actions of the conservative government of then prime minister Stephen Harper that impinged on First Nations treaty rights and threatened the environment and First Nations, Métis, and Inuit (FNMI) people. In an interview with Sarah Van Gelder, Sylvia McAdam (Cree) stated that when she returned home from law school, she was horrified by the conditions of the land and water on her father's property near the Whitefish reserve, because of logging and other environmental incursions. She began her own activism, nailing up signs around the reserve that read, "No Trespassing. Treaty 6 Territory."[30] McAdam began learning about Bill C-45, an omnibus bill that would change sixty-four legislative acts in Canada, among them the Indian Act; the Navigation Protection Act, once known as the Navigable Waters Protection Act; and the Environmental Protection Act. Because she realized this bill would put treaty lands and territory at risk in multiple ways—from environmental contamination and resource loss to complete loss of ownership of the land to the government—McAdam contacted her Facebook friends Jessica Gordon (Pasqua First Nation) and Nina Wilson (Kahkewistahaw First Nation). "I told them there's something in law called acquiescence," McAdam says. "That means that if you're silent, then your silence is taken as consent. All of us agreed that we couldn't be silent, that grassroots people have a right to know." She later asked Sheelah McLean, a non-FNMI instructor at the University of Saskatchewan, to join in their conversation. In a Facebook chat, Gordon coined the name the movement would eventually take on, later creating a Facebook page called Idle No More. The group also gave that name to their first teach-in at Station 20 West in Saskatoon, Saskatchewan, held to spread the message that action needed to be taken and to help people understand the proposed legislative changes, the infringements on treaty rights, and the environmental impact that not taking action would have. A national day of action, consisting of teachings, rallies, and protests, was organized for December 10, 2012, coinciding with Amnesty International's Human Rights Day. The day also was associated with Attawapiskat chief Theresa Spence's hunger strike, which she had announced she would begin on December 11, seeking meetings with the prime minister and the queen's representative to oppose Bill C-45. Idle No More flash mobs, round-dancing and armed with signs, began popping up at malls all across Canada and the United States before and after Christmas that year in support of the FNMI people's demands and of Chief Spence and additional fasting elders, such as Raymond Robinson from Cross Lake in Manitoba. Others held protest walks. Though not with the consent of the Idle No More founders, road, railway, and border crossing blockades also were held throughout Canada.

The FNMI student and young college-educated population was foundational in the early days of Idle No More. Taiaiake Alfred's work has had a great impact on the education of that generation in Canada, so it should be no surprise that the movement promotes grounding one's activism in "tradition" and spirituality, for Alfred suggests that this is the only way Indigenous activism can succeed. It is no accident that both education and social media sparked this movement—knowledge and relationships have always been primary sources of strength for Indigenous people. Universities, along with Facebook and other social media sites such as Twitter, simply provided the right conditions for Indigenous people to gain the knowledge needed of global corporate capitalism, the imperialism out of which it grew, and their historic and current threats to the lives of Indigenous people and the sustainability of life on the planet in general. Social media also allowed Indigenous people, as it has others, to develop and maintain relationships more easily than ever before with a wider group of people with shared experiences and interests.[31] Some Indigenous people see Idle No More as the revolutionary change prophesied by the Mayans to begin in December 2012, and the most radical branch of the movement vows to unite the condor and the eagle in fulfillment of these prophecies.

I first became involved at the unauthorized Penn Square Mall protest in Oklahoma City on December 29, 2012. It coincided with the authorized protest in Bricktown, a short distance away, and sparked the movement in Oklahoma, giving rise to several grassroots groups throughout the state that held flash mobs and rallies in varying locations from Oklahoma City to the University of Oklahoma in Norman to Tulsa, as well as on tribal lands. My former students from both the Kainai and the Piikani Bands of Blackfoot Indians in Canada, like many of their community members, were part of the early furor of the movement, and I felt a commitment to live up to my ideals and support their cause. Because I had maintained close relationships with them through Facebook, our posts, photos, and videos flew back and forth across the miles and the Medicine Line[32] between Oklahoma and Alberta, with the virtual world realizing our mental and spiritual world of a borderless Indian Country. As efforts became more organized, Idle No More leaders in Canada urged us to begin to address our local and tribally specific concerns. Larger Idle No More concerns that have emerged from the excavation of tar sands in Northern Alberta and affect not only surrounding communities (such as the Fort Chipewyan Reserve) but also the entire planet—for example, through the transport of the bitumen/tar sand blend in the proposed Keystone XL Pipeline—were certainly of interest to Native people in Oklahoma. The proposed path of the Keystone pipeline directly intersects tribal lands here, particularly in Cushing,[33] the hub that connects pipelines from all over the continent. Relationships with settler colonial allies and other oppressed groups were strengthened through common interests in global survival. The Tar Sands Blockade group[34] and members of the Occupy movement[35] have found common ground with Idle No More. Another important early issue was the renewal of the Violence Against Women Act to include special tribal provisions that transfer jurisdiction over sex crimes and domestic violence from the federal government to tribal authorities and to give tribes jurisdiction over non-Native perpetrators. The fight of the Choctaw and Chickasaw Nations with the State of Oklahoma over Sardis Lake water rights was supported by Idle No More groups in Oklahoma, particularly regarding concerns that the water might be used, not for human consumption, but for fracking, a possible cause of increased earthquakes.[36] Saving Hickory Ground in Alabama from development in support of traditional Muscogee people was also taken up by Idle No More, along with ending the racist land-run reenactments[37] that Native children have been subjected to in Oklahoma public schools for generations. In the meantime, on Facebook, Idle No More supporters began to appear holding signs of solidarity from around the world, largely from groups of Indigenous and/or oppressed people, but also from others of all walks of life who feel that unity is the only means humans have of surviving global corporate imperialism. Videos of protests and flash mobs proliferated on YouTube. A map created by Toronto freelance journalist Tim Groves and published in *The Huffington Post* on December 27, 2012, showed that actions had already been held not only all over North America but also in Hawaii, Nicaragua, Guatemala, Palestine, Egypt, Indonesia, Australia, New Zealand, five western European countries, and the Ukraine. The main Idle No More website displays this vision statement:

> Idle No More calls on all people to join in a peaceful revolution, to honour Indigenous sovereignty, and to protect the land and water.
>
> INM has and will continue to help build sovereignty & resurgence of nationhood.
>
> INM will continue to pressure government and industry to protect the environment.
>
> INM will continue to build allies in order to reframe the nation to nation relationship, this will be done by including grassroots perspectives, issues, and concern.[38] ("Vision")

Since that time, other Idle No More concerns in Oklahoma have been saving the Kiowa sacred site of Longhorn Mountain from being turned into gravel by developers to pave highways; helping Governor Mary Fallin understand that our need as Indigenous people to have sacred fires for our ceremonies is a religious right that supersedes statewide burn bans; and a growing concern over Monsanto's pesticides and genetically modified foods, as well as increasing warning signs of global environmental disaster, such as the mass die-offs of bees. Idle No More in Oklahoma supported Standing Our Ground for Veronica Brown and Standing Our Ground for Desirai, both on behalf of the two American Indian children involved, their birth families, and their sovereign tribal nations and as part of larger efforts toward protecting American Indian children in general from adoptions that violate the Indian Child Welfare Act and the UN Convention on the Prevention and Punishment of the Crime of Genocide. A number of Idle No More members protested the practice by Fallin's daughter, Christina, and by other privileged non-Native young people in the entertainment industry, of wearing traditional Plains chiefs' headdresses in a mockery of what is considered sacred. Likewise, many joined the efforts of the group Eradicating Offensive Native Mascots, renewing a battle a number of us, including me, were involved with in the first years of this millennium. This particular initiative had a great deal of success, with the hashtag #NotYourMascot being named one of the seven 2014 finalists for Digital Trend of the Year by the Digital Folklore Project at Utah State University. Social media spurred the kind of change that traditional texts had been unable to effect, resulting in an unprecedented number of entities ridding themselves of Indian monikers.

There is, however, a more radical movement that has sprung from Idle No More. On the summer solstice of 2013, Chase Iron Eyes—a Lakota activist and attorney who writes regularly for *Indian Country Today* and who ran as the 2016 North Dakota Democratic candidate for the U.S. House of Representatives—interviewed General Cha-O-Ha, self-described as the War Chief of the Amerindian Peoples Liberation Army of the Americas (APLA). The organization grew out of the Amerindian Peoples Liberation Front (APLF), a now defunct group that published a set of demands on the Last Real Indians website on January 16, 2013, beginning with this statement:

> DECLARATION #1
>
> In Solidarity with the IdleNoMore movement of North America, the Zapatista Army of National Liberation of Central America, the Movimento Xingu Vivo of South America, and the Siwa Lima Front of the Pacific:
>
> We the . . . Amerindian Peoples of Guyana, in Order to better serve our Creator, protect mother Earth, honor our ancestors, establish Justice, insure our domestic peace, provide for our common defence, promote our general welfare, preserve our cultural and biological identities, and secure the blessings of liberty that our ancestors once knew for ourselves and for our future generations yet unborn, do ordain and establish the Amerindian Peoples Liberation Front.

The APLF's demands included actual representation in the government in Guyana, not figurehead representation; the replacement of non-Indigenous law enforcement personnel in Amerindian communities with Indigenous personnel; the removal of unrelated settler colonials from and the revocation of their land ownership in Amerindian communities; a declaration of ownership of natural resources in Amerindian communities by Amerindian communities; the end of forced sex trafficking of Indigenous people; the demarcation of Amerindian lands and territories; a warning that Guyana Police and Defence Force members would be tried and punished by APLF "according to our laws and traditions" for incursions on tribal lands and for assaults, rapes, and murders; and a warning that the harming of the current chief, future chiefs, or any APLF members by the Guyana police for nonviolent actions in support of their internationally recognized human rights would be viewed as an act of war.

In the article that includes the summer solstice interview, Iron Eyes describes Cha-O-Ha as having a mother from an Amazonian tribe and a father from a Plains tribe.[39] Cha-O-Ha sees himself as someone who can unite the Land of the Eagle (North America) with the Land of the Condor (South America), as per prophecies. Iron Eyes asserts that Cha-O-Ha is also a prophet and a visionary in his own right. Though not an academic, Cha-O-Ha is educated regarding Indigenous rights within international human rights law, has memorized Sun Tzu's *The Art of War*, and has studied Che Guevara's book on the art of guerrilla warfare. Iron Eyes points out that Cha-O-Ha "has an ability to explain where Che was mistaken" and "has modified these teachings to be relevant and applicable to 21st century revolutionaries." When Iron Eyes met him for the interview, Cha-O-Ha and his field commanders had flown to Minneapolis to meet with a Mr. Gurung from Nepal to sign an agreement to train APLA warriors and to hire Gurkha warriors, "rated as the most feared fighting men on Earth by all the world's Armies," to fight as part of APLA units. The APLA purportedly has a concrete plan to fund, train, and supply their units and has issued a set of demands to the governments of Suriname, Belize, Dominica, and Guyana that build on their original demands to Guyana. Those governments were chosen partly because they have particularly small and ineffective armies. Cha-O-Ha says the APLF's goal is to create "autonomous Amerindian demilitarized states headed by Amerindian Governors—based on our perfected model of the Miskito Amerindian example in Eastern Nicaragua." The organization is planning for those states to work with current nation-states on a government-to-government basis and to achieve real sovereignty. Furthermore, APLF demands the full implementation of the UN Declaration on the Rights of Indigenous Peoples into the constitutions of the nation-states within whose borders Amerindian states lie. APLF has its eyes on the Navajo Nation to become the first such "demilitarized Indigenous state within the US itself." Iron Eyes says:

> This is what makes the APLA an unprecedented and in my opinion THE most exciting revolutionary phenomenon in the history of indigenous Guerrilla Armies of the world, not only because the existence of it was born on social media—but they are not restricted to one country or geographical area, and they are actively building forces to project enough power to protect Amerindian Tribes in various places in the Americas simultaneously; from Governments that have been treating them like second class citizens ever since these states gained their Independence from their Colonial masters—but then became Neo-Colonial masters in their treatment of the true indigenous landlords of their own countries . . . and we are seeing evidence that the emergence of the APLA is empowering and emboldening Indigenous peoples all over this Hemisphere and around the world to take increasingly stronger protest actions.[40]

On one hand, the APLA, an expanding force of alcohol- and drug-free, highly disciplined warriors, has promised to act only defensively. On the other hand, Indigenous activism evolved in an *exceedingly* rapid fashion from *ideas* expressed only half a year earlier when Sylvia McAdam started a conversation with her Facebook friends about Bill C-45 to the *action* of an intertribal army being organized. More and more, the world we Indigenous people inhabit looks like the world of Leslie Marmon Silko's *Almanac of the Dead,* a text that Subcomandante Marcos sees as coinciding with the Mayan prophecies that the mainstream made light of while our strength was growing (discussed in chapter 2 of this book). Environmental problems caused by global corporate capitalism and made possible by legislation that favors the rich forced issues of sovereignty and Indigenous rights to the forefront on social media, giving birth to activist movements that still utilize that medium for communications, fundraising, education and training, and increasing public awareness of their concerns.

However, grassroots Native activists must remember that like fire or water, social media can be at the same time our best friend and our worst enemy. In fact, because of the dangers social media creates in terms of security, APLF has deactivated its Facebook page, despite its birth and the birth of Idle No More on that social media site. There no longer is any presence of APLF online at all, just the original mentions in the work of Chase Iron Eyes and a few other articles leading up to 2014.[41] The reality is, however, that south of U.S. borders Indigenous leaders are being killed on a routine basis over conflicts regarding land and natural resources.

For those of us living within the borders of the United States, a murder related to extraction of Indian oil in North Dakota, as well as alleged threats against the life of Mandan, Hidatsa, and Arikara Nation tribal chairman Tex Hall, bring this kind of violence closer to home (Sontag and McDonald). More recently and also in North Dakota, peaceful water protectors standing up for concerns similar to those of Idle No More—an oil pipeline endangering tribal water supply as well as the water of those downstream in the watershed—have been repeatedly subjected to violent attacks by security forces in the ongoing occupation begun in 2016 at the Standing Rock Reservation, known best by its Internet hashtag #NoDAPL (meaning "No Dakota Access Pipeline"). The militarization of the law enforcement present and the security personnel hired by Energy Transfer Partners (the corporation behind the pipeline) included, but was not limited to, attack dogs, tear gas, helicopters, drones, water cannons, and snipers, reinforcing the reality that standing up for Indigenous people and the planet can be dangerous business. The water protectors make up several camps based on a number of divisions—Sacred Stone, Rosebud, Oceti Sakowin, and Red Warrior. The support base draws from the same demographic of Indigenous young people of Idle No More, substantially supplemented by non-Indigenous allies by the fervor of INM, the Tar Sands Brigade, and the Occupy Movement. Sylvia McAdam has spent quite a bit of time at Standing Rock and officially declared Idle No More's solidarity with the water protectors on November 6, 2016. With the help of social media, #NoDAPL became what is quite likely the largest intertribal and non-Native alliance in history, with more than two hundred tribes represented in camps that have held over ten thousand people at a time on more than one occasion during the duration of the occupation.[42] Sacred Stone, the original camp, was begun by Standing Rock tribal member and former historical preservation officer LaDonna Brave

Bull Allard and remains, along with Rosebud Camp, more moderate politically than Oceti Sakowin and Red Warrior Camp. A balance between the stability of the less radical camps on tribal land and the more direct-action-oriented camps on occupied Army Corps of Engineers land—frequently represented on social media by Chase Iron Eyes and comedian-activist Dallas Goldtooth—keeps the movement simultaneously productive and stable. Even if the Corps land is cleared of campers by force, the camp begun by Allard on tribal land will remain. Again, the wisdom of those who are more culturally authoritative—mothers and grandmothers in this case, as in Idle No More—seems to be the key to ongoing life for the movement, the people, and the planet.

Though Indigenous activism has moved beyond the bounds of this one movement, Idle No More—born on social media because McAdam, a First Nations woman trained in the word magic and rhetoric of the mainstream known as law, was angered at the verbiage she saw on a sign posted on treaty land—does give us a lot to think about in terms of rhetorical sovereignty and the power of words to change reality, because of how the movement manifested and the model it set for other Indigenous activist endeavors such as #NoDAPL. Idle No More was an idea, then words, then embodied protest and action *guided* by the words begun on social media that became mantra in signage; it is a battle against oppression created of words that become embodied as law and then govern our lives. That law, what we are told to accept as reality, conflicts with (1) the reality of nature (just because it is legal to destroy the environment doesn't mean there will be no consequences); (2) the reality of who we see ourselves to be as members of and descendants of sovereign nations that predate settler colonialism; and (3) the reality expressed by our ancestors in prophecy. As Métis Rebellion leader Louis Riel, a hero among First Nations people, said on July 4, 1885, "My people will sleep for one hundred years, but when they awake, it will be the artists who give them their spirit back." Not only has Idle No More spoken back to the empire, but it has also taken on the task of disseminating knowledge to the people in order to wake them up to action. What that action should be, and how radical that action should be, became a point of dissent very quickly, partly because of differing cosmologies and ontologies across Indian Country. Some simply radicalize the movement more than others, depending on personal grounding in tradition and prophecy, among other factors. Another element that added to radicalization of some who consider themselves part of the Idle No More movement was the almost immediate presence of individuals who have been at least perceived as agents provocateurs. Part of the ensuing politics in the official branch of the movement was an attempt to contain the grassroots movement by controlling what became considered the official discourse of Idle No More. This raises questions regarding the kind of rhetorical imperialism demonstrated in the analysis above of Cherokee rhetoric in the 1700s. How does the notion of who has the right and responsibility to speak on behalf of and/or to the people affect what discourse is perceived to be that of Idle No More? How have these divisions affected the rhetorical strategies being used in the movement now? How are the Indian activists from previous generations in the Red Power movement and AIM (American Indian Movement) contributing to the discourse, and do their contributions help shape the rhetoric? How are these rhetorical strategies related to those in traditional discourse and discourse like Occom's that is grounded in those traditions that we have carried with us across time, space, and language? And how are those strategies related to strategies in activist movements—like the Tar Sands Brigade and Occupy and the larger activist communities in Canada, in the United States, in the hemisphere, and in an international Transindigenous context—that have in some ways either supported or allied with Idle No More?

Conclusion

The late, respected CNO deputy chief Hastings Shade, a Cherokee philosopher and storyteller, plainly states in *Cherokee Stories of the Turtle Island Liars' Club* the appropriate ontological position for a Cherokee: "You're going to be right in the middle. . . . You're always in that middle. And they always say, 'Stand right in the middle.' *Ayetli hidogesdi.* 'Don't stand this side or stand on that side.' *Ayetli hidogesdi.* 'Stand right in the middle.' . . . That's our teaching. Whether it's something we like to do or don't like to do, we still take on that responsibility" (C. Teuton et al. 34). This ontology—based directly in the material rhetoric of the Belt That Would Not Burn, discussed in chapter 1—advocates for both balance and cultural groundedness. Of all people, those who lead and who are appointed to speak on behalf of others should be culturally grounded and centered. How else can they lead a people as a culturally distinct sovereign people? How else are they worthy of respect and authority in any traditional sense? If examining politics and traditional ceremonial cultures in

Indian Country over any length of time teaches us anything, surely it is that the traditional structures still have the respect of the people because the ceremonies *still work* in ways people can be proud of; people should be able to say the same of tribal politics.

Brotherlike relationships have developed between Indian leaders and non-Natives in many social contexts, most recently through investment in and the running of tribal nations as multi-enterprise businesses, with the bond of kinship being the almighty American dollar. Often the "brothers" of these Indian leaders have not acted in the best interests of American Indian people, and sometimes Indian leaders have followed along. Historically, brother relationships with settler colonials who stand to profit from Indian Country and/or Indian people have sometimes led a handful of Indian people in cahoots with their non-Indian brothers to make decisions that benefit themselves to the detriment of the tribe, rather than the people of the tribe making decisions on behalf of the people. It is the rare American Indian leader who has taken relationships with outside forces and yet has been able to balance those relationships in ways that allowed him or her to put the people's needs first. Rather, not only do leaders allied with outside forces occasionally mislead their people with their words, but they sometimes have not even bothered to try to persuade their people to support their decisions, seemingly indifferent to their people's opinions and concerns. The leasing of the central Blackfoot sacred site, Chief Mountain, by the Blackfeet Nation in Montana for oil fracking purposes against the wishes of the many of the Aamsskáápipikáni enrolled there, as well as many people in the confederated Blackfoot bands across the Medicine Line—Aapátohsipikáni, Káínaa, and Siksikáwa—is an apt example of how the values of leaders often differ from those of the people they are supposed to represent. But this is the way things work in the Western world, in mainstream culture, in the ways of settler colonialism. Today such conduct is replicated internally. Indian people in the communities should take into consideration whether their leaders merely "talk good" or whether they truly have the best interests of Indian people besides themselves in mind. Native leaders, like anyone else, are perfectly capable of "talking real good" in order to convince Indian people of things that aren't necessarily good for them or for future generations. Indigenous people need to be mindful of both the words and the values of those who attempt to persuade us to go along with their wishes. Our relations across the world, allied through the Idle No More grassroots collective and other activist organizations, Native and non-Native alike, offer a chance, yet again, for us to resist, survive, and thrive, whether our oppressors come from within or outside Indian Country. As Tsi'yugûnsi'ni said to the Shawnee delegation seeking alliance, "We are not yet conquered" (qtd. in Nash 440).

Conclusion

> In the autumn Chal set out for the University. . . . Running Elk and Sun-on-His-Wings had decided to go, despite the young man from the University who appeared in town that summer and talked of the many allurements, not the least of which was football. Most of the things which this young man said did not appeal to them, because the young representative had "talked from the teeth," they agreed. . . . Afraid-of-Bear, who played tackle at Carlisle, [had] come up to them one day at the village, very drunk. He had smiled vacuously, and after several attempts to get his arms around Running Elk's neck, kept repeating, "Yu ma frien,' yu ma frien,' ain't it?" Running Elk had looked over at Sun-on-His-Wings and said quietly, with amusement, "He talks from teeth—mus' be from the University." They laughed.
>
> —*John Joseph Mathews,* Sundown *(87)*

Ultimately, everything that I have written here I have written for the American Indian Studies students and American Indian and Indigenous college students in all disciplines of the future. While this volume posits a hermeneutic, examines traditional rhetorics, and posits a scholarly rhetoric, I have, for the most part, had to rely on the language of the academy to articulate this. The continued use of this sort of discourse is not what I envision for these students of the future. I don't want these students to have to justify their use of American Indian rhetorical structures in their work—in fact, I want to see them trained specifically in utilizing those structures so that when they leave the academy and go home, they can use language to effect change in the same ways great leaders among the tribal nations always have.

However, we are in a world where the idea of what and who a student is changes every day. The future generations of American Indians are likely to participate in postsecondary education through multiple venues that will reach ever-increasing numbers of people, some of whom will not have the goal of obtaining a college degree. There are many, many people in Indian Country who are interested in learning more in order to empower themselves and their people to improve the future. Some of these people will be traditional college students. Some will be tribal officials. Some will be grassroots activists. Some will be tribal employees. Some will work for corporate or governmental entities that want and need to do business in Indian Country for economic purposes. Some of these people will be Indian. Others will not. However, all of these people need education in order for us to work together.

We as American Indian studies scholars must strive to move our work from inside the classroom out into the communities through conduits that go above and beyond producing future teachers and passing around the few books that trickle back home to Indian Country from our classrooms; otherwise, the knowledge we produce in the academy cannot be used to facilitate change, whatever we envision that change to be. Social media has helped somewhat in this regard. For academics, gathering knowledge, writing, and disseminating information are second nature. Educated Indigenous people have, like Sylvia McAdam and Chase Iron Eyes, brought more knowledge home to Indian Country than ever before, through the use of Facebook, Twitter, blogging, and other digital venues. Still, the fruits of Native studies simply need to reach a wider audience of Indian people, and it is those people to whom we should be reporting as Native scholars and non-Native ally scholars as much as to our universities, regardless of our ancestry or citizenship. I believe that, ideally, we should work harder on promoting American Indian studies in Indian Country through a variety of initiatives, such as tribal libraries with bookmobiles and reading groups held through tribal colleges, libraries, community centers, Indian churches, and local universities. We need to establish summer and after-school youth literacy programs that include reading, storytelling, creative writing and performances, films, and multimedia presentations. We need to foster initiatives like the community-based theater work done by Blood Rez Playz on behalf of the Kainai and Piikani Bands in Alberta, which is written and performed to facilitate community healing. Sean Teuton's chapter in *Reasoning Together*, "The Callout: Writing American Indian Politics," focuses on his work with American Indian prisoners in the New York State Department of Corrections and is of particular note in regard to sending literature out from the academy in order to empower the people about and for whom it was written (Acoose et al. 105–25). I view this sort of community-based work as the future of organizations such as Wordcraft Circle of Native Writers and Storytellers and the Native Writers Circle of the Americas and would like to see similar initiatives created by tribes, tribal colleges, universities, the Native American and Indigenous Studies Association, and the Association for the Study of American Indian Literatures. The decision by the Vancouver Public Library to hire an Aboriginal storyteller in residence is a notable move in this regard by a non-Native entity. The Native Writers Circle of the Americas and Wordcraft partnered in 2016 with the Jacobson House Native Art Center in Norman, Oklahoma, to begin reviving the center's back-porch stage, which was originally utilized for American Indian theatrical performances, and to found an American Indian repertoire theater troupe for Oklahoma. As with Blood Rez Playz, the theater troupe housed at Jacobson will be community based, with a mission to promote paracolonial healing and cross-cultural understanding while celebrating all of the American Indian arts the Jacobson House has traditionally showcased and promoted. Additionally, the workshop approach to collective authorship promotes adult literacy and attentiveness, skills that are being lost as technological social interactions increase.

I see tribal nations, communities, colleges and universities, Native American/American Indian studies departments and programs, and teachers and professors all having a role in this sort of work. From those of us in the academy, more outreach is needed that does real work in Indian Country, not the kind of outreach that allows departments in tribal governments to check off boxes indicating employees received training when that training in reality does very little to improve anything for Indian people. Community-university research alliances like the one between the nations of the Blackfoot Confederacy and the University of Lethbridge offer models that other universities in the heart of Indian Country might follow. Partnerships like this will also improve the outcomes of grant writing and funded studies by both tribal nations and the academic institutions with which they ally. The institutes for tribal governance that I suggest be created in at least New Mexico, Washington, Oklahoma, California, and Alaska—states with significant Indian populations—offer other benefits. The kinds of partnerships and alliances that could be formed in order to more fully utilize our combined knowledge, skills, and abilities could strengthen our relationships and improve business, health, and general quality of life for all involved.

Likewise, relationships that already exist between the academy and Indian Country could be further strengthened by focusing the contributions Indian nations already often make to neighboring institutes of higher education where those nations have significant student populations. Tribal nations need to make significant investments in postsecondary education that are directly tied to Native American studies departments working in close partnership with those nations on (1) conducting research needed to inform decision making regarding policy and development and (2) educating a broader spectrum of tribal citizens in pragmatic programs under more networked Native American studies departments, in order to form further alliances and offer joint degrees in conjunction with education, health and medicine, social work, entrepreneurship, business, sustainability and natural resource management, tribal law, and governance. By doing this, we in the academy will produce students, Indian and non-Indian alike, who contribute to the betterment of the world around them, not just to tribal nations and the states within whose borders they lie. In short, the stakes are too high for us to be idle any longer. In the words of an often-quoted Cree prophecy: "Only after the last tree has been cut down. Only after the last river has been poisoned. Only after the last fish has been caught. Only then will you find that money cannot be eaten." Through tactical alliances that cross the lines between communities and the academy, we must work together to learn what we can from the rich oratorical and narrative heritage of Indian America. As the male voice says in Leslie Marmon Silko's *Ceremony* at the moment of the creation of our world, stories are more than mere entertainment. "They are all we have . . . to fight off illness and death," he says. "You don't have anything if you don't have the stories" (2).

Notes

Preface

1. "Paracolonial," here and throughout this book, refers to the condition of the culturally distinctive tribal nations and people who persist alongside mainstream culture despite ongoing colonialism. It also refers to the condition of unenrolled persons of American Indigenous descent who, despite their lack of legal status, are undeniably themselves the direct result of settler colonialism, and those who, because of "adopted" relationships, close friendships, or intermarriage, have become accepted as family, as members of tribal communities, and are thus socially and culturally tribal. I discuss this phenomenon more in the next note and discuss the term "paracolonial" at length in chapter 2.

   By privileging the term "paracolonial" over "postcolonial," I do not mean to dismiss postcolonial studies as a whole. Certainly, for the study of literature and other cultural production by peoples and nations no longer living under settler colonial or colonial governance, such as India and a number of African countries—whose circumstances gave rise to postcolonialism, the places where its founding scholars originated—postcolonial theory is an entirely appropriate approach. I do feel there are useful applications from postcolonial theory in Indigenous studies, while it has its limitations in regard to domestic dependent tribal nations under the governance of the United States and in regard to First Nations, Métis, and Inuit people whose bands are under the governance of Canada.
2. Throughout the Americas, the making of relatives took place in diplomacy, trade, and warfare traditionally, increasing both the extended kinship network and tribal nations themselves through a process that was the pre-Columbian version of naturalizing immigrants as citizens. Despite an entry into a culture though warfare and slavery, captives most often became kin and tribe. The culture of Comanches, for instance, was so integrally tied to this system during the height of their empire that as many new Comanches came from it at the time as did by birth. Today in Indian Country, those who are adopted or who marry in, either intertribally or as non-Natives, are made

kin through the same process, and colloquially these people are described only semi-jokingly as "captives." As Comanche Nation chairman Wallace Coffey says in Marthe Thorshaug's film *Comancheria*, "Today we have captives *everywhere*." Most of those captives are spouses, just as many Comanche wives were historically. However, some are non-Natives or members of other tribes who have become part of the "family" because of their fondness for Comanche culture, people, and spirituality. This notion is important to my arguments about relatedness, particularly in chapter 4.

3. This Blackfoot Beaver Bundle is one of a number of the sacred medicine bundles "held" by members of the Blackfoot Confederacy in Montana and Alberta. A bundle holder is not an owner per se but the person who keeps and maintains traditional responsibilities and rituals related to that sacred object. As the bundle holder, Grandma Elizabeth gave me specific permission to discuss the bundle. "There's nothing secret about this ceremony," she said. "Talk about it as much as you want. This ceremony is designed to make people *happy* and increase life." I hope that my discussion of this sacred object here is both respectful and in line with that objective.

   Only a handful of Beaver Bundles exist. They consist of a hide in which an array of ancient taxidermed animals and representations of animals made of their hide or other parts such as hooves are kept, brought out once a year in a ceremony after the first thunder of spring so that the animals that populate the Blackfoot ecosystem may return for the year. The ceremony lasts all day and contains many, many songs sung in Blackfoot and accompanied by Plains Sign Language. Blackfoot people say that at one time the bundles contained examples of every animal known to them, even tiny hummingbirds; however, some bundle contents have been lost while in private collections and museums. Traditionally, individuals who attended the annual ceremony for a bundle became "part of" that bundle and the people associated with it, through receiving one of the necklaces or bracelets belonging to the bundle. Because many of these items have also been lost over the years and because more people are involved today in this practice, Mrs. Crow Flag applied red paint (ocher) to supplicants in making them part of the ceremonial family.

4. I distinguish kinesthetic rhetorics, which are bodily enacted, from embodied rhetorics, which actually effect a change in or become part of the corpus; from material rhetorics, which are artifacts (that is, cultural production in the form of goods imbued with meaning such as baskets or moccasins); and from visual rhetorics, texts and carvings that utilize images rather than alphanumeric text.

5. At various points throughout this book, I make claims about some commonalities I have found in American Indian cultures on a widespread basis. I am aware of the charges I risk of "essentialism" here, particularly by those more familiar with academic discourse than with American Indian grassroots communities. In the academy, such claims have been common since the early years of American Indian literary studies, made popular by Arnold Krupat's "Scholarship and Native American Studies: A Response to Daniel Littlefield, Jr." However, both Dan Littlefield's "American Indians,

American Scholars and the American Literary Canon" (1992), which gave rise to Krupat's criticism at the time, and Craig Womack's comments in *Red on Red* on the subject subsequently argued that Indigenous people have the right to assert points of view grounded in their perspectives and experiences.

Others might claim that I am generalizing. Certainly, the possibility when dealing with many individual cultures as similar entities is that unnoticed exceptions will exist. Of course, not all American Indian cultures have identical ontologies and epistemologies. Each recognizes different spiritual entities and has unique rituals and other cultural expressions. However, I do in this book claim that traditional American Indian cultures share far greater similarities in the structures of their belief systems and ways of knowing than they do with Western culture. In this book, when such claims apply to specific tribal cultures, I always back them up with textual evidence of their existence in the discourse I analyze. I stand open to correction from culturally knowledgeable people from those nations, who have far more authority than I as an academic on such things, and I offer my apologies for any errors.

6. I teach "tradition" to my students as the "ever-shifting syncretic balance of continuity plus change accepted by a community in promoting its own survival as a culturally distinct Nation-People."
7. Previous to the publication of this book, I have used the terms "Indian," "American Indian," "Native American," "First Nations," and "Indigenous" interchangeably throughout my work, as none of these terms is more or less "correct" than the others. Indigenous people in the United States and Canada prefer to be referred to by their tribally specific names for their people, preferably in their own language, while some term must be used to address the ideas we as Indigenous peoples often share in common.

From my experiences living for four years in what is today Alberta, Canada, I find that most Indigenous people there prefer "First Nations" or "Indian" when needing a general term. The Canadian government uses the acronym "FNMI" for First Nations, Métis, and Inuit people. Also in my experience, most Indigenous people of what is today the United States prefer "American Indian" or "Indian" in such a situation, not only because "Indian" is the general term most people grew up with, but also because it is the word used in article 1, section 8, of the U.S. Constitution and is the word in which all legal rights are vested.

However, at the time of this writing, I can no longer use "American Indian" to refer to anyone who is not a member of a federally recognized tribe. Oklahoma House Bill 2261—sponsored by state senator John Sparks and state representative Chuck Hoskin, both Cherokee Nation members—was signed into law by Governor Mary Fallin on June 8, 2016, and promotes stricter measures for the state's Indian Arts and Crafts Act than does federal law. Specifically, HB 2261 restricts the use of the phrase "American Indian tribe" to references to federally recognized tribes and the term "American Indian" to refer to enrolled citizens of such nations, excluding unenrolled descendants, even those whose parents are citizens. Unlike federal law, HB 2261 also excludes members of state-recognized tribes or artists and craftspeople who are unenrolled but certified as Indian artisans by a federally or state-recognized tribe. The law also ands the products covered by the Indian Arts and Crafts Act to include "visual or performing arts or literature."

On the occasions in this book where I mean to be more broadly inclusive and refer to unenrolled and enrolled people as a group, I use the term "Native" or "Indigenous" (with or without the word "American"), "tribal," or "Amerindian," a term originating in the late nineteenth century and used mostly in anthropology and linguistics, most often to refer to Indigenous people of Mexico and Central and South America. The Oklahoma Indian Methodist Conference has spoken out against HB 2261, and the law has been controversial among writers of tribal descent, particularly first-generation descendants who are unable to enroll because of their blood quantum (an approximation, instituted by the U.S. government, of the percentage of an individual's Indian ancestry from a specific tribal nation) both in Oklahoma and in other states.

8. Big Eagle feels strongly enough about this to include it in "Notes for Teachers on Native American Cultures," written for publication in *Generations: Our People Say*, compiled for the California Department of Education.
9. Craig Womack also discusses this practice without using this terminology to describe it (*Red on Red* 78–79).
10. According to Dakota scholar Elizabeth Cook-Lynn, the First Convocation of American Indian Scholars, which was held in March 1970 at Princeton University, "called for the development by Indians of bodies of indigenous knowledge," and it referred to that development as "Native American Studies as an Academic Discipline" (9). Since that time, over one hundred programs and departments in the United States and at least twenty more in Canada have been founded with the philosophy that using Native perspectives to holistically approach knowledge that had originally been the province of disciplines such as English and anthropology in the academy would allow scholarship more aligned with the interests and rights of America's Indigenous people.
11. For instance, symbiotic relationships and the value of a low carbon footprint were part of traditional American Indian ways long before they were cornerstones of environmental and sustainability studies. Geographers took years to find out that Devil's Tower sprung up suddenly, as American Indian oral traditions claim, and did not erode from a mountain, as scientists had previously thought. American Indian holistic healing methods are recognized by many medical doctors as effective in treating diseases such as cancer. Quantum mechanics, the field that used to be quantum physics, acknowledges that molecules can appear or disappear from vacuums, depending on whether or not a scientific observer expects or wants them to. They call this discovery "observer-created reality." American Indians call this "medicine," acknowledging that human volition can affect the physical world for good or bad.
12. When the context is unclear, *Holisso Holitopa* is used.

Introduction

1. See Littlefield's *The Fus Fixico Letters: A Creek Humorist in Early Oklahoma*; Littlefield and Parins's *A Biobibliography of Native American Writers, 1772–1924*; and Peyer's *The Tutor'd Mind: Indian Missionary-Writers in Antebellum America*, *American Indian Nonfiction: An Anthology of Writings, 1760s–1930s*, and *"The Thinking Indian": Native American Writers, 1850s–1920s*. The Sequoyah National Research Center at the University of Arkansas at Little Rock, the lifework of Littlefield, Parins, and Robert Sanderson, offers rich resources for scholars interested in American Indian intellectual discourse in English, as do the Western History Collections at the University of Oklahoma.
2. This sort of thinking is indicative of Native logistical epistemologies as described in an ongoing conversation on logic, time, space, and memory in the works of LeAnne Howe, Donald Fixico, and Rain P. C. Goméz.
3. Donohue (Cherokee) uses information from an interview with the Reverend Mr. Randy Jacob, a Choctaw scholar from Broken Bow, Oklahoma, in explaining this aspect of Indigenous discourse.
4. Phillip Carrol Morgan, mentioned earlier, also relies on Howe's tribalography in constructing his work.
5. Self-deprecating remarks or declarations of humility are common in American Indian oratory. I talk more about this rhetorical device in chapter 3.
6. Alexander Longe was a white trader who lived among the Cherokee from sometime before 1710 until around 1724. His "A Small Postscript of the ways and maners of the Nashon of Indians called Charikees" provides the first description in English of Cherokee social practices, saying that traditionally "the women Rules the Rostt and weres the brichess and Some times will beate thire husbands within an Inch of thire life . . . the man will not Resesstt thire poure if the woman was to beate his breans out . . . for when shee has beate one sid like stalk fish . . . he will turne the other sid to her and beat till Shee is werrie sometimes they beat there husbands to that hight that they kill them out Right" (31–33).
7. This book builds on my earlier work on American Indian intertribal rhetorics. See Kimberly G. Roppolo, "An Incipient Study of the Indian Half of the Dialogic: Native Rhetoric and Occom's Use of Indirect Discourse," "Samson Occom as Writing Instructor: The Search for an Intertribal Rhetoric," "Towards a Tribal-Centered Reading of Native Literature: Using Indigenous Rhetoric(s) instead of Literary Analysis," and "Vision, Voice, and Intertribal Metanarrative: The Amerindian Visual-Rhetorical Tradition and Leslie Silko's *Almanac of the Dead*"; and Kimberly G. Wieser, "Who Is Cherokee? Federal Recognition, Culture, and Rhetorical Sovereignty."
8. I am also indebted to Cherokee scholar Daniel Justice for his extensive work on relatedness, much of which I draw on later in this book: "Currents of Trans/national Criticism in Indigenous Literary Studies"; "'Go Away, Water!' Kinship Criticism and the

Decolonization Imperative" (in Acoose et al.); "'To Look upon Thousands': Cherokee Transnationalism, at Home and Abroad"; and *Our Fire Survives the Storm: A Cherokee Literary History.*

9. The distinction between these two groups is that only enrolled tribal citizens are legally American Indian. "Resolution #08–08," issued by the Joint Council of the Cherokee Nation and the Eastern Band of Cherokee Indians, implies that making this distinction clear always is important.
10. The word "quipu" is both singular and plural in Quechua, the language that it comes from originally.

Chapter 1

1. In the NAISA Prize–winning and field-changing *Reasoning Together: The Native Critics Collective* (Acoose et al.), Oklahoma Creek/Cherokee scholar Craig S. Womack did as comprehensive of a job as anyone could have done in surveying book-length criticism authored by American Indian and American Indian–descended scholars from 1986 to 1997. (NAISA is the Native American and Indigenous Studies Association.)
2. Here, I use the term "Reading Red" as I did in the 2002 dissertation from which this book grew, not based on the work of any other scholar. My term references American Indian and Indigenous hermeneutical practices only and has no connotations of having violent or angry subtext or as being evidentiary of identity.
3. These are his words, not mine. Namšem viewed me through a lens of relatedness because of his traditional Tsis-tsis-tas ways.
4. For connections with mainstream rhetorical studies, see W. Benjamin Myers and Bryant Keith Alexander, "(Performance Is) Metaphors as Methodological Tools in Qualitative Inquiry."
5. NAGPRA is a federal law enacted on November 16, 1990, that requires federal agencies and entities that receive federal funding to return to the closest living descendants any American Indian or Native Hawaiian sacred objects, remains, or funerary items in their possession. The law also put forth protocols for dealing with such items when found on federal lands and made it illegal for individuals to market American Indian remains and cultural items without legal right to possession.
6. Here, as in my work elsewhere, I use the term "indirect discourse" to denote a common American Indian speech phenomenon in which the speaker avoids directly stating something to the listener or listeners, instead implying meaning and expecting those hearing to make meaning for themselves. Indian indirect discourse, rather than being merely subtext caused by polyphony as it is in Bakhtin, becomes polyvocal through intentionality because it is a socially learned behavior manifested in discourse. This practice was perhaps even directly taught in the days where speaking from the heart, speaking in a good way—that is, utilizing American Indian intertribal rhetorics—was taught to those whose roles included diplomacy, negotiation,

and leadership. For more on the practice of directly teaching intertribal rhetorics traditionally, see chapter 4.

7. Mary Brave Bird was rewarded for accomplishing a feat of courage in the face of the enemy, a practice traditionally engaged in by American Indians that brought empowerment and status. Both kills and coups earned war honors. "Counting coup" refers specifically to the practice of touching of an enemy on the field of battle and escaping unscathed, thereby symbolically and spiritually "unmanning" the opponent. Historically, this practice was considered even more honorable than a kill. After a kill, a number of warriors could even count coups on the remains of a fallen enemy as their comrades would be attempting to defend and recover the body.
8. This point is developed throughout *Reasoning Together* (Acoose et al.); see in particular the introduction and pp. 75, 150–51, and 205–6.
9. Elsewhere her tribal heritage is listed as Nez Perce (Bataille and Lisa 138).
10. I suggest that Occom's discourse—like all discourse—contains multiple voices. In *The Dialogic Imagination,* Bakhtin says that "fundamental heteroglossia" is "inherent in actual language" (327); he does not reserve this term for the polyphonic discourse of the novel.
11. I am not the first to work with the idea of the basket as a metaphor for explaining Native-perspective literary theories. Rain P. C. Goméz (Louisiana Choctaw/Creole/Muscogean/Métis descent) in "Brackish Bayou Blood: Weaving Mixed-Blood Creole-Indian Identity outside the Written Record," reads baskets as material culture. In two conference presentations, "Bayou Baskets: Weaving TriRacial Indian Narratives towards Cultural Sovereignty" and "Crawdad Baskets: Weaving Red Black Basketry Narratives in the Southeast," she uses baskets a metaphor for how cultures and stories are woven together and utilizes this concept in her hermeneutic to suggest that a dual discourse, with meaning on two levels and *between* those two levels, exists in discourse by "Red-Black," or Afro-Native, people. Qwo-Li Driskill (Cherokee descendant), in hir 2008 dissertation for Michigan State University, *Yelesalehe Hiwayona Dikanohogida Naiwodusv/God Taught Me This Song, It Is Beautiful: Cherokee Performance Rhetorics as Decolonization, Healing, and Continuance,* also employs baskets as metaphor, using Cherokee double weave to explain various strands and liminal zones through which Cherokees make meaning. The work of both scholars is discussed in *Back to the Blanket* as our work intersects at multiple points.

Chapter 2

1. For more on visual rhetorics, see the classic collection *Defining Visual Rhetorics,* edited by Charles A. Hill and Marguerite Helmers.
2. Children are considered by many tribes to be more in tune with spiritual knowledge. The Lakotas, for instance, call them Wakanheja, which loosely translates into "Sacred Ones." Close relatives may have special intuition regarding a person because of their blood relation.

3. Irwin ("Cherokee Healing") notes that knowledge can also be gained through fasting and the use of ceremonial space, particularly the *asi*, or Cherokee log hot house that some compare to a sweat lodge (250).
4. Some readers might note here that there is much overlap between Fixico's book and my work and wonder why I have not cited him more often. The early version of this book as my dissertation was completed in 2002, a year before Fixico's book came out. While I almost wholeheartedly agree with him, we arrived at our philosophical conclusions, our theorizing about American Indian thinking—and in my case, how this applies to hermeneutics, poetics, and rhetorics—independently of one another. I think this substantially supports the ideas that our conclusions are based on the Indian realities in which we are both immersed.
5. A relationship between this sign and the vulva-like shape of several sacred places is, in my opinion, no accident. My essay "Sacred Sexuality in Leslie Marmon Silko's *Ceremony*" explores this connection between the feminine and the holy further, as does my "'We've Got to Get Ourselves Back to the Garden': Indigenous Views of the Life-Death Cycle as Resistance in Silko's *Gardens in the Dunes*," in *Reading Leslie Marmon Silko: Critical Perspectives through* Gardens in the Dunes, ed. Laura Coltelli (75).
6. I have to say that based on my experiences with speech taboos still in effect among the Southern Cheyennes, I disagree with Kilroe's assertion that sign might have been used in regard to the in-law taboo. The in-law taboo is taken so seriously by those who still observe it today that even signing to one another would be deemed a violation of it. In fact, in light of the practice of attaching deer dewclaws and other noisemaking objects later to women's attire so that fathers-in-law could hear them coming and avoid them, it is highly unlikely that most daughters-in-law and their fathers-in-law would come into much contact to begin with. See Emil Her Many Horses, *Identity by Design: Tradition, Change, and Celebration in Native Women's Dresses* (24).
7. The Andean quipu, or *khipu*—the as yet incompletely deciphered system using a code similar to binary code to record information into knotted strings, which themselves were woven in patterns and with colors that held meaning—is yet another form of ancient American writing. Rasmussen says, "In the Andes, villages still use and maintain quipus, although their function has been dramatically altered since pre-colonial times" (13).
8. I would suggest that this crux in interpretation could be resolved if the CHS consulted even more Cheyenne sources, rather than asking a token few. I have witnessed a very strong oral tradition concerning Cheyenne warfare and have, in fact, even heard a detailed account of Custer's death. Seeking the proper approval for sharing these stories and consulting traditional oral historians, more of whom pass on each day, is paramount if scholars wish to have a more complete record.
9. At the 2006 Native American Literature Symposium in Michigan, Denise Low Weso presented an excellent study of images of women in Cheyenne ledger books that analyzed in depth how placement and direction affect meaning in this visual rhetoric, offering us a detailed hermeneutic for exploring this medium in further studies.

10. Luis Donaldo Colosio was the Institutional Revolutionary Party (PRI) candidate for president of Mexico when he was assassinated on March 23, 1994.
11. Jean-François Lyotard, who coined the term "metanarrative," uses it to describe totalizing narratives that reinforce hegemonic power structures. Here, I appropriate "metanarrative" to describe a unifying intertribal narrative that has evolved through urbanization and activism but is grounded in older intertribal movements such as Ghost Dance and specific tribal prophecies regarding liberation and renewal, such as the Anishinaabe Seven Fires prophecies, Hopi prophecies about the upcoming world, Cree prophecies about abuse of the earth, Sioux prophecies about the White Buffalo Calf, and Mayan prophecies about world cycles. It is within this intertribal metanarrative that the Amerindian Peoples Liberation Army of the Americas that I discuss in chapter 4 proposes to "unite the eagle and the condor." The power it legitimizes is not that of the state or of global corporate capitalism but that of Indigenous people to form alliances with others for the sake of life on Earth.
12. Robin Cohen has done a more in-depth study of Silko's tendency for the visual, from which she gave a brief presentation at the 1999 Southwest Symposium, "The Language, Literature, and Landscape of the Southwest," Albuquerque, N.Mex., April 16–17, 1999.
13. There are several films and screenplay drafts with the same story and alternate translations of the Laguna names for the title: "Estoyehmuut and the Kunideeyahs" (or "Estoyehmuut and the Ku ni deeyah"), "Arrowboy and the Witches," and "Stolen Rain" (Cummings 296n3).
14. For more on the Gorgon-Quetzal relationship, see Edith Hamilton, *Mythology* (43, 143).
15. Some of those relationships were of enemies, some were of allies, others were of confederacies of bands, and yet others were blood relations.
16. This quotation, from the transcript of the conversation between Boggs and Davis, has been edited to incorporate minor punctuation changes.
17. Rain P. C. Goméz suggests that this paracolonial woundedness today is sometimes marked with tattooing, piercing, or scarification, all of which are bodily or embodied rhetorics.
18. Roberto Cintli Rodríguez's *Our Sacred Maíz Is Our Mother: Indigeneity and Belonging in the Americas* is notable in this regard.
19. The ellipses and bracketed interpolation in the quotation are Stannard's.

Chapter 3

1. Kimberly Blaeser's article "Learning 'the Language the Presidents Speak': Images and Issues of Literacy in American Indian Literature" briefly discusses the othering created by colonial categories of "literacy" and "illiteracy" in regard to the privileging of English and some of the instances of the accompanying challenges and abuses of power faced by characters in works by Leslie Marmon Silko, Diane Glancy, N. Scott

Momaday, Linda Hogan, and Gerald Vizenor. Blaeser does not, however, directly examine the discourse of presidents or other colonial figures.

2. Smith's account is doubted by many scholars, partly because of his flattering depiction of himself and partly because in his writing he was saved no less than three times by exotic and beautiful young women. When quoting Powhatan, Smith's description of himself is less than flattering, however.
3. On May 28, 1830, during Andrew Jackson's presidency, the U.S. Congress passed this act, which called for the "Five Civilized Tribes"—Cherokees, Choctaws, Creeks, Chickasaws, and Seminoles—to be forced off of their already shrunken national land bases and removed to lands given in exchange that were west of the Mississippi, in the area designated as "Indian Territory," now known as Oklahoma. Those new tribal land bases would eventually also be largely lost through the practice known as "allotment," mandated by the Dawes Act (1887), and the later dissolution of Indian Territory with Oklahoma statehood (1907).
4. For more on this subject, consult Jason Black's *American Indians and the Rhetoric of Removal and Allotment.*
5. These cases are collectively known as the Marshall Trilogy, discussed in more detail later in the chapter.
6. While I greatly admire the work of Jason Black, I do want to note here that I find his assertion in "Authoritarian Fatherhood: Jackson's Early Lectures to America's Red Children"—that Jackson's use of the father/child dichotomy in addressing American Indians comes solely from a more general American paternalism—to be incomplete. Moreover, Black continues this frame of analysis in "Plenary Rhetoric in Indian Country: The *Lone Wolf v. Hitchcock* Case and the Codification of a Weakened Native Character," where he draws much the same conclusions. Black's other work shows he is aware of the history of American Indian use of relatedness terms in discourse with settler colonial officials. I do agree, however, with his assertions about the kind of "authoritarian fatherhood" predicated on a "hegemonic masculinity" embodied by Jackson and other presidents as representatives of Western culture. The differences between Western and American Indian fatherhood and in understandings of relatedness in general suggest that perhaps more studies examining American Indian/U.S. discourse from cross-cultural rhetorical perspectives would be useful.
7. The three Supreme Court cases of the Marshall Trilogy—*Johnson v. M'Intosh* (1823), *Cherokee Nation v. Georgia* (1831), and *Worcester v. Georgia* (1832)—serve as the basis for federal Indian law and define "domestic dependent nation" status along with the trust relationship that guides the federal government's obligations to the Indian nations.
8. According to Mark Trahant, Chester Arthur visited Wind River; Calvin Coolidge and Bill Clinton visited Pine Ridge, and Clinton also visited Shiprock; Harry Truman made a stop at Fort Peck and smoked a pipe with Assiniboine chiefs and headmen; Franklin Roosevelt visited the Quinault tribe in Washington State, the Blackfeet Nation in Montana, and the Eastern Band of Cherokee Indians in North Carolina. Trahant

argues that Warren Harding's trip to Alaska and Ronald Reagan's trip to Albuquerque count too. He also notes that Herbert Hoover lived in Pawhuska, Oklahoma, as a child and went to school with Osage children ("And Obama").

9. The Johnson-O'Malley Act, part of the "Indian New Deal," was passed in 1934 and provided subsidies to states for services such as medical care and education that the states administered to tribal citizens. Today this law primarily funds educational needs of American Indian students. Title VII refers to the section of the U.S. Department of Education code that addresses the federal obligation to "provide for not only the basic elementary and secondary educational needs, but also the unique educational and culturally related academic needs of these [American Indian, Native Hawaiian, and Native Alaskan] children." Tribal language programs in public schools, for instance, would be funded under Title VII.
10. Squanto was more properly known as Tisquantum, one of the last Patuxet Indians, who befriended the *Mayflower* pilgrims and lived with them for about a year.
11. Additionally, some of the non-Native notables Bush recognized and renewed relationships with have questionable histories as allies of Native people, in particular his Interior secretary, Gale Norton. A press release issued by the Blackfeet Reservation Development Fund on June 21, 2005, puts it well: "As anyone in Indian Country will tell you, when Interior Secretary Gale Norton and her appointees speak, it pays to check their facts." Norton and her cronies paid themselves a hefty sum in legal fees, defending themselves for not making good on their government's legal and financial obligations to American Indians instead of choosing to pay even this portion of America's debt to its First Nations. In truth, America owes Indians far more for all of the broken treaties and agreements that led to transfers of land and natural resources.
12. Known by Blackfoot/Blackfeet peoples as the Sweet Pine Hills, this area is a site sometimes used for fasting and thus, though not on tribal land, a sacred site.
13. See note 7 for chapter 1 for more information on the concept of "coup" in American Indian cultures.
14. A 2016 University of Arizona study debunks all of the myths and stereotypes regarding American Indians and alcohol, proving with a quantitative study that the majority of American Indians, 59.9%, abstain from drinking alcohol entirely, whereas only 43.1% of whites abstain. American Indians who drink lightly or moderately make up 4.5% of the population, while 32.7% of whites are light or moderate drinkers. The percentages of binge drinking were similar in both populations at 17.3% and 16.7%, respectively, as were the percentages of heavy drinking, 8.3% and 7.5% (Cunningham et al. 65).
15. Neither is its Canadian counterpart, the Assembly of First Nations.
16. The State of Sequoyah was a proposed union in 1905 between the Five Civilized Tribes—Cherokees, Choctaws, Creeks, Chickasaws, and Seminoles—in the old Indian Territory prior to Oklahoma statehood that would have allowed them to keep their land and live in a Native-controlled state guided by its own constitution.
17. Russell says he means postcolonial "in the worldwide sense": "We know the colonists could not now go home if they were so disposed. Our lot is intertwined with

the colonists as black South Africans are with the British and the Dutch. They have nowhere to go. While they have not historically been the best of neighbors, they are still our neighbors, and we must do our best to civilize them" (*Sequoyah* 148).

18. The Interior Alaska Campus of the University of Alaska Fairbanks does have a Tribal Management Program with some courses, such as "Federal Indian Law for Alaska Tribes," offered online with the content at least free.

Chapter 4

1. Ada-gal'kala is the name he was known by as an adult. In regard to spelling, I follow Cherokee theorist and novelist Daniel Justice in using Ada-gal'kala, first utilized by the late Cherokee novelist Robert J. Conley, whom I proudly called Uncle Bob for nearly twenty years. Sequoyah Guess, noted Cherokee storyteller, says that the appropriate pronunciation of the name is "Ada-galth-ga-la," while Geary Hobson said in an interview with me that pronunciation differs among the wide-ranging and highly localized Cherokee dialects. Hobson says the name means "to stack the wood with the tops leaning together in order to make our Sacred Fire."
2. While this was not traditional Cherokee practice, the people chose Moytoy as their "emperor" under pressure from Cumming, so that the Cherokees might have a representative with "power" to speak for them on a national basis in relation to the British crown. Prior to this, locally based leadership in a bifurcated system had addressed "White" issues (as Cherokee people designated issues within the community, "white" being symbolic in this case of the concept of "peace") and "Red" issues (as Cherokee people designated issues dealing with war, trade, and policy with groups outside the community). In other words, as culturally inappropriate as this was, recognizing Moytoy as emperor was a recognition of the sovereignty of the Cherokee Nation within the Westphalian nation-state system.
3. This is similar to but different from the "Transatlantic Moment" in African American studies, which is specifically used in reference to the transformative moment that occurred for African Americans during their transport from east to west as slaves, as described by scholar Michael A. Gomez in *Reversing Sail: A History of the African Diaspora* (71–72). Conversely, the crossing of the Atlantic as slaves from west to east happened for Indigenous American people in 1492 with Columbus's first return voyage. Diaspora through slavery continued throughout the Americas as different groups made contact with Europeans. For instance, Native American historian Dina Gilio-Whitaker says that the British colony of Carolina alone lost a minimum of fifty thousand Indians to Caribbean slavery from 1650 to 1730, according to colonial records ("Untold History"). While the Cherokee emissaries to the crown in 1730 were not enslaved, they were in effect giving up, without their *informed* consent, both their own personal freedom and the freedom of their nation, as they were asked to cross the Atlantic in order to represent Moytoy in submitting to the authority of King George.

From the perspective of the British, this literal "subjection" imposed upon the Cherokee people the European concepts of nationhood, sovereignty, and law. This imposition continues to this day for the Cherokee Nation, as well as the other federally recognized tribes in the United States and their First Nations counterparts in Canada.

4. This event may the source of Wiggan's Cherokee name, Tsi-s-du A-ga-yv-li, or Old Rabbit. Rabbit is the trickster figure in Cherokee oral tradition.
5. American naturalist and author William Bartram depicted Ada-gal'kala as speaking and understanding English quite well forty years or so later when Bartram met him on his travels shortly before the American Revolution (Rozema 607–709).
6. The Unanti, sometimes later called Kutani or Ani-Kutani, were the Cherokee priestly clan, those educated in specialized ceremonial knowledge and the ancient writing system used to record such things. Long ago, a member of this group is said to have to stolen the wife of the War Chief's son, some say to take her for his own woman; others say that he intended to use her as a human sacrifice. However, the other clans of Cherokee people rose up against the priestly clan, killing all of them. Since then, no one clan has been allowed to hold so much power over the rest.
7. "Inoli" (also spelled as Enoli or Inali) means "Badger" but was mistranslated as "Black Fox" by the English. Black Fox is used as a last name, however, by patrilineal descendants.
8. Food sovereignty is a concept expressed by an international movement that seeks to ensure that people have control over their own food and have culturally and nutritionally appropriate food. The movement encourages communities and individuals to reclaim production of their own food by healing their relationships with the land and nature through doing so. For Indigenous nations, food sovereignty has the potential for decolonial empowerment—that is, empowerment through reversing, whenever possible and to whatever extent possible, the effects of colonization—of both the literal body politic through improved health and of the tribal nations themselves through decreased dependence on the trust relationship with the federal government. Coupled with educational sovereignty and with energy sovereignty (possible today through alternative fuel sources and better utilization of natural resources in agreements with extratribal entities), food sovereignty could change international relations.
9. In building on my ideas about Intertribalism here from *Reasoning Together* (Roppolo, "Samson Occom"), I mean to be inclusive of coauthor Lisa Brooks's notions from that volume about "a historically and spatially specific Intertribalism—which is based on the actual relationships between individuals, families, nations, and places, as well as a continuous attempt to build and maintain communication and relations" (253).
10. In "'Go Away, Water!': Kinship Criticism and the Decolonization Imperative," Daniel Justice calls this concept "Cherokeeness." Despite our differences in terminology, I hope here to encompass the same diversity as Justice does in his "Rhetorics of Recognition," mentioned in the introduction.

11. One cannot "be" without "being" in relation to other entities—spirit, plant, animal, mineral, human, celestial, and so on. All are in constant flux. Actions are always interactions.
12. In his classes at the University of Oklahoma (all taught before the passage of HB 2261), Hobson further outlined his paradigm of what constitutes an "Indian," which he lays out in the introduction to *The People Who Stayed: Southeastern Indian Writing after Removal.* He suggests that there are four categories of characteristics that make up Indian identity—legal, social, cultural, and genetic.
13. The first version I saw of this document was listed as "Resolution #14–08."
14. I have never met David Cornsilk in person, and I have neither hired nor asked him, anyone else working for CNO, or anyone at all to do genealogical work for me. David Cornsilk has only corresponded with me informally in Facebook messages.
15. For traditional Indigenous thinkers, "time" is really just the movement of place in space, places holding meaning in the form of multiple narratives connected to those locations. Those layered narratives inform Indigenous perspectives on and understandings of place. This notion is key to Howe's tribalography. I have attempted to utilize some of Howe's praxis as well as her paradigmic understandings. This was my inspiration for beginning this chapter with historical fiction, including facsimiles of historical documents, and for including all of the disparate elements herein, from family history to a reading that takes what I can learn and share from my alleged relatives' experiences and applies it to the world's current political situation and environmental crisis.
16. I find that American Indian poetry and drama are grayer areas. Much American Indian poetry is self-expression, often performed by the poet. Especially in performance, I find this poetry to be less mediated than fiction, certainly, and much of it draws on poetics and structures grounded in American Indian cultural expression and material production. A good amount of American Indian drama was built with the technique of "storyweaving." Most frequently, this composition process is utilized by a group of people who begin with self-expression, by nature grounded in their own identities and cultures, rather than with mediated simulations of culture. This material is then "woven" together and *performed* in a mediated simulation that sometimes uses poetic elements of ritual expressions. Drama of this nature certainly draws heavily on cultural poetics, which shares much overlap with cultural rhetorics, making it have some commonality with both oratory and the oral tradition. Other poetry and dramatic production follow more mainstream conventions.
17. Out of respect, I am purposefully omitting the name of the society here, as many Blackfoot people feel is proper.
18. Byrd would go on to sire a son, Michael Byrd, whose son John Byrd would marry a Chickasaw woman, Mary Moore. Their son, William Leander Byrd, would eventually become governor of the Chickasaw Nation. For more information on this, see Phillip Carroll Morgan's *Riding Out the Storm: 19th Century Chickasaw Governors; Their Lives and Intellectual Legacy.* Stuart, who had a wife back home in the Highlands of

Scotland, took a Cherokee wife as well. The last name "Bushyhead" in the Cherokee Nation today is a result of that alliance.

19. This is Rozema's interpolation. In this context, Ada-gal'kala was referring to a yardstick.
20. For more information on this event that took place after the Anglo-Cherokee War (1758–61)—called by Cherokee people "the war with those in the red coats"—see Timberlake's *Memoirs* (D. King 18–20) and Barbara Duncan's chapter on the War Dance in *Culture, Crisis and Conflict: Cherokee British Relations, 1756–1765*, edited by Anne Rogers and Barbara Duncan.
21. Demere was later killed when Fort Loudon, which he was commanding, fell in the Cherokee War. By some reports, he was forced to dance until he died. Inarguably, his men were forced to watch while he was scalped and burned. Apparently, Cherokee people did not regard Demere very highly either.
22. Perhaps they actually said, "Howa," a word meaning "okay" or "it's all right" that can be used to indicate agreement or to substitute for "you're welcome" as a response to "wado" or "sgi" for "thank you."
23. Smoking a pipe, therefore, adds to one's ethos. From Native perspectives, no one but a fool would be untruthful, as lying would incur negative consequences to the speaker. For instance, according to Cheyenne oral tradition shared with me by Eugene Blackbear Sr., Custer smoked a pipe with Cheyenne leaders after the massacre he led against them at Washita, promising never to attack Cheyenne women and children again. Blackbear saw Custer's defeat at Little Big Horn as a direct result of his violating this promise.
24. The original of this letter, dictated to John Watts (Young Tassel) and marked with Ada-gal'kala's "X," has been lost. A note introducing a transcription of the letter in the January 1840 issue of the *Southern Literary Messenger* (vol. 40) reads: "'From the original, preserved at Berkley, James River. The original manuscript of the following letter, has been worn by time into a number of fragments—which to be made intelligible must be put together like the pieces of a Chinese puzzle'" (qtd. in Tinling 657). Interestingly, John Watts was Old Tassel's son and a Chickamauga who continued with his uncle Doublehead to attack settler colonial townships after Dragging Canoe's death in 1792.
25. Barbara Duncan notes, "This is clearly a reference to Oconostota, with garbled English spelling. Otoseita looks like one of the names for Ostenaco in London 1762, spelled there Outacite. I think they are both garbled, English versions of the war rank Asgayadihi, Man Killer. This was the next-to-highest war rank. The highest was Sgiagvsta" (Duncan e-mail).
26. The Cherokee Nation was divided into Upper, Lower, and Overhill towns. Ada-gal'kala was from the Overhill towns region.
27. Though many scholars have written on this complex series of historical events, I recommend John Oliphant's fine volume *Peace and War on the Anglo-Cherokee Frontier, 1756–63*.

28. Of the Six Nations of the Haudenosaunee Confederacy, the Senecas, Cayugas, Onondagas, and Mohawks sided with the British. The Oneidas, who at first tried to remain neutral, finally joined with the Tuscaroras in supporting the Americans.
29. According to Barbara Duncan, this is the eighteenth-century spelling in English phonetics for the Cherokee title of Beloved Woman, and the rendering of these English phonetics into the syllabary. She says that the more "correct phonetic Cherokee spelling is Tsi ge yu ha," or "I love her"—in other words, "beloved." Duncan asserts, "These are the syllables that should be rendered into the syllabary. . . . This is the word people in the Eastern Band use to speak of the Beloved Man or Woman today. I believe in the 18th century, the English speakers were pronouncing the G as a soft G or ji" (Duncan e-mail).
30. The relationships between FNMI people and the government of Canada are still guided by a series of eleven numbered treaties and their corresponding treaty areas, which commonly cover multiple "band" governments, the rough equivalent of tribal governments for American Indian people living in the United States.
31. For an examination of similar topics related to the 2011 protests in Egypt, see Laila Shereen Sakr's "A Digital Humanities Approach: Text, the Internet, and the Egyptian Uprising."
32. "Medicine Line" is a term American Indians have commonly used in English to refer the forty-ninth parallel, an informal name for the U.S.-Canadian border, since the drawing of this border after the War of 1812.
33. Cushing was established after the 1891 land run, one of a series of races from 1889 to 1907 to claim homesteads opened up by the federal government on Indian lands in Oklahoma. Cushing's founder was Billy Rae Little, who had been a government trader to the Sac and Fox and staked his claim immediately when their reservation was being broken up. During the 1912 oil boom, Cushing became a refining center. By 1915 the town, which was rich in oil itself, was nationally known and produced 17 percent of the nation's oil.
34. The Tar Sands Blockade began in the summer of 2012, unifying activists from all over North America in opposition to the TransCanada Keystone XL south tar sands pipeline and to the expensive, environmentally destructive, and unsustainable practice of extracting petroleum products from the tar sands in Northern Alberta. Tar Sands Blockade members work with members of frontline communities negatively affected by the extraction, transport, or refining of tar sand. Because all stages of the process have an impact on Indian communities and Indian people—whose lands are destroyed and whose health is jeopardized by extraction, and whose lands, waterways, and health are harmed by transport and refinement—Idle No More has been a natural ally. Activists have staged various forms of protest, including chaining themselves to sections of pipeline. Protests have ranged from Canada to Houston, Texas, where the toxic tar sand is refined to extract bitumen, a heavy, thick crude oil that must be mixed with other fossil fuels to be transported by pipeline. The refined oil yields 12 percent

more polluting emissions when burned than oil refined from traditionally extracted petroleum.

35. The Occupy movement was founded on September 17, 2011, by Micah White and is the international component that grew out of the Occupy Wall Street movement. It protests economic and political inequity and works to end the control exerted by the few over the many through global corporate capitalism. Protesters occupied sites around the world by setting up large camps. They were inspired by University of California student protests in 2009 and 2010 that proclaimed, "Occupy Everything, Demand Nothing." Though this global justice movement staged peaceful protests, on many occasions protesters were met with aggressive police actions. The most popular slogan of the movement was "We are the 99%," referring to the fact that the wealthiest 1 percent of Americans have an inequitable share of political power, money, and ownership in the means of production.
36. Fracking has become an increasing concern for Idle No More groups elsewhere as well. The Mi'kmaq people of the Elsipogtog First Nation in New Brunswick are just one example of tribal people being arrested for protesting exploration for fracking on their lands (Ball). After several months of ongoing protests over increasing encroachment by SWN Resources Canada, a company based in Houston, for the purposes of shale gas exploration, violence erupted between the Royal Canadian Mounted Police—accompanied by snipers in camouflage—and Indigenous people in the anti-fracking camp.
37. Celebrations of this loss of Indian land, prophesized by Dragging Canoe, began the very next year after the 1889 land run in Guthrie, Oklahoma, the original capital of Oklahoma Territory. Land run reenactments, a kinesthetic rhetorical tool, have been long held in Oklahoma public schools as a way of teaching this part of history through having children race to stake poles to mark their "claims" as "Sooners." In 2014, Oklahoma City Public Schools, one of the state's largest school districts, banned this practice. The same district banned the use of an Indian mascot at its Capitol Hill High School in 2015. Both of these initiatives were started by American Indian parents in the district, led by Choctaw activist Sarah Adams-Cornell, and facilitated by the Office of Indian Education and by visits with President Obama's White House Initiative on American Indian and Alaska Native Education Listening Tour of 2014.
38. The website continues to provide history, listings of events, and a variety of resources from articles to graphics to livestreams and webinars as the movement grows.
39. Cha-O-Ha (In the Wilderness) was also the birth name of Oglala Sioux warrior Crazy Horse, so I am supposing that the general is Lakota.
40. The ellipsis points are in the original.
41. Another movement, the Indigenous People's Liberation Front, sprung up around that time, creating a Facebook page and issuing a "12 Point Program" on September 15, 2014—the day before Mexican Independence Day, which marks the Grito de Dolores

(Cry of Dolores) that led to Mexico's successful revolt against Spain. This particular movement is even more intertribally inclusive in nature, being led by Indigenous people who proclaim, "We reject the terms 'hispanic' and 'latino' because these are terms created by colonial invaders! We are Indigenous People, from Alaska to Argentina and we are the only ones with the authority to identify ourselves!"

42. Though I myself spent only a few days at Oceti Sakowin with my family during the 2016 Thanksgiving holiday (when we brought supplies donated by our community), numerous people have been at the camp for varying degrees of time at one point or another. Some non-Native allies who have been to Oceti are quite famous, such as actor-activists Jane Fonda and Shailene Woodley, Green Party presidential candidate Jill Stein, journalist Amy Goodman, and former First Daughter Malia Obama, among others.

Works Cited

Ablavsky, Gregory. "Beyond the Indian Commerce Clause." *The Yale Law Journal* 124.4 (2015). www.yalelawjournal.org/article/beyond-the-indian-commerce-clause. Accessed 27 Dec. 2015.

Acoose, Janice, et al. *Reasoning Together: The Native Critics Collective.* Norman: U of Oklahoma P, 2008.

Alfred, Taiaiake. *Peace, Power, and Righteousness: An Indigenous Manifesto.* New York: Oxford UP, 1999.

———. "Sovereignty." *A Companion to American Indian History.* Ed. Philip Deloria and Neal Salisbury. New York: Blackwell, 2004, p. 466.

———. "Sovereignty." *Sovereignty Matters.* Ed. Joanne Barker. Lincoln: U of Nebraska P, 2005, pp. 33–50.

Allen, Chadwick. *Blood Narrative: Indigenous Identity in American Indian and Maori Literary and Activist Texts.* Durham, N.C.: Duke UP, 2002.

———. "A Trans*national* Native American Studies? Why Not Studies That Are Trans-*Indigenous?*" *Journal of Transnational Studies* 4.1 (2012): 1–22. escholarship.org/uc/item/82m5j3f5. Accessed 9 Aug. 2015.

Allen, Paula Gunn. *Spider Woman's Granddaughters: Traditional Tales and Contemporary Writings by Native American Women.* New York: Ballantine Books, 1990.

American Federation of Teachers. "Privatization Plan of Indian Schools Tabled: Rebuff of Ill-Advised Plan Makes Room for Real Reform." 23 May 2002. www.aft.org. Accessed 6 May 2006.

The American Indian's Sacred Ground. Videotape. Narrated by Cliff Robertson. 1977; Los Angeles: Freewheelin' Films and Wood Knapp Video, 1991.

Amerindian Peoples Liberation Front. "Breaking News: 9 Declarations to Those Who Will Not Listen—Amerindian Peoples Liberation Front (APLF) Communique." *Last Real Indians.* 16 Jan. 2013. lastrealindians.com/breaking-news-9-declarations-to-those-who-will-not-listen-amerindian-peoples-liberation-front-aplf-communique/. Accessed 11 July 2013.

Anaya, Rudolfo A. "The Myth of Quetzalcoatl in a Contemporary Setting: Mythical Dimensions/Political Reality." *Western American Literature* 23.3 (1988): 195–200.

Anzaldúa, Gloria. *Borderlands/La Frontera: The New Mestiza.* 2nd ed. San Francisco: Aunt Lute, 1999.

Argyle, Ashley. "The Secret to Survival? Code Narrative in Silko's *Almanac of the Dead.*" *American@* 3.2 (2005): 21–38. www.uhu.es/hum676/revista/argyle.pdf. Accessed 13 Feb. 2015.

Armstrong, Jeannette, ed. *Looking at the Words of Our People: First Nations Analysis of Literature.* Penticton, B.C.: Theytus Books, 1993.

Arnold, Ellen L., ed. *Conversations with Leslie Marmon Silko.* Jackson: UP of Mississippi, 2000.

———. "Listening to the Spirits: An Interview with Leslie Marmon Silko." *Studies in American Indian Literatures* 10.3 (1998): 1–34. *JSTOR*, www.jstor.org/stable/20739460. Accessed 13 Aug. 2005.

Bakhtin, M. M. *The Dialogic Imagination: Four Essays.* Austin: U of Texas P, 1982.

Ball, David P. "Fracking Troubles Atlantic First Nations after Two Dozen Protesters Arrested." *Indian Country Today Media Network.* 28 June 2013. indiancountrymedianetwork.com/news/first-nations/fracking-troubles-atlantic-first-nations-after-two-dozen-protesters-arrested/. Accessed 28 June 2013.

Barker, Joanne. "Recognition." *American Studies* 46.3–4 (2005): 133–61.

———. *Sovereignty Matters.* Lincoln: U of Nebraska P, 2005.

Barnes, Kim. "A Leslie Marmon Silko Interview." *"Yellow Woman": Leslie Marmon Silko.* Ed. Melody Graulich. New Brunswick, N.J.: Rutgers UP, 1993, pp. 47–65.

Bataille, Gretchen M., and Laurie Lisa, eds. *Native American Women: A Biographical Dictionary.* New York: Routledge, 2001.

Belleau, Lesley. "Nibi." *Kimiwan* 2 (2013): 17.

Belt, Tom. Interview by author. 13 Sept. 2012.

Berglund, Jeffrey. "Facing the Fire: American Indian Literature and the Pedagogy of Anger." *American Indian Quarterly* 27.1–2 (2003): 80–90.

Bevis, William. "Native American Novels: Homing In." *Critical Perspectives on Native American Fiction.* Ed. Richard F. Fleck. Washington, D.C.: Three Continents P, 1993, pp. 15–45.

Big Eagle, Duane. "Notes for Teachers on Native American Cultures." E-mail to the author. 26 Aug. 1999.

Billy, Rick. Interview by author. 19 July 2015.

Bird, Gloria, and Joy Harjo. *Reinventing the Enemy's Language: Contemporary Native Women's Writings of North America.* New York: Norton, 1988.

Birkerts, Sven. "Apocalypse Now." Review of *Almanac of the Dead,* by Leslie Marmon Silko. *The New Republic,* 4 Nov. 1991, pp. 39–41.

Bizzell, Patricia. "The 4th of July and the 22nd of December: The Function of Cultural Archives in Persuasion, as Shown by Frederick Douglass and William Apess." *College Composition and Communication* 48.1 (1997): 44–60.

Black, Jason Edward. *American Indians and the Rhetoric of Removal and Allotment.* Jackson: UP of Mississippi, 2015.

———. "Authoritarian Fatherhood: Jackson's Early Lectures to America's Red Children." *Journal of Family History* 30:3 (2005): 247–64. doi:10.1177/0363199005276946. Accessed 11 Nov. 2013.

———. "A Clash of Native Space and Institutional Place in a Local Choctaw–Upper Creek Memory Site: Decolonizing Critiques and Scholar-Activist Interventions." *American Indian Culture and Research Journal* 36:3 (2012): 1–22. doi:10.17953/aicr.36.3.c875884204q12h21. Accessed 11 Nov. 2013.

———. "Memories of the Alabama Creek War, 1813–1814: U.S. Governmental and Native Rhetorical Identities at the Horseshoe Bend National Military Park." *American Indian Quarterly* 33:2 (2009): 199–229. *JSTOR*, www.jstor.org/stable/25487928. Accessed 11 Nov. 2013.

———. "Native Resistive Rhetoric and the Decolonization of American Indian Removal Discourse." *Quarterly Journal of Speech* 95:1 (2009): 66–88. doi:10.1080/00335630802621052. Accessed 11 Nov. 2013.

———. "Plenary Rhetoric in Indian Country: The *Lone Wolf v. Hitchcock* Case and the Codification of a Weakened Native Character." *Advances in the History of Rhetoric* 11 (2011): 59–80. doi:10.1080/15362426.2009.10597380. Accessed 11 Nov. 2013.

———. "Symbolic Suicide as Mortification and Transformation: The Conciliatory (Yet) Resistant Surrender of Maka-tai-mesh-ekia-kiak." *Kenneth Burke Journal* 2.1 (2005). kbjournal.org/black. Accessed 11 Nov. 2013.

Blackbear, Eugene, Jr. Interview by author. 7 Sept. 2001.

Blackfeet Reservation Development Fund. "Indian Trust: Cobell v. Kempthorne." 21 June 2005. www.indiantrust.com. Accessed 19 May 2006.

Blaeser, Kimberly. "Learning 'the Language the Presidents Speak': Images and Issues of Literacy in American Indian Literature." *World Literature Today* 66.2 (1992): 230–36.

———. "Native Literature: Seeking a Critical Center." *Looking at the Words of Our People: First Nations Analysis of Literature.* Ed. Jeannette Armstrong. Penticton, B.C.: Theytus, 1993, pp. 51–62.

Blanchard, Paulette. Interview by author. 20 Feb. 2016.

Blanche, Jerry D. "Ignoring It Won't Make It Go Away." *Journal of American Indian Education* 12.1 (1972). *JSTOR*, www.jstor.org/stable/24397097. Accessed 31 July 2001.

Blodgett, Harold. *Samson Occom.* Dartmouth College Manuscript Series, no. 3. Hanover, N.H.: Dartmouth College P, 1935.

Boggs, Grace Lee. "Detroit Activist, Philosopher Grace Lee Boggs: 'The Only Way to Survive Is by Taking Care of One Another.'" *Democracy Now!* 2 Apr. 2010. www.democracynow.org/2010/4/2/grace_lee_boggs. Accessed 26 July 2013.

Boggs, Grace Lee, and Angela Davis. "On Revolution: A Conversation between Grace Lee Boggs and Angela Davis." *27th Empowering Women of Color Conference, 'A Holistic Approach: Justice, Access and Healing.'* Pauley Ballroom, University of California,

Berkeley, 2 Mar. 2012. www.radioproject.org/2012/02/grace-lee-boggs-berkeley/. Accessed 26 July 2013.

Boulware, Tyler. "'Our Mad Young Men': Authority and Violence in Cherokee Country." *Blood in the Hills: A History of Violence in Appalachia.* Ed. Bruce Stewart. Lexington: U of Kentucky P, 2011.

Bower, Bruce. "When Stones Come to Life: Researchers Ponder the Curious Human Tendency to View All Sorts of Things as Alive." *Science News*, 5 June 1999, pp. 360–63. doi:10.2307/4011344. Accessed 25 Jan. 2000.

Bradford, William. *Of Plymouth Plantation.* New York: Random House, 1981.

Brayboy, Bryan McKinley Jones. "Toward a Tribal Critical Race Theory in Education." *Urban Review* 37.5 (2005): 425–46. doi:10.1007/s11256-005-0018-y. Accessed 4 June 2013.

Brooks, Lisa. *The Common Pot: The Recovery of Native Space in the Northeast (Indigenous Americas).* Minneapolis: U of Minnesota P, 2008.

Brown, Carrie Budoff. "Dems Woo Native American Vote." *Politico*, 28 May 2008. www.politico.com/story/2008/05/dems-woo-native-american-vote-010676. Accessed 29 May 2008.

Brown, John P. "Eastern Cherokee Chiefs." *Chronicles of Oklahoma* 16.1 (1938): 3–35. digital.library.okstate.edu/Chronicles/v016/v016p003.html. Accessed 4 June 2013.

———. *Old Frontiers: The Story of the Cherokee Indians from Earliest Times to the Date of Their Removal to the West, 1838.* Kingsport, Tenn.: Southern Publishers, 1938.

Burke, Colleen. *Teaching American Indian Literature with* Black Elk Speaks. MA thesis, St. Cloud State University, 2001.

Burke, Kenneth. *A Rhetoric of Motives.* Berkeley: U of California P, 1950.

Burnett, Peter. "State of the State Address." *The Governor's Gallery: California State Library.* 6 January 1851. governors.library.ca.gov/addresses/s_01-Burnett2.html. Accessed 30 Jan. 2016.

Bush, George W. "Memorandum on Government-to-Government Relationship with Tribal Governments: September 23, 2004." *Weekly Compilation of Presidential Documents* 40 (39): 2105–6. www.gpo.gov/fdsys/pkg/WCPD-2004-09-27/html/WCPD-2004-09-27-Pg2106.htm. Accessed 10 Nov. 2005.

———. "National American Indian Heritage Month Proclamation 12 Nov. 2001. www.whitehouse.gov/news/releases/2001/11/20011112-4.html. Accessed 17 May 2006.

———. "National American Indian Heritage Month, 2005: A Proclamation." 2 Nov. 2005. www.whitehouse.gov/news/releases/2005/11/20051102-16.html. Accessed 10 Nov. 2005.

———. "Remarks on the Opening of the National Museum of the American Indian: September 23, 2004." *Weekly Compilation of Presidential Documents* 40 (39): 2105–6. www.gpo.gov/fdsys/pkg/WCPD-2004-09-27/pdf/WCPD-2004-09-27-Pg2105.pdf. Accessed 10 Nov. 2005.

———. "Statement of Administration Policy: H.R. 4241—Deficit Reduction Act of 2005." *The American Presidency Project.* 17 Nov. 2005. www.presidency.ucsb.edu/ws/?pid=24891. Accessed 20 Feb. 2016.

Byrd, William. "From History of the Dividing Line." *Norton Anthology of American Literature.* Ed. Nina Baym et al. 5th ed. Vol. 1. New York: Norton, 1998, pp. 428–39.

Cajete, Gregory. *Native Science: Natural Laws of Interdependence.* Albuquerque, N.Mex.: Clear Light, 1998.

Caldwell, E. K. "Protect Endangered Peoples, Protect Endangered Species: Honor the Earth Tour in 1995." *News from Indian Country,* 15 July 1995. *Ethnic NewsWatch,* search-proquest-com.ezproxy.lib.ou.edu/docview/367686732?accountid=12964. Accessed 13 Oct. 1995.

Calloway, Colin G. "Declaring Independence and Rebuilding a Nation: Dragging Canoe and the Chickamauga Revolution." *Revolutionary Founders: Rebels, Radicals, and Reformers in the Making of a Nation.* Ed. Alfred F. Young, Gary B. Nash, and Ray Raphael. New York: Alfred A. Knopf, 2011, pp. 185–98.

———. *White People, Indians and Highlanders: Tribal Peoples and Colonial Encounters in Scotland and America.* New York: Oxford UP, 2008.

Campbell, Joseph. *The Power of Myth.* New York: Doubleday, 1988.

Capriccioso, Rob. "American Indians Make Voices Heard This Election Cycle." *PBS.* 24 Oct. 2012. www.pbs.org/wnet/need-to-know/opinion/american-indians-make-voices -heard-this-election-cycle/15207/. Accessed 6 Feb. 2016.

Césaire, Aimé. "Culture and Colonisation." *Présence Africaine: The First International Congress of Negro Writers and Artists.* Sorbonne, Paris, 19–22 Sept. 1956. www.freedomarchives.org/Documents/Finder/Black%20Liberation%20Disk/Black%20Power!/SugahData/Journals/Presence.S.pdf. Accessed 25 June 2013.

Cobb, Amanda J. "Understanding Tribal Sovereignty: Definitions, Conceptualizations, and Interpretations." *American Studies* 46.3–4 (2005): 115–32.

Cohen, Robin. Interview by author. Albuquerque, N.Mex., 16 Apr. 1999.

Cook-Lynn, Elizabeth. "Who Stole Native American Studies?" *Wicazo Sa Review* 12.1 (1997): 9–28. *JSTOR,* doi:10.2307/1409161. Accessed 9 Aug. 2015.

Cooper, Thomas W. *A Time before Deception: Truth in Communications, Culture, and Ethics; Native Worldviews, Traditional Expression, Sacred Ecology.* Santa Fe, N.Mex.: Clear Light Books, 1998.

Cooter, Robert D., and Robert K. Thomas. *The People and the Strangers: Narratives and a Theory of Native American Life.* 1995. *Anthropology Commons.* works.bepress.com/robert_thomas/1/. Accessed 1 Feb. 2015.

Corkran, David H. *The Cherokee Frontier: Conflict and Survival, 1740–62.* Norman: U of Oklahoma P, 1962.

Cornell, Stephen, and Joseph P. Kalt. "Reloading the Dice: Improving the Chances for Economic Development on American Indian Reservations." *What Can Tribes Do? Strategies and Institutions in American Economic Development.* American Indian

Manual and Handbook Series, no. 4. Eds. Stephen Cornell and Joseph P. Kalt. Los Angeles: American Indian Studies Center, UCLA, 1992, pp. 1–59.

Crow Dog, Mary. *Lakota Woman*. New York: Harper Perennial, 1991.

Cummings, Denise K. "Indigenous American Cinema." *The Oxford Handbook of Indigenous American Literature*. Ed. James H. Cox and Daniel Heath Justice. New York: Oxford University Press, 2014, pp. 284–98.

Cunningham, James K., Teshia A. Solomon, and Myra L. Muramoto. "Alcohol Use among Native Americans Compared to Whites: Examining the Veracity of the 'Native American Elevated Alcohol Consumption' Belief." *Drug and Alcohol Dependence* 160 (2016): 65–75. doi:10.1016/j.drugalcdep.2015.12.015. Accessed 7 Mar. 2016.

Cushman, Ellen. "Toward a Rhetoric of Self-Representation: Identity Politics in Indian Country and Rhetoric and Composition." *College Composition and Communication* 60.2 (2008): 321–65.

DataCenter, Research Justice. "Decolonizing Knowledge: A Conversation between Dr. Linda Tuhiwai Smith, Dr. Michelle Fine, and Dr. Andrew Jolivette." *YouTube*. 22 July 2013. youtube.com/watch?v=7lb7edhWghY. Accessed 27 July 2013.

Davis, Jeffrey. "A Historical Linguistic Account of Sign Language among North American Indian Groups." *Multilingualism and Sign Languages: From the Great Plains to Australia: Sociolinguistics of the Deaf Community*. Vol. 12. Ed. C. Lucas. Washington, D.C.: Gallaudet UP, 2006, pp. 3–35.

DeBruyne, Nese F., and Anne Leland. "American War and Military Operations Casualties: Lists and Statistics." Congressional Research Service. 2 January 2015. fas.org/sgp/crs/natsec/RL32492.pdf. Accessed 17 Dec. 2015.

Deloria, Philip S. "The Era of Indian Self-Determination: An Overview." *Indian Self-Rule: First-hand Accounts of Indian-White Relations from Roosevelt to Reagan*. Ed. Kenneth R. Philp. Logan: Utah State UP, 1995.

Deloria, Vine, Jr. *For This Land: Writings on Religion in America*. New York: Routledge, 1999.

———. *Spirit and Reason*. Golden, Colo.: Fulcrum, 1999.

DePasquale, Ron. "Politics: Native Power." *Newsweek*, 6 Sept. 2004, p. 12.

Diamond, Jared. *Guns, Germs, and Steel: The Fate of Human Societies*. New York: W. W. Norton, 1999.

Dinome, William. "Laguna Woman: An Annotated Leslie Silko Bibliography." *American Indian Culture and Research Journal* 21.1 (1997): 207–80.

Dippie, Brian W. *The Vanishing American: White Attitudes and U.S. Indian Policy*. Middletown, Conn.: Wesleyan UP, 1982.

Donohue, Betty Booth. "Observations of Another Trotline Runner: A Critical Discussion of D. L. Birchfield's *Oklahoma Basic Intelligence Test*." *Studies in American Indian Literatures* 11.3 (1999): 66–79.

Driskill, Qwo-Li. "Paracolonial." *Beyond Greco-Roman Rhetorics*. 20 Feb. 2011. breakingprecedent.wikifoundry.com/page/Paracolonial. Accessed 24 June 2013.

———. *Yelesalehe Hiwayona Dikanohogida Naiwodusv/God Taught Me This Song, It Is Beautiful: Cherokee Performance Rhetorics as Decolonization, Healing, and Continuance.* Diss., Michigan State University, 2008. *ProQuest Dissertations and Theses Global,* search-proquest-com.ezproxy.lib.ou.edu/docview/304580493?accountid=12964. Accessed 11 July 2013.

Duncan, Barbara, ed. *Living Stories of the Cherokee.* Chapel Hill: U of North Carolina P, 1998.

———. E-mail to author. 17 July 2015.

Dunham, Richard S., and Aaron Bernstein. "Campaign Reform Loophole." *Business Week,* 15 Apr. 2002, p. 51.

Elliott, Michael. "'This Indian Bait': Samson Occom and the Voice of Liminality." *Early American Literature* 29.3 (1994): 233–53.

Elrod, Eileen Razzari. "'I Did Not Make Myself So . . .': Samson Occom and American Religious Autobiography." *Christian Encounters with the Other.* Ed. John C. Hawley. New York: New York UP, 1998, pp. 135–49.

Fixico, Donald. *The American Indian Mind in a Linear World: American Indian Studies and Traditional Knowledge.* New York: Routledge, 2003.

Forbes, Jack D. *Black Africans and Native Americans: Color, Race and Caste in the Evolution of Red-Black Peoples.* New York: Basil Blackwell, 1988.

Fowler, Loretta. *Tribal Sovereignty and the Historical Imagination: Cheyenne-Arapaho Tribal Politics.* Lincoln: U of Nebraska P, 2002.

Francis, Lee, IV. Interview by author. 6 Feb. 2012.

Galvin, Robert Free. "Venezuela's Oil Program Is a Gesture of Solidarity." 12 Oct. 2006. indiancountrymedianetwork.com/news/venezuelas-oil-program-is-a-gesture-of-solidarity. Accessed 17 May 2007.

Gerstaecker, Friedrich. *Wild Sports in the Far West.* Philadelphia: J. B. Lippincott and Co., 1884. archive.org/details/wildsportsinfarw00gers_0. Accessed 6 Feb. 2016.

Gibson, Danna. "The Community of the Eastern Cherokee: Enacting Community via Discourse." *American Communication Journal* 2.1 (2000). ac-journal.org/journal/vol2/Iss1/essays/gibson.htm. Accessed 30 Apr. 2001.

Gilio-Whitaker, Dina. "Indian Self-Determination and Sovereignty." *Indian Country Today Media Network.* 17 Jan. 2013. indiancountrymedianetwork.com/news/opinions/indian-self-determination-and-sovereignty/. Accessed 26 Dec. 2015.

———. "The Untold History of American Indian Slavery." *About Education.* 10 Dec. 2014. nativeamericanhistory.about.com/od/controversies/a/The-Untold-History-Of-American-Indian-Slavery.htm. Accessed 21 Feb. 2016.

Gomez, Michael A. *Reversing Sail: A History of the African Diaspora.* New York: Cambridge UP, 2005.

Goméz, Rain P. C. "Bayou Baskets: Weaving TriRacial Indian Narratives towards Cultural Sovereignty." CIC American Indian Studies Consortium, Michigan State University, East Lansing. 2007.

———. [Cranford-Gomez, L. Rain]. "Brackish Bayou Blood: Weaving Mixed-Blood Creole-Indian Identity outside the Written Record." *American Indian Culture and Research Journal* 32.2 (2008): 93–108.

———. [Cranford-Goméz, Letha Rain A.] *Gumbo Banaha Stories: Louisiana Indigeneities and Decolonizing the Transnational South.* Diss., University of Oklahoma, 2014.

———. [Goméz, Rain P. C.] "Crawdad Baskets: Weaving Red Black Basketry Narratives in the Southeast." SW/TX Regional PCAACA Native American/Indigenous Studies, Albuquerque, N.Mex. 2007.

Goodpasture, Albert V. "Indian Wars and Warriors of the Old Southwest, 1730–1807." *Tennessee Historical Magazine* 4.1 (1918): 3–49.

———. "Indian Wars and Warriors of the Old Southwest, 1730–1807 (Continued)." *Tennessee Historical Magazine* 4.3 (1918): 161–210.

Gross, Lawrence W. *Anishinaabe Ways of Knowing and Being.* Surrey, UK: Ashgate, 2014.

Haag, Marcia, ed. *A Listening Wind: Native Literature from the Southeast.* Lincoln: U of Nebraska P, 2016.

Haas, Angela. *A Rhetoric of Alliance: What American Indians Can Tell Us about Digital and Visual Rhetoric.* Diss., Michigan State University, 2008. *ProQuest Dissertations and Theses Global,* search-proquest-com.ezproxy.lib.ou.edu/docview/304580933?accountid=12964. Accessed 11 July 2013.

Hamilton, Edith. *Mythology.* New York: Mentor, 1969.

Harjo, Joy. Interview by author. Waco, Tex., 27 Mar. 2000.

———. *She Had Some Horses.* New York: Thunder's Mouth, 1983.

Her Many Horses, Emil. *Identity by Design: Tradition, Change, and Celebration in Native Women's Dresses.* New York: HarperCollins / National Museum of the American Indian, 2007.

Hester, Thurman Lee, Jr. "*Pishukchi*: One Choctaw's Examination of the Differences in English and Choctaw Language Use." *Ayaangwaamizin: The International Journal of Indigenous Philosophy* 1.1 (1997): 81–90.

Hilden, Patricia Penn. "Ritchie Valens Is Dead: *E Pluribus Unum.*" *As We Are Now: Mixblood Essays on Race and Identity.* Ed. William S. Penn. Berkeley: U of California P, 1997, pp. 219–52.

Hill, Charles A., and Marguerite Helmers, eds. *Defining Visual Rhetorics.* New York: Taylor and Francis e-Library, 2008.

Hobson, Geary. Interview by author. 14 June 2015.

Hobson, Geary, Janet McAdams, and Kathryn Walkiewicz. *The People Who Stayed: Southeastern Indian Writing after Removal.* Norman: U of Oklahoma P, 2010.

Holland, Sharon P. "'If You Know I Have a History, You Will Respect Me': A Perspective on Afro-Native American Literature." *Callaloo* 17.1 (1994): 334–50.

Hollrah, Patrice. "Sherman Alexie's Challenge to the Academy's Teaching of Native American Literature, Non-Native Writers, and Critics." *Studies in American Indian Literatures* 13.2–3 (2001): 23–35.

Holm, Tom, J. Diane Pearson, and Ben Chavis. "Peoplehood: A Model for the Extension of Sovereignty in American Indian Studies." *Wicazo Sa Review* 18.1 (2003): 7–24. *JSTOR*, www.jstor.org/stable/1409431. Accessed 29 July 2012.

Hoover, Dwight W. *The Red and the Black.* The Rand McNally Series on the History of American Thought and Culture, no. 4. Chicago: Rand McNally College Publishing, 1976.

Howe, LeAnne. "The Story of America: A Tribalography." *Clearing a Path: Theorizing the Past in Native American Studies.* Ed. Nancy Shoemaker. New York: Routledge, 2002, pp. 29–48.

ICTMN (Indian Country Today Media Network) staff. "4th Largest Tribe in US? Mexicans Who Call Themselves American Indian." *Indian Country Today Media Network.* 5 Aug. 2013.

"Idle No More Map Reveals Movement's Global Reach." *The Huffington Post,* 27 Dec. 2012. www.huffingtonpost.ca/2012/12/27/idle-no-more-global-map_n_2372718.html. Accessed 11 July 2013.

Iron Eyes, Chase. "Interview with the General Cha-O-Ha, War Chief of the Amerindian Peoples Liberation Army of the Americas." *Last Real Indians.* 23 June 2013. last realindians.com/interview-with-the-general-cha-o-ha-war-chief-of-the-amerindian-peoples-liberation-army-of-the-americas-by-chase-iron-eyes/. Accessed 11 July 2013.

Irwin, Lee. "Cherokee Healing: Myth, Dreams, and Medicine." *American Indian Quarterly* 16.2 (1992): 237–58.

———. "Dreams, Theory, and Culture: The Plains Vision Quest Paradigm." *American Indian Quarterly* 18.2 (1994): 229–45.

Jackson, Andrew. "First Annual Message to Congress, December 8, 1829." *The Nomadic Spirit: Tracking Western Expansion and the Trail of Tears.* 1995. www.synaptic.bc.ca/ejournal/JacksonFirstAnnualMessage.htm. Accessed 17 May 2007.

———. "First Inaugural Address, March 4, 1829." *The Nomadic Spirit: Tracking Western Expansion and the Trail of Tears.* 1995. www.synaptic.bc.ca/ejournal/JacksonFirstInauguralAddress.htm. Accessed 17 May 2007.

———. "Second Annual Message to Congress, December 6, 1830." *The Nomadic Spirit: Tracking Western Expansion and the Trail of Tears.* 1995. www.synaptic.bc.ca/ejournal/JacksonSecondAnnualMessage.htm. Accessed 17 May 2007.

Jacobs, Don Trent. *Unlearning the Language of Conquest: Scholars Expose Anti-Indianism in America.* Austin: U of Texas P, 2006.

Jefferson, Thomas. *Notes on the State of Virginia.* Boston: Lilly and Wait, 1832.

Joint Council of the Cherokee Nation and the Eastern Band of Cherokee Indians. "Resolution #08-08." Apr. 2008. taskforce.cherokee.org/Portals/3/Exhibits/Fabricated%20Tribes%20Resolution.pdf. Accessed 29 July 2012.

Justice, Daniel Heath. "Currents of Trans/national Criticism in Indigenous Literary Studies." *American Indian Quarterly* 35.3 (2011): 334–52. *JSTOR*, www.jstor.org/stable/10.5250/amerindiquar.35.3.0334. Accessed 15 June 2015.

———. "'Go Away, Water!': Kinship Criticism and the Decolonization Imperative." Acoose et al. 2008, pp. 147–68.

———. *Our Fire Survives the Storm: A Cherokee Literary History.* Minneapolis: U of Minnesota P, 2006.

———. "Rhetorics of Recognition." *The Kenyon Review* 32.1 (2010): 236–61.

———. "'To Look Upon Thousands': Cherokee Transnationalism, at Home and Abroad." *The New Centennial Review* 10.1 (2010): 169–78.

Katanski, Amelia V. *Learning to Write "Indian": The Boarding School Experience and American Indian Literature.* Norman: U of Oklahoma P, 2005.

Kauder, Rob. "Bad Blood, Black Gold and the Death of Doug Carlile." *KXLY News.* 15 Jan. 2014. www.kxly.com/news/local-news/spokane/bad-blood-black-gold-and-the-death-of-doug-carlile_2016112108131926/177553111. Accessed 26 Jan. 2014.

Kelly, James C. "Notable Persons in Cherokee History: Attakullakulla." *Journal of Cherokee Studies* 3.1 (1978): 2–34.

Kennedy, George A. *Comparative Rhetoric: An Historical and Cross-Cultural Introduction.* Oxford: Oxford UP, 1998.

Kilroe, Patricia. "On the Probable Origin of Plains Indian Sign Language." *In Search of Language Origins: Selected Papers from the Seventh Meeting of the Language Origins Society, DeKalb, Illinois.* Ed. Edward Callary. 30 Dec. 2001. baserv.uci.kun.nl/~Los/Meetings/Dekalb/ (site discontinued). Accessed 16 Jan. 2002.

King, Duane H., ed. *The Memoirs of Lt. Henry Timberlake: The Story of a Soldier, Adventurer, and Emissary to the Cherokees, 1756–1765.* Chapel Hill: U of North Carolina P, 2007.

King, Lisa, Rose Gubele, and Joyce Rain Anderson, eds. *Survivance, Sovereignty, and Story: Teaching American Indian Rhetorics.* Logan: Utah State UP, 2015. Kindle edition.

King, Thomas. *Medicine River.* Toronto: Penguin, 1991.

———. *The Truth about Stories: A Native Narrative.* Toronto: House of Anansi P, 2003. Minneapolis: U of Minnesota P, 2008.

Krupat, Arnold. "Scholarship and Native American Studies: A Response to Daniel Littlefield, Jr." *American Studies* 34.2 (1993): 81–100. *JSTOR*, www.jstor.org/stable/40643668. Accessed 20 Aug. 2015.

Lastrealindians. Post on *Last Real Indians* (Facebook page). 24 July 2013. www.facebook.com/lastrealindians/posts/614830081871959. Accessed 25 July 2013.

Leap, William L. *American Indian English.* Salt Lake City: U of Utah P, 1993.

Littlefield, Daniel F., Jr. "American Indians, American Scholars and the American Literary Canon." *American Studies* 33.2 (1992): 95–111. *JSTOR*, www.jstor.org/stable/40642474. Accessed 20 Aug. 2015.

———. *The Fus Fixico Letters: A Creek Humorist in Early Oklahoma.* Norman: U of Oklahoma, 2002.

Littlefield, Daniel F., Jr., and James W. Parins. *A Biobibliography of Native American Writers, 1772–1924.* Metuchen, N.J.: Scarecrow, 1985.

Longe, Alexander. "A Small Postscript on the ways and maners of the Nashon of Indians called Charikees, the contents of the whole soe that you may find everything by the peages." *Southern Indian Studies* 21 (1969): 7–49. www.rla.unc.edu/Publications/NCArch/SIS_21.pdf. Accessed 11 Feb. 2017.

Low Weso, Denise. "Cheyenne Women in a Western Oklahoma 19th-Century Ledger Account." 2006 Native American Literature Symposium, Soaring Eagle Casino and Resort, Mt. Pleasant, Mich., 6–8 Apr. 2006.

Lyons, Scott Richard. "Rhetorical Sovereignty: What Do American Indians Want from Writing?" *College Composition and Communication* 52.3 (2000): 447–67.

———. *X-Marks: Native Signatures of Assent.* Minneapolis: U of Minnesota P, 2010. Kindle edition.

Martínez, David. *The American Indian Intellectual Tradition: An Anthology of Writings from 1772 to 1972.* Ithaca, N.Y.: Cornell UP, 2010. 15 Aug. 2015.

———. "Neither Chief nor Medicine Man: The Historical Role of the 'Intellectual' in the American Indian Community." *Studies in American Indian Literatures* 26.1 (2014): 29–53. *JSTOR*, www.jstor.org/stable/10.5250/studamerindilite.26.1.0029. Accessed 11 Feb. 2017.

Masich, Andrew E., et al. *Cheyenne Dog Soldiers: A Courageous Warrior History.* CD-ROM. Colorado Historical Society, 1999.

Mathews, John Joseph. *Sundown.* Norman: U of Oklahoma P, 1988.

McCrady, Edward. *The History of South Carolina under the Royal Government, 1719–1776.* London: Macmillan, 1899.

McFarland, Ron. "Sherman Alexie's Polemical Stories." *Studies in American Indian Literatures* 9.4 (1997). *JSTOR*, www.jstor.org/stable/20739423. Accessed 1 Aug. 2001.

McKegney, Sam. "Strategies for Ethical Engagement: An Open Letter concerning Non-Native Scholars of Native Literatures." *Studies in American Indian Literatures* 20.4 (2008): 56–67.

Melmer, David. "Federal Sale May Include Treaty Lands." *Indian Country Today*, 11 Nov. 2005. indiancountrymedianetwork.com/news/federal-sale-may-include-treaty-lands/. Accessed 11 Nov. 2006.

———. "Indian Country Not a Priority for Bush Administration, Johnson Says." *Indian Country Today*, 15 May 2006. www.indiancountry.com/content.cfm?id=1096413006 (page discontinued). Accessed 11 Nov. 2006.

Miller, Arthur G. Introduction to *The Codex Nuttall.* Ed. Zelia Nuttall. New York: Dover, 1975, pp. vii–xviii.

Miller, Brad. "Draining the Life from the Land: Mining and Indigenous People." *Earth Island Journal* 17.3 (2002): 26–27. www.thefreelibrary.com/Draining+the+life+from+the+land.+(mining+and+indigenous+people)-a089392642. Accessed 10 Nov. 2005.

Miller, Mark Edwin. *Claiming Tribal Identity: The Five Tribes and the Politics of Federal Acknowledgment.* Norman: U of Oklahoma P, 2013.

Milligan, George. *A Short Description of the Province of South-Carolina, with an Account of the Air, Weather, and Diseases, at Charles-town.* London: J. Hinton, 1770. *Early*

Encounters in North America: Peoples, Cultures, and the Environment, solomon.eena .alexanderstreet.com.ezproxy.lib.ou.edu/cgi-bin/asp/philo/navigate.pl?eena.299. Accessed 26 Feb. 2015.

Minges, Patrick Neal. *Slavery in the Cherokee Nation: The Keetoowah Society and the Defining of a People, 1855–1867*. New York: Routledge, 2003.

Momaday, N. Scott. *The Man Made of Words: Essays, Stories, Passages*. New York: St. Martin's, 1997.

Morgan, Phillip Carroll. *Riding Out the Storm: 19th Century Chickasaw Governors; Their Lives and Intellectual Legacy*. Ada, Okla.: Chickasaw Nation P, 2013.

Morrison, Scott Kayla. "An Apokni by Any Other Name Is Still a Kakoo." Bird and Harjo, pp. 88–102.

Moulder, M. Amanda. "Cherokee Practice, Missionary Intentions: Literacy Learning among Early Nineteenth-Century Cherokee Women." *College Composition and Communication* 63.1 (2011): 75–97. *JSTOR*, www.jstor.org/stable/23006897. Accessed 23 July 2013.

Murray, David. *Forked Tongues: Speech, Writing, and Representation in North American Indian Texts*. Bloomington: Indiana UP, 1991.

Myers, W. Benjamin, and Bryant Keith Alexander. "(Performance Is) Metaphors as Methodological Tools in Qualitative Inquiry." *International Review of Qualitative Research* 3.2 (2010): 163–72. *JSTOR*, www.jstor.org/stable/10.1525/irqr.2010.3.2.163. Accessed 12 Feb. 2015.

Mygatt, Matt. "Two Worlds Collide." *Albuquerque Journal*, 5 Feb. 2000. www.albuquerque journal.com. Accessed 6 Feb. 2000.

Nash, Gary B. *The Unknown American Revolution: The Unruly Birth of Democracy and the Struggle to Create America*. New York: Penguin, 2006.

National Indian Education Association. "NIEA Appropriations Priorities for the FY 2007 Continuing Resolution and for FY 2008: Fighting for Funding on Two Fronts at the Same Time." 6 Feb. 2007. www.niea.org/sa/uploads/legislativetracking/29.8 (page discontinued). Accessed 17 May 2007.

Neihardt, John G. *Black Elk Speaks: The Complete Edition*. Lincoln: U of Nebraska P, 2014.

Nelson, Dana D. "'(I Speak Like a Fool but I Am Constrained)': Samson Occom's *Short Narrative* and Economies of the Racial Self." *Early Native American Writing: New Critical Essays*. Ed. Helen Jaskoski. Cambridge: Cambridge UP, 1996: 42–65.

———. "Reading the Written Selves of Colonial America: Franklin, Occom, Equiano, and Palou/Serra." *Resources for American Literary Study* 19. 2 (1993): 246–59.

Nelson, Joshua, Daniel Swan, and Lizz Toombs. *Native Peoples of Oklahoma*. Janux Interactive Learning Community. 2013. janux.ou.edu. Accessed 28 Jan. 2013.

Nelson, Robert. E-mail to author. 29 July 2013.

NHPRC (National Historical Publications and Records Commission). "From George Washington to Major General John Sullivan, 31 May 1779." founders.archives.gov /documents/Washington/03-20-02-0661. Accessed 17 May 2007.

———. "From George Washington to the Seneca Chiefs, 29 December 1790." founders.archives.gov/documents/Washington/05-07-02-0080. Accessed 17 May 2007.

———. "Proclamation on Recent Crimes against the Cherokees, 12 December 1792." founders.archives.gov/documents/Washington/05-11-02-0303. Accessed 17 May 2007.

———. "To George Washington from the Seneca Chiefs, 1 December 1790." founders.archives.gov/documents/Washington/05-07-02-0005. Accessed 6 Feb. 2016.

Niatum, Duane. "History, Nature, Family, Dream: The Musical Colors of Their Poems." Armstrong 1993, pp. 63–81.

Nichols, John L. "John Stuart: Beloved Father of the Cherokees." *Highlander*, Sept.–Oct. 1993. www.thepeoplespaths.net/lit/bushyhd.html. Accessed 9 Feb. 2015.

Norris, Tina, Paula L. Vines, and Elizabeth M. Hoeffel. "The American Indian and Alaska Native Population: 2010." *2010 Census Briefs*. Jan. 2012. www.census.gov/prod/cen2010/briefs/c2010br-10.pdf. Accessed 9 Feb. 2015.

Nuttall, Zelia, ed. *The Codex Nuttall*. New York: Dover, 1975.

Occom, Samson. "A Short Narrative of My Life." *The Norton Anthology of American Literature*. Ed. Nina Baym et al. 5th ed., vol. 1. New York: Norton, 1998, pp. 612–19.

Oliphant, John. *Peace and War on the Anglo-Cherokee Frontier, 1756–63*. Baton Rouge: Louisiana State UP, 2001.

Ortiz, Simon J. *From Sand Creek*. Tucson: U of Arizona P, 2000.

———. "Towards a National Indian Literature: Cultural Authenticity in Nationalism." 1981. *Nothing but the Truth: An Anthology of Native American Literature*. Ed. John L. Purdy and James Ruppert. Upper Saddle River, N.J.: Prentice Hall, 2001, pp. 120–25.

"Over to You, George." *The Economist*, 26 Aug. 2000. *ABI/INFORM Collection*, search-proquest-com.ezproxy.lib.ou.edu/docview/922240596?accountid=12964. Accessed 10 Nov. 2005.

Parker, Robert Dale. *Changing Is Not Vanishing; A Collection of American Indian Poetry to 1930*. Philadelphia: U of Pennsylvania P, 2011.

Payne, David. Review of *Mixed-Blood Messages: Literature, Film, Family, Place*, by Louis Owens, and *Off the Reservation: Reflections on Boundary-Busting, Border-Crossing, and Loose Canons*, by Paula Gunn Allen. *Studies in American Indian Literatures* 11.2 (1999): 84–89.

Penn, William S., ed. *As We Are Now: Mixblood Essays on Race and Identity*. Berkeley: U of California P, 1997.

Perry, Donna. *Backtalk: Women Writers Speak Out: Interviews by Donna Perry*. New Brunswick, N.J.: Rutgers UP, 1993.

Peyer, Bernd C. *American Indian Nonfiction: An Anthology of Writings, 1760s–1930s*. Norman: U of Oklahoma P, 2007.

———. *"The Thinking Indian": Native American Writers, 1850s–1920s*. Frankfurt: Peter Lang, 2007.

———. *The Tutor'd Mind: Indian Missionary-Writers in Antebellum America*. Amherst: U of Massachusetts P, 1997.

Pound, Edward T. "The Man in the Hat Sings: Who Else Will Lobbyist Jack Abramoff Take Down with Him?" *U.S. News and World Report,* 8 Jan. 2006. www.usnews.com/usnews/news/articles/060116/16abramoff.htm. Accessed 17 May 2007.

Powell, Malea. "Blood and Scholarship: One Mixed-Blood's Story." *Race, Rhetoric, and Composition.* Ed. Keith Gilyard. Portsmouth, N.H.: Heinemann-Boynton/Cook, 1999, pp. 1–16.

———. "Growing Our Discipline: An Interview with Malea Powell." Interview by Andréa D. Davis. *Composition Forum* 23 (Spring 2011). compositionforum.com/issue/23/malea-powell-interview.php. Accessed 24 June 2013.

———. *"I Write These Words with Blood and Bone": Two Nineteenth Century American Indian Intellectuals and a Rhetoric of Survivance.* Diss., Miami U, 1998. *ProQuest Dissertations and Theses Global,* search-proquest-com.ezproxy.lib.ou.edu/docview/304432118?accountid=12964. Accessed 23 July 2013.

———. "Rhetorics of Survivance: How American Indians Use Writing." *College Composition and Communication* 53.3 (2002): 396–434. *JSTOR,* www.jstor.org/stable/1512132. Accessed 16 Feb. 2011.

Pratt, Stephanie. "Reynolds' 'King of the Cherokees' and Other Mistaken Identities in the Portraiture of Native American Delegations, 1710–1762." *Oxford Art Journal* 21.2 (1998): 135–50. *JSTOR,* www.jstor.org/stable/1360618. Accessed 15 Jan. 2015.

Price, Steve. "Critical Discourse Analysis: Discourse Acquisition and Discourse Practices." *TESOL Quarterly* 33.3 (1999): 581–95.

Progler, J. A. "Honesty, Integrity Hallmarks of Native Indian Communication Discourse." *Crescent International,* 1–15 June 1998. www.muslimedia.com/archives/book98/deceptbk.htm. Accessed 22 Nov. 2005.

Rasmussen, Birgit Brander. *Queequeg's Coffin: Indigenous Literacies and Early American Literature.* Durham, N.C.: Duke UP, 2012.

Reyhner, Jon. "American Indian/Alaska Native Education: An Overview." *American Indian* Education. 2006. www2.nau.edu/jar/AIE/Ind_Ed.html. Accessed 26 Dec. 2015.

———. "Plans for Dropout Prevention and Special School Support Services for American Indian and Alaska Native Students." *American Indian Education.* 1992. jan.ucc.nau.edu/~jar/INAR.html#1. Accessed 10 Nov. 2005.

Reynolds, Jerry. "Even Start Literacy Program Could Lose Funding, Dems Warn." *Indian Country Today,* 19 May 2006. indiancountrymedianetwork.com/news/even-start-literacy-program-could-lose-funding-dems-warn/. Accessed 11 Nov. 2006.

Rodríguez, Roberto Cintli. *Our Sacred Maíz Is Our Mother: Indigeneity and Belonging in the Americas.* Tucson: U of Arizona P, 2014.

Rogers, Anne, and Barbara Duncan, eds. *Culture, Crisis and Conflict: Cherokee British Relations, 1756–1765.* Cherokee, N.C.: Museum of the Cherokee Indian P, 2009.

Romero, Channette. "Envisioning a 'Network of Tribal Coalitions.'" *American Indian Quarterly* 26.4 (2002): 623–40.

———. "Expanding Tribal Identities and Sovereignty through LeAnne Howe's 'Tribalography.'" *Studies in American Indian Literature* 26.2 (2014): 13–25.

Roppolo, Kimberly G. "An Incipient Study of the Indian Half of the Dialogic: Native Rhetoric and Occom's Use of Indirect Discourse." *"Stealing/Steeling the Spirit: American Indian Identities" and "Smoke Screens/Smoke Signals: Looking through Two Worlds": Proceedings of the Third and Fourth Native American Symposiums.* Ed. Lucretia Scoufos, Mark Spencer, and Chad Litton. Durant: Southeastern Oklahoma State UP, 2003–2004: 41–47.

———. "Sacred Sexuality in Leslie Marmon Silko's *Ceremony.*" *Red Ink* 11.11 (2002): 70–77.

———. "Samson Occom as Writing Instructor: The Search for an Intertribal Rhetoric." Acoose et al. 2008, pp. 303–24.

———. "Selections from *Breeds and Outlaws.*" *Children of the Dragonfly: Native American Voices on Child Custody and Education.* Ed. Robert Bensen. Tucson: U of Arizona P, 2001, pp. 191–95.

———. "Towards a Tribal-Centered Reading of Native Literature: Using Indigenous Rhetoric(s) instead of Literary Analysis." *Paradoxa* 15 (2001): 263–74.

———. "Vision, Voice, and Intertribal Metanarrative: The Amerindian Visual-Rhetorical Tradition and Leslie Silko's *Almanac of the Dead.*" *American Indian Quarterly* 31.4 (2007): 534–58.

———. "'We've Got to Get Ourselves Back to the Garden': Indigenous Views of the Life-Death Cycle as Resistance in Silko's *Gardens in the Dunes.*" *Reading Leslie Marmon Silko: Critical Perspectives through* Gardens in the Dunes. Ed. Laura Coltelli. Pisa, Italy: Edizioni Plus/Pisa University Press, 2007, pp. 74–89.

Rozema, Vicki. *Cherokee Voices: Early Accounts of Cherokee Life in the East.* Winston-Salem, N.C.: John F. Blair, 2002. Kindle edition.

Rubin, Hannah Gladfelter. "Dropout Rates Fueling Debate over Testing." *Education Daily*, 16 Sept. 2002, pp. 1–3.

Ruoff, A. LaVonne Brown. *American Indian Literatures.* New York: MLA, 1990.

Russell, Steve. "The Racial Paradox of Tribal Citizenship." *American Studies* 46.3–4 (2005): 163–85.

———. *Sequoyah Rising: Problems in Post-Colonial Tribal Governance.* Durham, N.C.: Carolina Academic P, 2010.

Sakr, Laila Shereen. "A Digital Humanities Approach: Text, the Internet, and the Egyptian Uprising." *Middle East Critique* 22.3 (2013): 247–63. doi:10.1080/19436149.2013.822241. Accessed 17 Apr. 2014.

Salyer, Gregory. *Leslie Marmon Silko.* New York: Simon and Schuster Macmillan, 1997.

Sarris, Greg. *Keeping Slug Woman Alive: A Holistic Approach to American Texts.* Berkeley: U of California P, 1993.

Schuetz, Janice. *Episodes in the Rhetoric of Government-Indian Relations.* Westport, Conn.: Praeger, 2002.

Sealy, Leroy. Interview by author. 16 June 2016.

"Senators, Tribal Leaders Bash Bush's Latest Budget." *Indianz.com.* 15 Feb. 2006. www.indianz.com/News/2006/012533.asp. Accessed 17 May 2007.

Sheehy, Kelsey. "Graduation Rates Dropping among Native American Students: Latino and Black Students Are Gaining Ground, but American Indians Are Slipping, a New Report Shows." *U.S. News and World Report,* 6 June 2013. www.usnews.com /education/high-schools/articles/2013/06/06/graduation-rates-dropping-among -native-american-students. Accessed 29 July 2013.

Sherzer, Joel, and Anthony C. Woodbury. *Native American Discourse: Poetics and Rhetoric.* New York: Cambridge UP, 1987.

Silko, Leslie Marmon. *Almanac of the Dead.* New York: Penguin, 1991.

———. *Ceremony.* New York: Penguin, 1986.

———. Reading at the University of New Mexico Bookstore, Albuquerque. 16 Apr. 1999.

———. *Yellow Woman and a Beauty of the Spirit: Essays on Native American Life Today.* New York: Simon and Schuster, 1996.

Simpson, Audra. *Mohawk Interruptus: Political Life across the Borders of Settler States.* Durham, N.C.: Duke UP, 2014. Kindle edition.

Simpson, Leann. "Stories, Dreams, and Ceremonies: Anishinaabe Ways of Learning." *Tribal College* 11.4 (2000): 26–30. web.b.ebscohost.com.ezproxy.lib.ou.edu/ehost /detail/detail?vid=3&sid=9eedff1`8f9-44ab-b428-68c03a7302af%40sessionmgr104 &hid=116&bdata=JnNpdGU9ZWhvc3QtbGl2ZQ%3d%3d#AN=3334495&db=aph. Accessed 11 Feb. 2001.

Skow, John. "People of the Monkey Wrench." Review of *Almanac of the Dead,* by Leslie Marmon Silko. *Time,* 9 Dec. 1991: 86. web.b.ebscohost.com.ezproxy.lib.ou.edu/ehost /detail/detail?vid=5&sid=9eedff19-68f9-44ab-b428-68c03a7302af%40sessionmgr104 &hid=116&bdata=JnNpdGU9ZWhvc3QtbGl2ZQ%3d%3d#AN=9112090797&db=aph. Accessed 11 Feb. 2001.

Smallwood, James M., and Steven K. Gragert, eds. *Will Rogers' Weekly Articles.* Vol. 4. Stillwater: Oklahoma State UP, 1980.

Smith, Andrea. *Conquest: Sexual Violence and American Indian Genocide.* Cambridge, UK: South End P, 2005.

Smith, John. *The Generall Historie of Virginia, New-England, and The Summer Isles: With the Names of the Adventurers, Planters, and Governours from Their First Beginning, Ano: 1584. To This Present 1624. With The Procedings of Those Severall Colonies and the Accidents That Befell Them in All Their Journyes and Discoveries. Also the Maps and Descriptions of All Those Countryes, Their Commodities, People, Government, Customes, and Religion Yet Knowne. Divided into Sixe Bookes. By Captaine John Smith, Sometymes Governour in Those Countryes & Admirall of New England.* London, 1624; electronic ed., Chapel Hill: University of North Carolina Library, 2004. docsouth.unc.edu/southlit/smith/smith.html. Accessed 26 Jan. 2007.

Smith, Linda Tuhiwai. *Decolonizing Methodologies: Research and Indigenous Peoples.* London: Zed, 1999.

Sol, Adam. "The Story as It's Told: Prodigious Revisions in Leslie Marmon Silko's *Almanac of the Dead.*" *American Indian Quarterly* 23.3–4 (1999): 24–48.

Sontag, Deborah, and Brent McDonald. "In North Dakota, a Tale of Oil, Corruption and Death." *The New York Times,* 28 Dec. 2014. www.nytimes.com/2014/12/29/us/in-north-dakota-where-oil-corruption-and-bodies-surface.html?_r=0. Accessed 15 Jan. 2015.

Standing Bear, Luther. *Land of the Spotted Eagle.* Lincoln, Neb.: Bison, 1978. First published in 1933.

Stanford, Ann Folwell. "'Human Debris': Border Politics, Body Parts, and the Reclamation of the Americas in Leslie Marmon Silko's *Almanac of the Dead.*" *Literature and Medicine* 16.1 (1997): 23–42. *Project MUSE,* doi:10.1353/lm.1997.0008. Accessed 11 Feb. 2001.

Stannard, David E. *American Holocaust: Columbus and the Conquest of the New World.* New York: Oxford UP, 1992.

Starnes, Bobby Ann. "Same Story, Different Century." *Phi Delta Kappan,* Dec. 2003, pp. 330–31.

Starr, Emmet. *History of the Cherokee Indians and Their Legends and Folklore.* Oklahoma City: Warden, 1921.

Stromberg, Ernest, ed. *American Indian Rhetorics of Survivance: Word Medicine, Word Magic.* Pittsburg: U of Pittsburgh P, 2006.

Szasz, Margaret Connell. "Samson Occom: Mohegan as Spiritual Intermediary." *Between Indian and White Worlds: The Cultural Broker.* Ed. Margaret Connell Szasz. Norman: U of Oklahoma P, 1994, pp. 61–78.

Tapahonso, Luci. "The Snakeman." *Children of the Dragonfly: Native American Voices on Child Custody and Education.* Ed. Robert Bensen. Tucson: U of Arizona P, 2001, pp. 92–96.

Tarbet, Thomas V., Jr. E-mail to Wordcraft Circle of Native Writers and Storytellers discussion list. 23 Feb. 1999.

Taylor, Paul Beekman. "Silko's Reappropriation of Secrecy." *Leslie Marmon Silko: A Collection of Critical Essays.* Ed. Louise K. Barnett and James L. Thorson. Albuquerque: U of New Mexico P, 1999, pp. 23–62.

Tecumseh. "Speech of the Shawnoes, Kikapoos & Winibiegoes, deilvered [*sic*] by Teekhumthia [Tecumseh] at Machekethie, on the Wabash, in answer to the Message I [Col. M. Elliott] sent to them by the Hurons last Winter." *Documents relating to the Invasion of Canada and the Surrender of Detroit, 1812.* Ed. E. A. Cruikshank. Ottawa: Government Printing Bureau, 1912, pp. 33–35. archive.org/details/cu31924032759742. Accessed 28 Feb. 2017.

———. "Tecumseh's Speech to the Osages (Winter 1811–12)." *Voices of a People's History of the United States.* 2nd ed. Ed. Howard Zinn and Anthony. New York: Seven Stories Press, pp. 134–35.

Teuton, Christopher B., et al. *Cherokee Stories of the Turtle Island Liars' Club.* Chapel Hill: U of North Carolina P, 2012. Kindle edition.

Teuton, Sean. "The Callout: Writing American Indian Politics." Acoose et al. 2008, pp. 105–25.

Tillet, Rebecca, ed. *Howling for Justice: New Perspectives on Leslie Marmon Silko's* Almanac of the Dead. Tucson: U of Arizona P, 2014.

Tinling, Marion, ed. *The Correspondence of the Three William Byrds of Westover, Virginia, 1684–1776.* Charlottesville: UP of Virginia, 1977.

Trahant, Mark. "And Obama Makes Eight: Presidents Who Visited Indian Country." *Indian Country Today Media Network.* 17 June 2014. indiancountrymedianetwork.com/news/politics/and-obama-makes-eight-presidents-who-visited-indian-country/. Accessed 26 June 2016.

———. "Confused by the 2016 Presidential Campaign?" *Indian Country Today Media Network.* 18 Dec. 2015. indiancountrymedianetwork.com/news/politics/confused-by-the-2016-presidential-campaign/. Accessed 6 Feb. 2016.

Treuer, David. *Native American Fiction: A User's Manual.* Saint Paul, Minn.: Graywolf, 2006.

UCTP [United Confederation of Taino] Taino News. "Bolivian Indigenous President to Meet with North American Native American Leaders." *The Voice of the Taino People Online.* 18 Sept. 2006. uctp.blogspot.com/2006/09/bolivian-indigenous-president-to-meet.html. Accessed 20 Aug. 2007.

U.S. Census Bureau. *Profile America Facts for Features: American Indian and Alaska Native Heritage Month: November 2012.* Report CB12-FF.22. www.census.gov/newsroom/releases/pdf/cb12ff-22_aian.pdf.

"Unraveling Abramoff." *The Washington Post,* 13 Oct. 2006. www.washingtonpost.com/wp-dyn/content/custom/2005/12/23/CU2005122300939.html. Accessed 17 May 2007.

Van Gelder, Sarah. "Speaking with the Founders of Idle No More." *The Huffington Post,* 21 Feb. 2013. www.huffingtonpost.ca/sarah-van-gelder/idle-no-more-founders_b_2708644.html. Accessed 11 July 2013.

Vest, J. L. "Comparative African and American Indian Philosophy." Presentation at the American Philosophical Association Pacific Division Conference. Albuquerque, 5–8 Apr., 2000.

"The Vision." *Idle No More.* www.idlenomore.ca. Accessed 11 July 2013.

Vizenor, Gerald. *Crossbloods: Bone Courts, Bingo, and Other Reports.* Minneapolis: U of Minnesota P, 1990.

———. *Manifest Manners.* Hanover, N.H.: U of New England P, 1994.

———. *Narrative Chance: Postmodern Discourse on Native American Indian Literatures.* Norman: U of Oklahoma P, 1993.

Walters, Anna Lee. *Talking Indian: Reflections on Survival and Writing.* Ithaca, N.Y.: Firebrand, 1992.

Warrior, Robert. *The People and the Word: Reading Native Nonfiction.* Minneapolis: U of Minnesota P, 2005.

———. *Tribal Secrets: Recovering American Indian Intellectual Traditions.* Minneapolis: U of Minnesota P, 1995.

Washington, George. "Talk to the Cherokee Nation, City of Philadelphia, August 29, 1796." *The Writings of George Washington from the Original Manuscript Sources, 1745–1799.* Ed. John C. Fitzpatrick. Washington, D.C.: GPO, December 1940, pp. 193–98. archive.org/details/writingsofgeorge35wash. Accessed 17 May 2007.

Waters, Anne. *American Indian Thought.* Malden, Mass.: Blackwell, 2004.

Weaver, Jace. *Other Words: American Indian Literature, Law, and Culture.* Norman: U of Oklahoma P, 2001.

———. *That the People Might Live: Native American Literatures and Native American Community.* New York: Oxford UP, 1997.

Weaver, Jace, Craig Womack, and Robert Warrior. *American Indian Literary Nationalism.* Albuquerque: U of New Mexico P, 2006.

Webster, Anthony K. "Sam Kenoi's Coyote Stories: Poetics and Rhetoric in Some Chiricahua Apache Narratives." *American Indian Culture and Research Journal* 23.1 (1999): 137–63.

Welch, James. *Fools Crow.* New York: QPB, 1995.

Western Shoshone Defense Project. "Western Shoshone Victorious at United Nations: U.S. Found in Violation of Human Rights of Native Americans—Urged to Take Immediate Action." Press release. 10 Mar. 2006. law2.arizona.edu/iplp/outreach/shoshone/documents/WSDPPressRelease.pdf. Accessed 28 Feb. 2017.

Wieser, Kimberly G. "Who Is Cherokee? Federal Recognition, Culture, and Rhetorical Sovereignty." *A Listening Wind: Native Literature from the Southeast.* Ed. Marcia Haag. Lincoln: U of Nebraska P, 2016, pp. 251–60.

Wilkins, David Eugene, and Heidi Kiiwetinepinesiik Stark. *American Indian Politics and the American Political System.* Lanham, Md.: Rowman and Littlefield, 2007.

Womack, Craig S. *Red on Red: Native American Literary Separatism.* Minneapolis: U of Minnesota P, 1999.

Yellow Bird, Michael. "Why Are Indigenous (American Indian) Soldiers Serving in Iraq?" Open letter to all Indigenous Peoples. Personal copy. 10 Oct. 2006.

"Yesterday's Outlaw, Willie Nelson, Warily Follows His Potholed Highway to Hollywood Stardom." *People*, 1 Sept. 1980, pp. 35–38.

Index

References to illustrations are in italic *type.*